PERCEPTIONS OF LANGUAGE PEDAGOGY

Perceptions of Language Pedagogy

N. S. Prabhu

Edited by

Geetha Durairajan

Orient BlackSwan

PERCEPTIONS OF LANGUAGE PEDAGOGY

ORIENT BLACKSWAN PRIVATE LIMITED

Registered Office
3-6-752 Himayatnagar, Hyderabad 500 029, Telangana, India
e-mail: centraloffice@orientblackswan.com

Other Offices
Bengaluru, Bhopal, Chennai, Guwahati, Hyderabad, Jaipur, Kolkata, Lucknow, Mumbai, New Delhi, Noida, Patna, Visakhapatnam

First published 2019

ISBN 978-93-5287-639-6

Typeset in Adobe Garamond Pro 11.5/13.5 *by*
Shine Graphics, Delhi 110 094

030153

Printed at
Yash Printographics, Noida

Published by
Orient Blackswan Private Limited
3-6-752, Himayatnagar,
Hyderabad 500 029, Telangana, India
e-mail: info@orientblackswan.com

For

PRAPHULLA

my wife of sixty years

Contents

Author's Note

The last two chapters of this book present my most recent understanding of language learning and teaching. I am grateful to Professor Geetha Durairajan for helping me to state it so clearly.

Geetha also offered to edit a collection of my various papers from past decades, mostly written for conferences, into book-form. While looking back at those papers, we both realised that a majority of them showed successive stages of continuing thought on two or three aspects of pedagogy, before coming together and coalescing in the two recently written chapters. That led to the idea of arranging the papers in chronological order.

I am very grateful to Geetha for helping to organise the book with a genuine sense of involvement and also acknowledge with gratitude the editorial assistance provided by Dr Deepesh Chandrasekharan and Mr Vikas Kadam.

I also appreciate greatly the care and quality with which Ms Padmaja Anant of Orient Blackswan has edited and managed the production of the book.

N. S. Prabhu

Editor's Note

The twenty-nine articles of this volume encapsulate a lifetime of contemplation and articulation on language pedagogy. Spanning more than half a century, Dr N. S. Prabhu's articles offer theoretical discussion, and analysis of existing situations, assumptions and practices, often leading to radical proposals for change, in successively more convergent and persuasive stages. They also offer several new concepts and associated terms, such as enabling–equipping, deployment–acquisition, cerebration–imitation, simulation–reproduction, ideation–ideology, which can lead to sharper insights into and a deeper understanding of language pedagogy. For these reasons, editing this volume has been a memorably challenging and educative experience.

Four of the articles in this collection have an academic addendum at the end, consisting of questions asked by the editor during the process of compiling this book, and answers by the author. The questions deal with some specific issues/arguments which continue to be of concern in India and happen not to be addressed either in the article concerned or elsewhere in the book.

The articles are arranged chronologically by the date of first publication (mentioned on the opening page of each article). It was decided not to try modernising matters such as gender reference, spelling and time references ('recent developments', 'last half of the century', 'in the past months') referring to time frames of twenty, thirty or even forty years ago. In-text citation references and bibliography entries have been standardised for ease of reading.

GEETHA DURAIRAJAN

Publisher's Acknowledgements

1. "Rational Approach to English Teaching." First published in *The Hindu*, 13 April 1966. © N.S. Prabhu 1966. Reproduced with permission.
2. "The Teaching of English and Notions about Communication," in *Applications of Linguistics to Language Teaching: Selected Papers from the RELC Seminar on Recent Developments in Linguistics Research Relevant to Language Teaching in Southeast Asia, Singapore*, Anthology Series 6, edited by Jack C. Richards, pp. 73–81. First published by Singapore University Press for the Southeast Asian Ministers of Education Organization (SEAMEO) Regional Language Center (RELC), 1979. Reproduced with permission of SEAMEO.
3. "Alternative Strategies in Educational Reform: An ELT Practitioner's Views," *Journal of Indian Association of Programmed Learning and Educational Innovation*, 1979, pp. 39–44. Reproduced with permission of Champa Tickoo.
4. "Procedural Syllabuses," in *Trends in Language Syllabus Design*, Anthology Series 13, edited by John A. S. Read, pp. 272–80. First published by Singapore University Press for the Southeast Asian Ministers of Education Organization (SEAMEO) Regional Language Center (RELC), 1984. Reproduced with permission of SEAMEO.
5. "Communicative Teaching: "Communicative" in What Sense?" in *Communicative Language Teaching: Selected Papers from the RELC Seminar on "Communicative Language Teaching, Singapore*, Anthology Series 14, edited by Bikram C. Das, pp. 32–40. First published by Singapore University Press for the Southeast Asian Ministers of Education Organization (SEAMEO) Regional Language Center (RELC), 1985. Reproduced with permission of SEAMEO.
6. "Coping with the Unknown in Language Pedagogy," in *English in the World: Teaching and Learning the Language and Literatures,*

edited by Randolph Quirk, H. G. Widdowson, pp. 164–73. © The British Council 1985, published by Cambridge University Press. Reproduced with permission of the copyright holder and publisher.

7. "Language Education: Equipping or Enabling?" in *Language Education in Human Resource Development,* Anthology Series 20, edited by Bikram C. Das, pp. 190–201. Published by Singapore University Press for the Southeast Asian Ministers of Education Organization (SEAMEO) Regional Language Center (RELC), 1987. Reproduced with permission of SEAMEO.
8. "A World Language in Education: Defining the Domain," in *Languages in Education in a Bilingual or Multilingual Setting,* edited by Verner Bickley, pp. 161–67. Published by Hong Kong Education Department, 1988.
9. "Materials as Support: Materials as Constraint," *Guidelines: A Periodical for Classroom Language Teachers,* vol. 11 (1), 1989, pp. 66–74. Reproduced with permission of SEAMEO.
10. "Acquisition Through Comprehension: Three Procedures," in *Focus on English 5/4.* Reproduced with permission of the British Council. This paper was also presented at TESOL Conference, Athens, Greece, April 1989. © 1989 Reprinted with permission from TESOL International Association. All rights reserved.
11. "Three Models in Second Language Pedagogy," *Journal of English and Foreign Languages,* vol. no. 3, 1989, pp. 1–14. Reproduced with permission of The English and Foreign Languages University, Hyderabad.
12. "There is no best method – Why?" *TESOL Quarterly* 24(2), 1990, pp. 161–76. Reproduced with permission of Wiley-Blackwell. A version of this paper was presented as plenary address to the 23rd annual meeting of the IATEFL held in Coventry, England, April 1989.
13. "The Learner's Effort in the Language Classroom," in *Language Acquisition and the Second/Foreign Language Classroom,* Anthology Series 28, edited by Eugenius Sadtono, pp. 49–58. First published by Singapore University Press for the Southeast Asian Ministers of

Education Organization (SEAMEO) Regional Language Center (RELC), 1991. Reproduced with permission of SEAMEO.

14. "Dynamics of the Language Lesson," *TESOL Quarterly*, 26(2), 1992, pp. 225–41. Reproduced with permission of Wiley-Blackwell.
15. "Descriptive and Prescriptive Approaches to the Norms of English in Singapore," in *The English Language in Singapore: Standards and Norms*, edited by Anne Pakir, pp. 1–5. Published by Singapore University Press, 1993.
16. "English Language as a University Discipline." This paper was presented at the Department of English Language and Literature, National University of Singapore, 1993. © N. S. Prabhu 1993.
17. "Communicative Language Teaching: Three Perceptions," *Language and Communication Review* 1, 1994, pp. 39–42.
18. "Mathetic Function of English as a World Language," *Journal of English and Foreign Languages*, no. 13 and 14 (June and December 1994). Special Issue on Pedagogical Linguistics, edited by V Prakasam, pp. 53–66. Reproduced with permission of The English and Foreign Languages University, Hyderabad.
19. "Attempting Educational Change." This lecture was delivered at the H. M. Patel Institute, Vallabh Vidyanagar, Gujarat, 1995. Reproduced with permission of Dr N. V. Bose, Principal, H. M. Patel Institute of English Training and Research.
20. "Teaching is at Most Hoping for the Best," in *Language Teaching: New Insights for the Language Teacher*, Anthology Series 40, edited by Christopher Ward and Willy Renandya, pp. 48–57. First published by Singapore University Press for the Southeast Asian Ministers of Education Organization (SEAMEO) Regional Language Center (RELC), 1999. Reproduced with permission of SEAMEO.
21. "Should Materials be Prescribed?" in *The Language Curriculum: Dynamics of Change. The Outsider Perspective: Report of the International Seminar*, vol. 1, edited by Rama Mathew, R Lalitha Eapen, Jacob Tharu, CIEFL Hyderabad, pp. 22–27. First published by Orient Blackswan Pvt Ltd., 1995. Reproduced with permission of The English and Foreign Languages University, Hyderabad.

22. "Ideation and Ideology," in *Teaching English in Non-native Contexts: Essays Presented to V. Saraswathi*, edited by S. C. Chaudhury, 2002, pp. 12–22. Chennai: Prof. V. Saraswathi Felicitation Committee. Reproduced with permission of S. C. Chaudhury.
23. "The Appropriation of ELT," *Readings: A Biannual Journal of English Studies*, 1 (2), 2003, pp. 1–10. Reproduced with permission of Rizwan Khan.
24. "Misapplied linguistics" in *Language, Context and Culture: Essays in Honour of Professor Shivendra Kumar*, edited by S. C. Chaudhury, 175–82. Published by Gurukul Publications, Lucknow, 2002. Reproduced with permission of Shradha Dwivedi.
25. "Teacher's Growth." Originally published in *Indian Voices in ELT*, edited by Francis Peter, pp. 1–6. New Delhi: Viva Books, 2012. Reproduced with permission of Viva Books.
26. "A Case Against Practice." This lecture was delivered at Asian TEFL, 4–6 October 2012 at Hotel Leela Kempinski, Gurgaon. © N.S. Prabhu 2012. Reproduced with permission.
27. "Evaluation in ELT: Six Levels." This paper is the summary of a plenary address given at the All-India Seminar 'Trends in Second Language Evaluation' in 2013 at the Regional Institute of English, Bengaluru.
28. "Rethinking Language Pedagogy." An earlier and shorter version of this interview was published in *Language and Language Teaching*, 7 (14) no. 2. Reproduced with permission of Ramakant Agnihotri.

1

Rational Approach to English Teaching

English teaching in India today presents an anomalous situation: it no longer serves the purpose which it was once designed to serve and it fails to meet the minimum needs of the new situation that has arisen since Independence.

In the past, English teaching in schools had the objective of giving a thorough grounding in the language; and English teaching in colleges was meant to enable the student to develop a style for expression, an appreciation of English literature leading to aesthetic enlightenment and the cultivation of critical judgment. To quote the Report of the English Review Committee of the University Grants Commission: "All along, in our universities, the student in the under-graduate classes was made to write essays and was taught to express himself in good English, to organise his thoughts logically, to present them clearly and to argue persuasively".

TEACHING METHODS

The schools have been aiming at the Direct Method, but for various reasons, in practice, following the Grammar and Translation Method, laying down "rules", emphasising "exceptions" and drilling through exercises. College teachers have been delivering "lectures", explaining, summarising, analysing, comparing and eulogising English classics which are invariably the textbooks. The students are expected to write essays containing logical thought and effective expression and to comment on given passages of the text revealing close study and critical ability.

This essay was first published in *The Hindu* on 13 April 1966. The author has stated that it was written before he had received any specialist training in ELT but its publication happened to lead directly to such specialisation.

The weak point of the system is that it calls for total implementation of the plan at the school as well as the college level. Indeed, the success of teaching in college depends entirely on the effective groundwork of language laid at school. If the school fails to do its work, college teaching fails entirely, neither serving its purpose nor helping to make good the deficiency in school-teaching.

Owing to a variety of causes English teaching in schools has deteriorated disastrously over the past quarter century. With the change-over to the mother-tongue as the medium of instruction, the pupil ceased to receive any help from his study of other subjects. English itself lost its importance as a subject when it became the "second language" and received fewer hours of teaching. The rapid expansion of school education in recent years has inevitably led to a deterioration of standards, including English standards. Not only are there not enough qualified teachers; the teaching profession itself has ceased to attract talented men.

When deterioration sets in, its pace is doubled by the fact that the very products of low-standard instruction—and the least talented among them in the present circumstances—come back to teaching within some five years. There is, finally, the fact that the study of English has lost its former status and importance in the public mind.

The result is alarming. College entrants can neither understand lectures delivered in English nor read with profit books written in English. Since English is largely the medium of instruction in colleges, this has a very adverse effect on their study of all subjects. A kind of pidgin English is fast evolving among the student community—English which is barely within the limits of common comprehension.

It is not surprising that, faced with this situation, students have come to depend heavily on bazaar notes, guides, etc. in the subject of English chiefly and in other humanities increasingly. What is more, lecturers themselves dictate pre-fabricated "essays" and "annotations" in a bid to make students memorise better answers than are found in printed notes and to obtain a satisfactory percentage of examination results. It is amusing that, having delivered a lecture to his students, the English lecturer hastens to dictate a prepared note on the subject of his lecture thus acknowledging to himself the futility of his lecture.

COLLEGE TEACHERS' ROLE

For this situation, most college teachers put the responsibility on defective teaching in schools. This is perhaps justifiable as far as apportioning responsibility goes. But it is not a constructive approach inasmuch as they are not doing much to set right the defect either in the interest of the students or in recognition of the fact that their own teaching is rendered entirely useless unless the language groundwork is laid firmly. Part of the reason is their inability to do the language work, for, while the teacher at school has been trained to teach English, the lecturer in college has received no training in the matter.

Added to this, there is a widespread feeling among lecturers and professors of English that their job, both by qualification and by declared objective, is lecturing on English literature, not teaching the English language. This amounts to a refusal to see facts.

The English Review Committee takes the easy way out of this controversy, "There can be no inherent conflict", it states, "between the claims of literature and those of language. Literature cannot be properly appreciated by those who do not know the English language well and the English language cannot be taught in a vacuum. In fact, the best way to teach it after the necessary structures are learned and the elementary vocabulary is acquired is through the reading of samples of good English writing in prose and verse, which will widen vocabulary and establish the structure of the language in the mind of the student".

OBJECTIVES IN VIEW

This is a harmless, theoretical position to take, although one may wonder whether "the claims of literature" are met when good prose and verse are read for the purpose of widening the vocabulary and establishing the structures in the learner's mind. One may also ask when exactly a student is expected to have "learned the necessary structures and acquired the elementary vocabulary." The Committee itself admits that "until such time as the teaching of this subject in the schools is radically re-organised and considerably improved, the universities will have to take upon themselves the task of remedying the defects in the English of the students." If the college teacher claims, that his job is to sponsor literary appreciation, there is a direct conflict between "the claims of language and those of literature" in the undergraduate class.

What is necessary is to re-define, clearly, the objectives of English teaching at each level, particularly the undergraduate level, keeping in mind both the limitations of our educational system and the changed status of English in post-Independence India. It is useless to hanker back nostalgically to a period when English enjoyed the pride of place in school and college curricula—when literary appreciation of certain classics of English literature was considered a basic necessity for the award of any degree. If English lives in future India, it will do so only as an international language which cannot be dispensed with in certain spheres of activity—knowledge of science and technology; international contacts, collaboration and diplomacy; a national medium in India itself, at least till another language is able to serve that purpose. One cannot persuade the public that literary appreciation is one such activity.

The English Review Committee itself defines the objective of English teaching quite realistically. It says: "The urgent, pressing, over-riding problem is to teach the students enough to enable them to read simple books on the one hand and to express themselves in correct English on the other." In other words, English is needed as a means to acquiring knowledge and as a tool of communication in spheres where the relevant Indian language cannot fulfill these functions. Literature itself will have to be left to the postgraduate level, though even here half the emphasis has to be on methods of teaching the English language, since most men who do the postgraduate course take up teaching at the undergraduate level. The rest of the students will have to depend on their own language for an aesthetic enjoyment of literature.

Having defined the objective, one has to find the best method of achieving it. Much good work is being done in this matter at the Central Institute of English and at various regional Institutes of English, though its impact is yet to be felt in schools and colleges generally. The structural approach, which is the most modern approach adopted in the West, seems to offer the quickest and most scientific way of achieving results. What is more, it can be geared to a given objective since the objective itself can be translated into a certain vocabulary, a certain number of structures and certain skills of comprehension and communication. Actual achievement of students in this direction can be measured and demonstrated. Further, a single expert can design a course which can be given to a large number of students by a group of teachers possessing only some knowledge of the technique. This, therefore, seems to be the method best suited to the new position of English as a tool of knowledge and communication.

WITHOUT SENTIMENT

There are, however, many hurdles to cross in its general adoption and implementation in colleges; teachers will have to undergo special training; each college will have to employ a larger number of teachers and provide a larger number of classrooms, since students have to be handled in small groups. Equipment like a duplicating machine and a tape recorder will be needed in each college.

Much sentiment—misconceived nationalism as well as misdirected attachment to English literature—has been wasted on the question of the future status of English in India. It seems time that a rational, utilitarian approach is adopted, so that objectives are clearly defined, methods are decided upon and quick steps are taken to implement a programmme. The task of retaining enough knowledge of the English language in India to serve the cause of national progress is big enough, without its being complicated by sentiment either way.

2

The Teaching of English and Notions about Communication

The following is, I think, a possible categorisation of recent developments in linguistics and their probable relevance to language-teaching:

1. *Linguistic development*: Meaning, in at least some senses of the term, can be specified independently of syntax and can be analysed with some degree of comprehensiveness.
   Pedagogic claim: It is both possible and, at least for certain purposes, desirable to design language courses in semantic, rather than structural, terms.
2. *Linguistic development*: Some aspects of language performance are, contrary to earlier belief, rule-governed, just as a large part of language structure is known to be; there is, therefore, a communicative competence distinct from grammatical competence.
   Pedagogic claim: These aspects of language performance can and need to be taught deliberately, that is to say, communicative competence does not necessarily result from an acquisition of grammatical competence.
3. *Linguistic development*: The form and order of sentences in a piece of discourse are subject to a higher-level ("rhetorical")

This essay was first published in 1979. *Source*: Prabhu, N. S. (1979). The teaching of English and notions about communication. In Jack C. Richards (Ed.), *Applications of linguistics to language teaching*, Anthology Series 6 (pp. 73–81). Singapore: Singapore University Press.

structure, just as the form and order of words in a sentence are subject to syntactic structure.

Pedagogic claim: Such discourse-structure can and needs to be taught deliberately and systematically.

The potential influence of these pedagogic claims on language-teaching practice can be viewed from three points of view: as offering alternative principles of course-construction; as extending the scope of language-instruction; and as providing a new principle of language-teaching methodology.

In contrast to the past few decades when the only meta-language available for syllabus-specification was grammar, it seems possible today—though not provenly feasible yet—to state syllabuses in terms of "notions" (as suggested by Wilkins) or particular aspects of situations such as roles, settings and themes (as indicated, for instance, by van Ek). On the face of it, this looks like little more than an exercise in novelty for novelty's sake: given the fact that there is no one-to-one correspondence between the forms of a language and the meanings/functions associated with them, one can use either the forms as the basis of systematisation of a course (thus leaving the meaning/functions to be dealt with in an essentially unsystematic progression) or use some available specification of meanings/functions as the principle of systematisation (thus leaving the forms to be dealt with in a less than systematic progression). The difference between a structural and a semantic syllabus is thus similar to that between a dictionary and a thesaurus, with neither being inclusive of (hence, superior to) the other and indeed the balance of advantage appearing to rest, in each case, with the former on the grounds of its greater specificity.

However, just as it is an advantage to have available a thesaurus as well as a dictionary and to be able to use it for certain purposes in preference to a dictionary, the availability of a principle of course organisation other than the structural is an advantage in at least certain teaching situations. For instance, there has in recent years been an increasing dissatisfaction—in countries such as India, and quite independently of the possibility of semantic syllabuses—with the degree of linguistic control (in classroom work and in coursebooks) demanded by structural syllabuses and a growing desire for a relaxation of such control. Suggestions that have been made in this connection are all in the nature of *ad hoc* modifications of the structural approach, such as an acceleration of structural progression, early structural "decontrol" in regard to reading alone, regulated use of the mother-tongue in the classroom, etc. The fact, however, is that structural "decontrol" makes little sense while the systematicity of a course is seen in terms of a structural progression: it is only when one is able to use some other principle of course-organisation that one can ignore—or relax—structural control; and a semantic syllabus can perhaps provide just such an alternative. A second, and more limited, situation where a non-structural syllabus is felt to be necessary is that of courses which are primarily revisional or remedial in nature. Learners' motivation on such courses is seen to suffer if the course looks to them like a repetition; and a different principle of organisation can, among other things, be a useful means of disguising the inevitable repetition.

A second view of the implications of recent ideas is that they enlarge the scope of language-teaching, by taking in one or both of two new areas:

i. an aspect of meaning hitherto neglected—the social meaning ("communicative value") as distinct from verbal and cognitive meaning ("signification" [Widdowson, 1971]) of language forms; and
ii. a level of structure not systematically taught in the past—rhetorical (as distinct from syntactic) structure.

The former can conceivably be brought in within the framework of a structural syllabus and will probably be of special importance where there is a high priority on learners being able to use the language in social—especially oral—interaction, while the latter represents a stage of learning beyond the structural and is particularly relevant where reading and writing (for academic or professional purposes) are among the chief aims. Both have resulted from new insights about language use, and have brought about a widening of our view of what is involved in successful language-acquisition. Explorations in rhetorical structure have, in particular, indicated possible answers to two existing questions in language-teaching. First, the attractive concept of English for Specific Purposes (especially English for Science and Technology) led, as we know, to a search for features of language peculiar to particular fields of activity, but the results produced, in terms of structural and lexical items, have been neither very illuminating nor very usable. As Widdowson's work has shown (1973), the search promises to be much more revealing and usable when one investigates the rhetorical structure of different types of text. Secondly, there has always been an awkward gap—felt widely though acknowledged only occasionally—between controlled practice of sentences and free use of the language by the learner: when the language teacher felt ready to lift syntactic and lexical controls (in, say, the reading texts and writing tasks on a course), he assumed that learners were then ready to read and write freely and competently; and if he found that they weren't, he moved back to syntactic and lexical controls. The frequency with which such retracing of steps occurred suggested that some essential part of language-ability was being missed out in the pedagogic process, but there was no clear identification of the ability involved. It looks plausible now that what was being missed was the ability to handle rhetorical structure and, further, that a stage of teaching organised in terms of rhetorical structure can provide a much-needed bridge between linguistic control and complete freedom.

A third possible consequence of recent ideas has to do with language-teaching methodology, in the narrow sense of classroom procedures and techniques, as distinct from the scope and organisation of courses. The basic proposal that is made here is that classroom interaction should possess certain essential features of real-life communication such as

i. a genuine information gap between speaker/writer and hearer/reader,

ii. perceived options and deliberate choices between alternative linguistic formulations,
iii. a consequence to the choice made in terms of success in communication (and not merely in terms of teacher's approval or disapproval), and
iv. arising from these factors, an element of challenge to the learner's mind and a sense of achievement in successful performance.

What is envisaged, in general, is a preoccupation, on the learner's part, with meaning (or "message") rather than with forms of language as such. It is to achieve these aims that forms of classroom activity such as games, simulations and role-play are currently receiving renewed attention. Such techniques differ from the ones favoured in the past in important respects such as that the heavy premium placed so far on "correctness" (of language) now shifts largely to success in communication, and that past emphasis on the prevention of errors is now replaced by a concern to make the learner perceive the consequence of errors. It is possible that we shall discover a number of limitations on the feasibility of the new techniques—they seem to demand, for instance, a much smaller class-size and a much higher level of teacher's proficiency in the language than the structural approach did—but they do represent, I think, a genuine new strategy in language-teaching and are likely to influence, if not replace, present procedures in significant ways.

This view of recent proposals as constituting a methodological innovation receives further support when we attempt to relate those proposals to felt needs of a more general kind, in countries (such as India) where English is widely taught as a part of the formal educational systems.

What recorded evidence we have of actual implementation of the proposals comes at present from situations in which adult learners who had already had years of instruction in English (within the older pedagogic framework) were receiving a further course in the language in a native-speaker environment (for example, Essex,

Lancaster, Reading). The fact that such further instruction was needed at all has been taken to confirm the view that grammatical competence is not enough for learners, while such success as has been claimed for those courses seems to show the merit of the new approach. The question that arises, however, is: do these experiments imply that teaching for communicative competence is subsequent to successful teaching for grammatical competence? Or do they have implications for the process by which grammatical competence itself is sought to be imparted, to millions of young learners in, say, the Asian countries? A few instances have been pointed out above where some of the new proposals promise to meet some of the felt needs within a structural framework, but the general question of how fundamental and widely applicable the new ideas are remains.

Notice that most of the expressed dissatisfaction with structural syllabuses and audio-lingual classroom procedures is not that learners, after mastering the grammatical structure, fail to communicate successfully but that many learners fail to acquire the grammatical system itself. Even when one hears complaints about students' weaknesses in English from, say, teachers of science and technology or from employers, one finds that the evidence cited is nearly all in the form of grammar (or spelling) errors. It is of course possible that one's pre-occupation with grammatical errors prevents one from seeing other types of deficiency, but even on the new-concept courses referred to above at British universities—where the perspective was not grammatical—a component of remedial grammar often seems to have been found necessary. Notice now that all proposals for teaching communicative competence involve less attention to, and a less systematic teaching of, grammatical structure than in the past (since course-organisation as well as classroom technique are now guided by considerations other than grammar). We thus have something of a paradoxical situation as follows:

a. Courses based on grammatical structure often fail to achieve their aim of imparting grammatical competence.

b. It is now realised that learners need to go beyond grammatical competence to acquire communicative competence.
c. Teaching for communicative competence necessarily involves a less systematic teaching of grammatical structure (and therefore appears less likely to succeed in imparting grammatical competence).

It is this anomaly, I think, which ELT practitioners in ESL/EFL countries find disturbing in considering recent approaches. Arguments such as that "linguistic competence is, in general, a part of communicative competence" and that, therefore, "we would be well-advised to focus on communicative skills, in the knowledge that this will necessarily involve developing most areas of linguistic competence as an essential part of the product" (Allwright, 1976, p. 3) do not seem to me to face the issue—(i) that there is, in Wilkins' words, "a lack of congruence between grammatical and semantic systems" (1976, p. 66) and (ii) consequently, organisation of teaching in terms of one of these systems involves a corresponding sacrifice of systematicity in terms of the other. Nor can I take seriously the view that grammatical competence is relatively unimportant because "good communicators with a poor command of English may be better able to cope with communication problems in English than fluent speakers who are poor comunicators" (Allwright, p. 10) or because "some occasions call for being appropriately ungrammatical" (Hymes,1972, p. 60): the evidence pointed to here is anecdotally true but does not sustain the generalisation made (or implied). Wilkins seems to me right in insisting that "the acquisition of the grammatical system of a language remains a most important element of any language learning" and that "an inadequate knowledge of the grammar would lead to a serious limitation on the capacity for communication" (p. 66).

Some suggestions have appeared in the literature on possible ways of reconciling grammatical and semantic organisations—for instance, (i) using a grammatical syllabus in the early stages, and introducing a semantic organisation in later—"post-intermediate" stages, (ii) merely increasing the weight given to semantic criteria in ordering grammatical items (even in the early stages) (Wilkins, p. 66), or even (iii) making no change in the grammatical syllabus but ensuring that teaching in the classroom goes beyond the "signification" of the item being dealt with to take in its communicative value, employing appropriate techniques (Johnson, 1977). I think there is a basic pedagogic claim, made hesitantly, in such proposals, that the linguistic code is learnt better if, in the process of learning it, learners' attention is not on the code itself but on some problem of meaning or message involving the use of the code. There is a parallel here to the essential pedagogic claim that was involved in the earlier transition from language teaching through rules of grammar to merely the presentation and practice of (sets of) similar sentences: the claim was that the rules of grammar are learnt ("internalised") better if, in the process of learning them, learners' attention is not on the rules but on the actual forms which exemplify them. As a result, teaching based on structural syllabuses concentrated attention on (selected and ordered) forms, in association with their lexis- and syntax-based meanings, using explicit analysis only incidentally, minimally and less systematically than in earlier practice. What is being claimed now is not only that one should teach "meanings" other than those derivable from lexis and syntax but—in a way comparable to the earlier claim—that the forms (and their interrelationships) will themselves be learnt better if the teaching concentrates on these other meanings, paying only incidental, minimal and, of necessity, much less systematic attention to the forms as such. There is thus, from this point of view, a progression from explicit grammar (in the classroom) to exemplificatory forms alone to meaning and use—from a direct learning of the theory (grammar) to its indirect acquisition through evidence to an indirect perception of the evidence itself through meaning-centred activity.

To the extent this claim is justified, recent proposals in language-teaching can be seen to contain an important pedagogic insight, fundamental in nature (since it concerns one's concept of how a language is best learnt) and very general in applicability.

The new principles of course-organisation and syllabus-specification mentioned above can now be judged or justified by one overriding criterion, namely, how far they facilitate, or constitute a necessary condition to, the new methodology. Further, the consequence of employing such non-structural modes of organisation, a sacrifice of systematicity in teaching the grammatical structure, can be seen to be more apparent than real (in the light of the claim that the forms themselves are better learnt in the process). All this, of course, puts a high stake on the validity of the pedagogic claim, and although one finds in the literature an occasional assertion of such validity, based on experimental teaching, one also finds, along with it, some degree of hesitation or some form of alibi. Thus, Richard Allwright asserts that "communication practice can be expected to develop linguistic skills" and that "if the language-teacher's management of activities is directed exclusively in involving the learners in solving communication problems in the target language, then language-learning will take care of itself" (1976, p. 5). He also suggests, elsewhere in the same paper, that "the strain on most learners will be considerable if they are faced with the twin problems of developing linguistic accuracy and achieving communicative self-confidence" and that, therefore, "it would seem more helpful to concentrate on developing their communicative ease first…and thus to clear the way for a subsequent development of such linguistic accuracy as they may desire" (p. 11). One therefore needs more unqualified evidence—based perhaps on larger-scale projects—in support of the claim, but there seems no reason at present to suppose it implausible, or any less likely to be true than the earlier claim cited above as a parallel. Indeed, the "ring of truth" one often finds in statements of the new proposals arises, I think, from a shared pedagogic instinct in the profession about the truth of the claim. At any rate, it seems to me important that we see the claim clearly and realise that

a. if it is justified
    i. recent proposals in language-teaching contain, most essentially, a new methodological insight, and

ii. for that reason, they have relevance to language-teaching at all stages and in all places;

and

b. if it is not justified,

i. recent proposals are relevant only to later stages of language-teaching and only for certain specific purposes;

ii. they have little to offer on one of our persistent problems, namely, that of remedial teaching to improve learners' grammatical competence; and

iii. their application at a stage of teaching where the linguistic code has not yet been mastered by learners is likely to hamper the mastery of the linguistic code—and thus aggravate the problems of remedial teaching.

References

Allwright, Richard. (1976). Language learning through communication practice. *ELT Documents*, 76(3), 3–15.

Hymes, D. H. (1972). On communicative competence. In J. B. Pride and J. Holmes (Eds.), *Sociolinguistics* (pp. 269–94). New York: Penguin Books.

Johnson, Keith. (1977). Adult beginners: A functional or just a communicative approach? Paper presented at the BAAL Annual General Meeting, at University of Essex, Colchester.

van Ek, J. A. (1975). *The threshold level.* Strasbourg: The Council of Europe.

Widdowson, H. G. (1971). The teaching of rhetoric to students of science and technology. *CILT Reports and Papers*, 7, 31–41.

Widdowson, H. G. (1973). An applied linguistic approach to discourse analysis. Ph.D. Diss., University of Edinburgh.

Wilkins, D. A. (1976). *Notional syllabuses.* Oxford: Oxford University Press.

3

Alternative Strategies in Educational Reform: An ELT Practitioner's Views

The purpose of this paper is to examine two alternative strategies of educational reform from the point of view of their potential impact. The discussion is done with specific reference to English Language Teaching (ELT) in India, but the general argument is likely to be relevant to other programmes of instructional reform as well.

The two strategies may broadly be called Direct Contact and Remote Control, respectively. Essentially, the Direct Contact strategy seeks to influence every element in the educational system—teacher, syllabus, textbook, examination—discretely, hoping thereby for a cumulative effect amounting to overall change. In particular—and, in practice, most often—it concentrates effort on teacher-training (or re-training) and treats the reconstruction of syllabuses, course-materials and examinations as additional effort meant to support the trained teacher. The Remote Control strategy, in contrast, attempts to identify the most crucial element in the system and to manipulate it in such a way that the other elements are automatically influenced and the system as a whole begins to change in the desired direction. Direct Control here does not necessarily mean face-to-face interaction between reform-designer and classroom-teacher: a tiered system of teacher-orientation (for example,

---

This essay was first published in 1979. *Source*: Prabhu, N. S. (1979). Alternative strategies in educational reform: an ELT practitioner's views. *Journal of the Indian Association of Programmed Learning and Educational Innovation*, 3, 39–44.

designer to resource person to teacher-trainer to classroom-teacher) would also be a form of the Direct Control strategy.

Let us now relate this to ELT reform in India. There has, over the past twenty years, been considerable organised effort in bringing about better teaching of English in our schools and colleges. Between 1956 and 1966, ten specialist ELT Institutes—at the national, regional and state levels—were established by the central and state governments; from 1965, summer courses for teachers of English have been conducted every year at a number of places in the country; fixed-duration "campaigns" and "crash programmes" (for example, the Madras English Language Teaching Campaign, 1959–63; the Bridge Intensive Course Programme, 1966–1970) have been attempted from time to time, with the aim of retraining every teacher at a certain level (for example, Primary School, Pre-University) in a certain geographical area (for example, a State; a University) within a relatively short period; and extension centres in various forms have been set up by ELT Institutes to spread the teacher-training effort and to multiply the number of teachers trained. There have also been several recommendations (at state and national levels) on desirable syllabuses, as well as a few actual syllabuses and a number of innovative coursebooks. Two large Study Groups, constituted by the Government of India, have produced elaborate reports on the question, not to mention the much larger number of committees, seminars and conferences. British specialists in the subject have been brought to India to assist with teacher training or textbook production, either on short courses or on longer-term attachment to important institutions; and Indian teachers have been sent to Britain or the US for further training in ELT or linguistics.

The broad strategy involved in all this effort is what we have called Direct Contact, analysable further as involving three main approaches:

i. *exhortation* (that is, reports and recommendations; incentives such as financial grants and academic degrees;

the use of experts on committees or Boards of Studies; pronouncements of most so-called 'seminars' etc);

ii. *dissemination of expertise* (that is, teacher-training; resource-person training; campaigns and crash programmes; the publication of journals and monographs, etc); and

iii. *the production of tools* (that is, new syllabuses and coursebooks; radio lessons and tapes meant for learners; localised or low-cost teaching aids, etc).

The result of this strategy—in terms of its ultimate objective, viz. improved teaching and learning in the classrooms—is at best ambiguous. Thus, the total number of teachers trained in India (with varying degrees of sophistication) is said to be over a hundred thousand but that is barely a third of the actual number of people in the profession, and there is very little evidence to show that those trained teachers are in fact teaching the language better—or any differently from others—in the classrooms. Specialist ELT Institutes repeatedly complain that their expertise is not adequately used, and their advice not sufficiently heeded, by Education Departments and Universities. New syllabuses and coursebooks, even when they are accepted and 'prescribed' by the authorities at the top, are frequently distorted or misused in the classroom either because teachers are uninformed or (more importantly) because there is not enough motivation for teachers, learners and academic bodies to counteract the other influences in the system, a variety of vested interests and the sheer weight of tradition. Radio lessons are broadcast more and more widely but the people who prepare them also complain that the lessons are not listened to or made use of in the way intended. More disturbingly, plans and projects for future work seem to seek, on the one hand, an expansion of the same kind of work as done hitherto (for example, larger-scale teacher-training to cover all teachers) and, on the other, various

> elements of compulsion (for example, making the training obligatory for certain posts) or incentives (for example, increments or promotions to trained teachers) to reinforce it, thus neglecting the question of whether such work is in fact the best strategy for achieving results and ignoring available evidence that it probably is not.

Why is this strategy proving so disappointing in its result? First, because what is being offered (viz. the advice, the expertise, and the tools) is not essential for the education system to keep itself going. That system is a self-contained one where, whatever the quality of teaching and real success in learning, an acceptable percentage of students pass the examination and receive public certification. It does not matter to the teacher whether he teaches well or badly, since the system itself defines teaching merely in terms such as meeting the class so many times a week, and views success in terms of examination passes, which it takes care, by various means, to maintain at a socially acceptable level. A pragmatic teacher, therefore, does in the classroom what it is easiest for him to do, and the pragmatic learner takes the shortest route he can to examination passing. What the Direct Contact strategy attempts to do is to counter pragmatism with idealism—to urge the teacher to make an additional effort in teaching which he does not have to, which his learners do not see the need for and which examination-passing does not call for. Secondly, (and relatedly) there is no recognisable relationship between success in examinations and real-life abilities—which is what enables the system to maintain examination results at a certain level irrespective of the equality of teaching and learning. There is, that is to say, no proficiency level in English which the society recognises or demands in, say, every school leaver or every graduate that comes out of the system. This is evident—if evidence were needed—from the fact that those employers who seriously demand certain levels of proficiency in their recruits have for some time now been administering their own tests of proficiency to applicants, thus declaring their lack of faith in the certification done by the educational system.

What we have here is something of a double paradox, as follows:

1. Teaching takes place in the educational system because learners wish to obtain public certification; and they wish to have such certificates because they hope to get employment on the strength of it.
2. But the educational system is unable to maintain a constant relationship between its certification and real ability; and the employer who demands real ability has started ignoring public certification.
3. Yet, the educational system rejects reforms in teaching because it is by now used to public certification unrelated to ability and can afford to regard reform as inessential idealism.

It is this paradox that suggests to us a different strategy for reform, on the lines of what we have called Remote Control. Suppose that we evolve a new system of public certification (based on proficiency-tests), which is unrelated to any course of instruction, but which does reflect actual ability. Suppose, further, that this new certification proves its merit and gets accepted by employers—at least in those fields of employment where there is a serious insistence on proficiency and where, as it happens, the more desirable jobs lie—as being a more reliable guide than school and university certificates. Learners in schools and colleges will then wish to acquire the new certification and will inevitably begin to judge the years they spend at an educational institution by their usefulness in achieving that objective; and that will force the educational system to model its certification on the new system and, more importantly, to look for ways of imparting the proficiency required for the purpose. What the ELT specialists have to offer will then be eagerly examined, tried out and accepted, as essential and important from a purely pragmatic point of view; and if what is offered is either unsound or inadequate (as shown by results in relation to the new objective), the system itself will undertake exploration and experimentation—as large industries undertake research relevant to their activity—

to find or develop a more efficient pedagogy and to have its teachers trained in it.

The difference between current strategy in ELT reform and the one just proposed can perhaps be brought out best through a parallel, having to do with driving licenses. Driving instructors (or driving schools) prepare learners for a driving test which leads to a public certification of those who succeed in it. Driving schools are naturally interested in the most effective and economical means of teaching people to drive, since it is only those who have acquired the ability to drive that can succeed in the test. Suppose now that there is some collusion between driving schools and the authorities that administer the driving test, with the result that the schools are able to ensure the success of an acceptable number of its students regardless of how proficient they have become in driving. This will mean first, that the driving test and the resultant license no longer reflect real ability in driving; and, secondly, that the driving schools are no longer interested in efficient techniques of imparting driving ability. Traffic accidents will of course increase alarmingly and the government—or enlightened public bodies—will wish to do something about it. They now have two alternative strategies available: (a) to exhort driving schools to improve their courses, to train (or retrain) an increasing number of instructors, and to make available useful manuals or aids in driving instruction; or (b) to set up a new driving test which will really assess driving and certify only those who possess that ability. The first is a Direct Contact strategy, which is likely to be looked on as a piece of inessential idealism by driving schools since they do not need it to obtain public certification for their students. The second is a Remote Control strategy, which—given that the new driving test is really reliable and receives public recognition as such—will force driving schools to look for better techniques of instruction and will motivate them to accept what expertise is offered—or to develop it on their own.

One can of course argue that the second strategy can achieve its objective by reforming the existing test in driving, instead of setting up a new test and, by analogy, that the Remote Control strategy in ELT should concentrate on improving existing examinations rather than setting up a new examination system. This is true in principle—and does not affect the contrast made here between the two strategies—but facts such as the multiplicity of existing examination bodies, the firmly established links between their examinations and courses of instruction, the habitual resistance of these systems to change in any of their aspects all suggest that a new system of examination and certification might be easier and more effective. After all, such systems already exist in areas such as secretarial skills (for example, typing and shorthand), accounting skills (for example, Chartered Accountancy) engineering skills (for example, AMIE) and, internationally, in English (for example, the Cambridge Certificate in English).

It will no doubt be a difficult task to set up the suggested system of testing and certification—both professionally (to ensure that the tests in fact measure real proficiency) and logistically (to make sure that they acquire the kind of prestige that the CA or the AMIE tests have done). However, the existing operation in ELT reform, briefly described earlier in this paper, would hardly have been possible on that scale if the country did not possess at least a hardcore of high-quality expertise and did not regard ELT as a matter of national importance. What is called for by the Remote Control strategy suggested here, therefore, is merely a fruitful redeployment of existing expertise and public commitment. Further, the number of high-quality professionals required for this operation is incomparably smaller than the number needed and deployed in the existing operation; and the quality of the entire operation will now derive directly from that small number of good professionals, instead of depending, as at present, on the varying quality of a large army of "experts" at different levels. The money and physical facilities needed will also, of course be only a fraction of those already employed in the Direct Contact Operation.

There is also a genuine professional advantage to the Remote Control strategy, in comparison with the Direct Contact strategy. Approaches such as exhortation, dissemination and tool-production demand, by their very nature, insistence on a certain fixed pedagogy, its repeated justification before different audiences and, almost inevitably a certain degree of professional dogmatism and rigidity of outlook, which are all harmful to a field of activity—perhaps any field of activity—where openness, experimentation and continual refinement of techniques are the only guarantee against obsolescence or prolonged misdirection. The Remote Control strategy, on the other hand, throws the possibility of innovation and experimentation wide open: every teacher of English is now not only free but positively motivated (from what to him is a purely pragmatic interest, viz. enabling learners to acquire the new certification) to examine, experiment with or develop what seem likely to be—and in practice prove to be—the most effective techniques of teaching, unhampered by dogma or some official policy. What the Remote Control strategy will thus do is to tap the inventiveness and imagination of every individual engaged in teaching English, instead of seeking to impose the faith of a few (viz. the experts) on all the rest as the Direct Contact strategy does.

There are two tendencies to guard against in educational reform. First, it tends to be assumed that the most obvious and direct means are also the most effective in achieving an objective. If teaching is to improve, teachers have to be trained first; and this seems so obvious that all other less obvious possibilities escape one's attention. Secondly—and somewhat paradoxically—the largeness of a task seems to make it all the more attractive to the reformer. It is, by any account, a stupendous task to train all the 4,00,000 teachers of English (on a rough estimate) in the country, and this fact gives the task a very challenging nature—indeed, promotes it from no more than a possible means to an absolute objective by itself. A periodical exercise in standing back and weighing the larger options can be a useful corrective to both tendencies.

***GD:** In this article written nearly three decades ago, you have made the case for a 'remote control strategy' to improve ELT in India through proficiency testing. Today, there have been international and national forays into this domain.*

However, we do not have a pan Indian test of English proficiency yet. What do we need to do to make this a reality?

A related question is about proficiency level descriptors. Most descriptors construe all four skills at the same level, but we find that Indians are able to comprehend spoken and written texts at a much higher level than what they are able to produce. What would be a solution to this dilemma?

NSP: This paper was written at a time when I was vaguely thinking of the Bangalore Project, and my concept of proficiency then was the ability to say what one wants to say in the language, with the mind occupied with meaning/content, not the language itself. I was dissatisfied with a language being taught, learnt and tested, all with attention on the language itself.

Since the Bangalore Project was about getting learners occupied with comprehension, that is, with meaning/content, and to absorb the language in that process, there was no longer a wide difference between language learning and language using: using was, instead, direct evidence of success in learning. That is to say, task-based language teaching is meant to develop the ability which will manifest itself in a task-based test—both processes being meaning-focussed. It is when learning is not task-based (that is, not meaning-focussed) that we need the 'Alternative Strategy'.

Task-based testing can be used to get evidence on levels of comprehension and production separately and, from the latter, evidence of the level of internal grammar-construction arrived at. As a big bonus, the evidence will all be genuine, since it will all be focused on given meaning/content, not predictable or 'muggable'.

4

Procedural Syllabuses

This paper is in two parts. The first is a discussion of two different perspectives on language-acquisition and their implications for a language-teaching syllabus. The second part is a description of a teaching experiment based on one of the two perspectives.

A syllabus can be seen to have either or both of two major roles. It is, on the one hand, an articulation of what is intended to be taught and, on the other, an indication of what is proposed to be done in the classroom. In its first role, the syllabus is an analysis of the objectives or content of teaching and may be said to be product based. This is of interest essentially to educational administrators and perhaps to the public. In its second role, by contrast, the syllabus is a specification of the means envisaged for achieving those objectives and may therefore be said to be process-based. This is essentially a form of guidance to classroom teachers and writers of course materials. It is of course, possible to take the view that only the first of the two roles, viz. specification of what is to be taught, is the proper function of a syllabus and that what is to be done in the classroom is a matter of methodology; but that assumes, rather than ensures, compatibility between syllabus and methodology. It is much more useful, I think, to relate the two roles of a syllabus to relevant perspectives on language acquisition and to ask which of those roles is primary for a given perspective and how the other can then be made compatible with it.

One perspective on language acquisition—the one that has been dominant in the past half-century—is that it is a process

---

This essay was first published in 1984. *Source*: Prabhu N. S. (1984). Procedural syllabuses.In John A. S. Read (Ed.), *Trends in Language Syllabus Design*, Anthology Series 13 (pp. 272–80). Singapore: Singapore University Press.

of successive input-assimilation and that the sequence in which inputs are assimilated can be determined or manipulated by the teacher. This is the belief that supports a structural syllabus—or any syllabus (including a notional/functional one) which envisages the teaching of pre-selected language-items in particular lessons. It makes us concentrate on the analysis, selection and organisation of content—that is to say, on the specification and sequencing of inputs. The principles which guide that organisation may be varied: for a structural syllabus as such, the guiding principles are systematicity and increasing complexity, implying the belief that what is perceived to be systematic is learnt more easily; while, for a functional or "communicative" syllabus, the organising principles are economy and perceptible need, implying beliefs such as that what is found to be useful is learnt more efficiently. There are also, of course, methodological consequences—resulting at least in a difference in emphasis—to adopting a structural or a functional syllabus, but both kinds of syllabus have the fundamental similarity that they look on language acquisition as a planned process of input-assimilation. They both rely on the validity of the equation: What is taught = what is (or ought to be) learnt.

Given this view of language acquisition, the primary function of a syllabus is indeed to specify what is to be taught and in what order; and all syllabuses which are stated in terms of components of language structure (whether or not solely in those terms) are, from this point of view, product-based. What is to be done in the classroom is then a matter of applying a given methodology to the syllabus.

A quite different perspective on language acquisition is that it is a process of organic development, furthered by effort by the learner to deploy his communicative resources—that acquisition takes place, not through planned assimilation, but through *ad hoc* deployment. This view denies that the sequence in which different parts of language structure are acquired can either be determined or manipulated by the teacher—indeed it does not consider it useful at all to look on language acquisition as a matter of assimilating one piece of input at a time. It also denies the equation between what is taught and what is learnt and holds instead that what is learnt at any given point is both unpredictable and nearly always, imperceptible. It does believe that there is a system to language-structure and that language-acquisition involves the construction of a grammar by the learner but it does not accept that particular models and descriptions of language structure produced by linguists (and simplified in various ways for pedagogic purposes) can be taken to be isomorphic with what is acquired—or, more importantly, be usefully employed to guide the learner in his grammar-construction.

Stated thus, this view may appear to be unacceptably radical and unsupported by past experience or the instincts of fellow-professionals. It is, however, possible to see it as the cumulative outcome of the major ideas and insights that have emerged in the last fifteen years or so, as a reaction to the structural approach. That deployment leads to acquisition is, I think, a part of the instinct, though articulated differently, behind Widdowson's distinction between "use" and "usage" and it is much more directly related to Brumfit's emphasis on the need for and value of fluency activity in language teaching. I take the professional—as distinct from the commercial—perceptions that led to the ESP movement to be a vague awareness of the value of deployment for acquisition, and one can easily point to both interlanguage studies and second-language acquisition research in the US (for example, Krashen's distinction between learning and acquisition) as forms of evidence that generally support the view. Indeed one can go right back to the days (for example, of Harold Palmer) when language was asserted to be a matter of skill rather than of knowledge and see in that assertion a first perception of the importance of deployment for language-acquisition. What prevented the pursuit of that perception at that time was, I think, the roughly simultaneous realisation that language-structure can be reduced to a systematic inventory and that systematicity in input-assimilation was therefore feasible. The result was a syllabus and a methodology which were in tension rather than in harmony: the methodology called for situations of naturalistic deployment while the syllabus called for linguistic manipulation of classroom discourse in a way that reduced deployment to repetition, recall or cued response.

If we wish to bring about acquisition through deployment, we have to focus not on what language to teach at this point or that, but on how to cause deployment in the classroom and how to ensure that the deployment that takes place is genuine. A precondition for genuine deployment is mind-engagement and the resultant need to communicate—a genuine preoccupation with understanding, thinking out, doing or saying something. The focus here for the course-designer is entirely on what to do in the classroom, not on what (piece of language) to teach; and the only syllabus that is compatible with such teaching and can be supportive to it is a specification not of language-items but of kinds of classroom activity—that is to say, a process-based syllabus. I am calling such syllabuses procedural syllabuses and will describe, in the rest of this paper, an attempt to evolve and try out such a syllabus.

The Communicational Teaching Project in South India started in June 1979 and has involved the regular teaching by the project team of particular classes of children in ordinary, mother-tongue medium schools. Seven classes have so far been taught for durations of fifteen months to three years, the classes themselves representing different levels (first year to fourth year of English), age-groups (seven-year-olds to fifteen-year-olds) and environments (for example, rural as well as urban schools, government as well as missionary schools). The total number of lessons taught so far is about 1,350, though no single class of children has been taught more than about 275 lessons. The state education authorities support the project as an interesting experiment but have not so far examined the possibility of any large-scale implementation of its outcome. Indeed the project team wishes to continue the project for at least a year more—hence a total of five years—before any recommendations are thought of on the strength of it. The project team consists of six teacher-trainers at the school level, two tertiary-level teachers, two staff of the British Council in Madras and five teachers from different schools: fifteen persons in all. In the first two years of the project, detailed reports on the teaching done were made available to anyone interested in the form of a series of newsletters, and an annual review seminar has been held at the end of each year's teaching.

The main hypothesis of the experiment is that language-structure is best acquired when the learner's attention is on meaning—when, that is to say, the learner is preoccupied with understanding, working out, relating or conveying messages, and copes in the process, as well as he can, with the language involved. This coping—or deployment—is seen to be central to the process of language-acquisition—that is, grammar-construction by the learner—and any attempt to guide that process more directly (and whether or not explicitly) is rejected as being unprofitable and probably harmful. There is therefore no syllabus in terms of vocabulary or structure, no pre-selection of language items for any given lesson or activity and no stage in the lesson when language-items are practised or sentence-production as such is demanded. The basis of each lesson is a problem or a task, and the conduct of the lesson consists of setting the task, demonstrating ways of tackling it and in the process giving some pupils a chance to attempt it, then getting all pupils to attempt it and finally giving each pupil a rough indication of the measure of his or her success. In practice this means using two closely similar tasks in a lesson—the first (which we call a pre-task) for public, collective handling (by the teacher as necessary but by some of the learners as well) and the second for each pupil's individual effort. The functions of the pre-task are to make known the nature of the task, to let the language relevant to it come into play, to allow some pupils to learn from attempts made by others to tackle it, to indicate criteria of success and the forms in which solutions are to be stated and, finally, to allow the teacher to assess the difficulty of the task for the class and if necessary to modify it quickly to the extent possible.

The function of the task is to bring about a sustained period of self-reliant effort by the learners (whether successful or not) to achieve a clearly perceived goal, viz. success on the task. Tasks consist of such things as: interpreting a schedule, a map or a set of rules; giving a set of directions; deciding which statement/action is right and why; making travel arrangements; drawing pictures from instructions; inferring where something must have happened or who something was done by; and working out where it is cheaper to buy certain things. Tasks of the same kind (for example, instructions for drawing) are called a task sequence and there is a rough, subjective grading of tasks by complexity within the same sequence. Not all tasks in the same sequence are, however, done in a single row of lessons; different task sequences interrupt each other, so that only about five consecutive lessons are based, at any stage of the teaching, on tasks of the same kind. To give one example, tasks based on the map of a village may be as follows:

1. Finding and describing location of places (where is the bus stop? the hospital?);
2. Marking new places on the map from a description of their locations;
3. Finding and stating the best route for someone to go from one place to another;
4. Deciding on the best form of transport (bus, auto-rickshaw, walk) for someone (from the point of view of cost or time);
5. Deciding on the need for new bus routes or roads;
6. Making choices between alternative sites for a new hospital, school or post office.

The choice of task for a given class is subject to the condition that it should present a reasonable challenge to learners. A task is unsuitable if its challenge is so low that success does not seem to learners to represent an achievement. A task is also unsuitable if its challenge is so high that learners do not see success as a possibility. A suitable task is one on which success seems to learners to be difficult but attainable—whether or not they succeed in it in the actual event. In practice, of course, the teacher can learn only by trial and error to assess the challenge of a task and its suitability for the class—and this was especially true of the teaching done on the project in the first year. A rough measure of reasonable challenge for us is that at least half the class should be successful with at least half the task. Tasks which proved suitable for one class have been reused with others, in the past four years, and we now have a repertoire of about 400 tasks which have proved generally suitable for two or more classes.

A part of the challenge of a task is, of course, the level of language use which it demands and the teacher takes this into consideration both in choosing the task and in using it in the classroom. A possible task may be avoided because it involves linguistic formulations which are predictably beyond the learner's ability to process; and even when a task is chosen as being linguistically feasible, the teacher has to simplify his language as necessary when he uses it in the classroom. This is not planned language control in the classroom, of the kind envisaged under the Structural Approach—that is, the teacher's language to be confined to the language items he has taught so far and the item or items he is teaching now. The simplification used in conducting a task is similar to that used by any speaker of a language when he has to communicate with someone whose language-competence is lower than his. It is responsive to actual need, regulated by ongoing evidence and is of a kind which all language users seem to be able to exercise when necessary.

Explicit attention to language as such in the course of the teaching is entirely incidental. Grammatically incorrect responses from learners are accepted for their content but often restated by the teacher; spelling is corrected when things are written on the blackboard; errors in learners' scripts are corrected, to the extent possible, but ignored in assessing the scripts themselves. In general such incidental correction is comparable to that which occurs in the classroom in the teaching of subjects other than language. No attempt is made at any stage to tackle an error—through explanation, paradigmatic illustration or an exercise for the whole class.

The tasks used are nearly always those that call for a little thinking, relating or working out. The presentation of tasks is done both orally and in writing, within the same cycle, orally presented tasks generally preceding those presented in writing. The teaching aids used are confined to those which can be expected to be available in most Indian schools—blackboard, chalk, paper and pencil.

The principle of acquisition through deployment would seem to imply that learners ought to have acquired some competence in the language—that is to say, they have to have something to deploy—before the principle can be applied. This would mean that a procedural syllabus and methodology could be used only with post-initial learners, not with beginners. Indeed, the classes selected for teaching in the first two years of the project were all in their fourth year of English, which seemed to reinforce that conclusion. However, a class of beginners was in fact taken up for teaching in the third year of the project and two other classes of beginners were added to it in the fourth year. It was clear, in teaching beginners, that although they had little or no linguistic resource in the target language to deploy, they had a range of other communicative resources (for example, guessing, gestures, mother-tongue, actions) whose deployment easily led to the acquisition of some target-language resource—that there was, from the point of view of communicative resources, no 'zero-level' at all. We have therefore found this approach as feasible with beginners as with post-initial learners.

The aim of the project has been both to develop a new approach to English-teaching in India and to test it out in the classroom. We are able to say with some confidence now that communicational teaching does represent a new approach, with its own principles, procedures and now a body of tested material. The pedagogic hunch with which the project team started has been steadily strengthened in the course of the teaching and classroom experience has led to increasing clarity and conviction in the evolving methodology. Evidence of progress in learning—in terms of learners' ability to handle increasingly complex tasks—has been uniformly encouraging and learners' interest in the classroom has been surprisingly high, in varied circumstances and over long stretches of teaching. Beginners have, at the end of about a hundred lessons, been able to tackle tasks which were appropriately challenging to fourth-year learners in the normal school system; and when project classes have, after a year or two's teaching by the project team, gone back to the normal teaching in the school, teachers at the school have remarked on the clear advantage they had over their peers. The project team has not, however, attempted a formal evaluation which can yield quantified outcomes; nor have there been any control groups to compare the project classes with, other than the existing classes in the schools concerned. A seminar on possibilities for a formal evaluation was held in Madras in March 1983 and some proposals have emerged from it for use over the next twelve months.

Communicational teaching cannot use a language syllabus since that would be unprofitable and, indeed, detrimental to desired forms of teaching. A semantic (or "functional") syllabus would be equally detrimental if the semantic categorisation were a means of selecting and grouping relevant language items—and a needless distraction if they weren't. The only form of syllabus which is compatible with and can support communicational teaching seems to be a purely procedural one—which lists, in more or less detail, the types of task to be attempted in the classroom and suggests an order of complexity for tasks of the same kind. The list of six tasks on the map of a village given above is a rough example. Such a syllabus seems to me to give at least as much help to teachers on what to do in the classroom as a product-based syllabus does on what to teach—and it can of course be supported with a coursebook which is a repertoire of actual tasks, with partial ordering. Teachers will perhaps find it strange not to know what piece of language they are teaching at a given point but then the main hypothesis of this approach is that language is best taught and learnt when neither the teacher nor the learner is worrying about pieces of language.

5

Communicative Teaching: "Communicative" in What Sense?

This paper is an attempt to identify and discuss the different senses in which the term "communicative" has been used in recent proposals and materials for language teaching. The analysis is conceptual, not historical.

The first concept I want to discuss is that communicative teaching consists of adding a new component to existing pedagogic procedures and perhaps also a redistribution of emphases in those procedures. Specifically, the practice stage of a lesson or teaching unit based on a pre-selected linguistic input (for example, a structural item) should, it is thought, not rely any more on drill-like exercises or sets of parallel but semantically unrelated contexts but should employ, instead, communicative exercises. A communicative exercise is defined, for this purpose, either loosely in terms of larger contexts, texts instead of sentences, games, simulations and role-play, or more precisely, as in Johnson (1982, pp. 163–75) in terms of an information-gap, information-transfer, task-dependency, etc. What is considered important is that the learner is engaged in a meaning-focused activity and handles the language-form he has been taught a little earlier with a purpose other than merely the handling of it. The learner, that is to say, is now using the form, not merely practising it.

This essay was first published in 1985. *Source*: Prabhu, N. S. (1985). Communicative teaching: "Communicative" in what sense? In Bikram K. Das (Ed.) *Communicative language teaching*, Anthology Series 14 (pp. 32–40). Singapore: Singapore University Press.

When teachers or educational administrators say that they wish to incorporate communicative teaching within the existing framework of a structural syllabus—and when specialists claim that a communicative methodology can in fact be reconciled with a linguistic syllabus—this is the sense in which they must be using the term "communicative", viz. the addition of a component of communicative exercises to the practice stage of each teaching unit. The reconciliation involved is essentially that between a pre-selected language item which is deliberately being taught and some meaning-focused activity which brings that item into use. One can therefore ask two questions: What is the possible value of such a reconciliation? What is likely to be its pedagogic cost?

The value of introducing communicative exercises in the teaching of a structural syllabus would presumably be that such meaning-focused activity can mitigate the unwanted effects of a structural syllabus. There has always been a tension in the structural approach between the principle of systematicity and the principle of naturalness; it is thought that a deliberate regulation of linguistic inputs to the learner—both in terms of an overall order and in terms of concentration on one language item at a time—will facilitate the learner's construction of a grammar of the language for himself; and it is, at the same time, realised that natural language use is an activity in which the user's internal grammar is being deployed without any deliberation. A linguistic regulation of inputs leads to pedagogic activities which involve linguistic deliberation in classroom transactions and therefore runs the risk of promoting an ability which does not approximate to natural language use. The problem then is: how can one make a deliberate linguistic input in such a way that it becomes available for non-deliberate deployment by the learner? How, that is to say, can one ensure that something that is learnt through form-focused activity is deployable in meaning-focused use? One answer which suggests itself readily is that meaning-focused activity should be employed within the classroom as a supplement—indeed, a corrective—to form-focused activity; and a communicative exercise at the end of each teaching unit is meant to serve this function. The model of language acquisition which operated in such thinking is one of deliberate language inputs being first received and handled deliberately by the learner and then being made to sink below the level of linguistic consciousness. The value of communicative exercises, then, is that, by focusing the learner's attention on things other than language, they create conditions in which the learner engages in a non-deliberate use of the language input received earlier.

Against this perceived advantage, we should consider the pedagogic cost of attempting to reconcile a structural syllabus with a communicative methodology. A structural syllabus by its nature demands that classroom activity be designed to bring into play a pre-selected language item and, if communicative exercises are to be employed in the process, those exercises too will have to meet that demand. Natural language use, however, does not in general allow prediction of particular language and any genuine meaning-focused activity in the classroom cannot, consequently, be expected to bring into play a pre-selected language item. Indeed, this is an essential part of the distinction we make between form-focused and meaning-focused activities: the more dependable the prediction of particular language, the more form-focused the activity is and vice versa. Language drills are activities in which the language aimed at is most predictable and contextualisation is a process which proportionately reduces that predictability. A communicative exercise—that is to say, a meaning-focused activity—is therefore one in which particular language is least predictable and yet adherence to a structural syllabus requires that particular language be predicted in it. This is a very real conflict and its practical consequences in the classroom can be either the use of activities which are communicative only in appearance (but fulfill linguistic prediction) or the use of activities which are genuinely meaning-focused (but do not conform to the linguistic syllabus). The former is what one sees in a large majority of the so-called communicative exercises (including games, role-play etc.) suggested or provided in the literature; and the latter is what is involved in Brumfit's straightforward proposal to provide time in the classroom for fluency activity, quite independently of language-focused accuracy activity—that is to say, a disassociation of the communicative activity from the structural syllabus (Brumfit, 1981) not an integration of the two. There is a further point to make about predicting particular language in meaning-focused activities. When one has made a pre-selection of language there is an inevitable attempt to ensure its occurrence in the activity being set up and an accompanying uncertainty (hence, anxiety) about it in conducting the activity. This leads to an effort to monitor and scan the language that is being brought into play even while it is being brought into play—an effort to combine deliberation with non-deliberate deployment. This is a process which is very unlike language use and is sure to produce a distortion, in varying degrees, of the discourse that emerges from the activity. The issue therefore is not only that particular language is largely unpredictable for genuinely meaning-focused activity; it is also that, even when it is predictable to some extent, the act of making the prediction has consequences which are detrimental to the quality of meaning-focused activity.

Let me now move to a second concept of what communicative teaching is. This is based on the familiar distinction between grammatical and communicative competence—or between "usage" and "use". It is asserted that natural language use involves an ability which goes beyond the deployment of an internalised language-system and that this additional ability can also be analysed as a system and developed deliberately in learners. The analyses attempted are both in terms of rhetorical functions which make discourse coherent and in terms of interactional functions which make interpersonal communication possible. The claim is that these functions tend to occur in identifiable patterns and that the ability to operate these patterns can and should be developed in language-learners. What is involved here therefore is not a claim about the acquisition of language-structure but the claim that it is not enough to acquire language-structure. Consequently, this notion of communicative teaching is relevant only to intermediate—or advanced—level courses, not to initial language teaching. It has accordingly been used mainly on what are called language-activation, extension or acculturation courses, which aim to teach people how to use the language they already know. In practice, of course, such courses very often attempt to teach some elements of language-structure as well—or to remedy certain gaps in the earlier acquisition of language-structure—and that leads to a conflict between deliberate linguistic inputs and a message-focused operation of discourse patterns (or to a disassociation of the two kinds of activity), in the same way as has been discussed above. It is also possible to make a much larger claim for this particular concept of communicative teaching, viz. that message-focused activity, which develops the ability to operate discourse patterns, is at the same time a good way of bringing about the acquisition of language-structure itself. This would be a radical development of the concept we are dealing with and is in fact close to a different concept which I will discuss later in this paper.

A third concept of what makes language-teaching communicative is that which underlies notional syllabuses. It involves three related claims: first, that the world of meaning can be analysed sufficiently for us to state language-teaching syllabuses in semantic, instead of structural, terms; second, that a syllabus-statement in semantic terms is likely to have a beneficial effect on classroom activity, by making it more meaning-focused; and third, that such a syllabus-statement permits a more purposeful or pragmatic selection and organisation of teaching items than does a structural syllabus (Wilkins, 1981). The first claim is obviously vulnerable if taken on its own but what it refers to is not the world of meaning as such but the sorts of meaning units which are identifiable in recurrent situations of language use and which can, more importantly, be associated with the items of language structure that are normally employed to articulate them. It is this association of semantic and structural items that sustains the second claim, viz. that the resulting classroom activity is then likely to be more meaning-focused.

The assumption is that each structural item in the syllabus will then appear under a conspicuous semantic label which will act as a constant reminder that the item is to be handled meaningfully in the classroom and will also perhaps help to suggest certain actual contexts which can be employed for the purpose. The third claim—that of purposeful selection—is based on the assumption that learners can be equipped with specific language for specific situations and is related to the perceived desirability of graded objectives, modular courses and surrender values.

The first comment to make on this concept is that it is concerned with modes of making and justifying statements about language courses, not with modes of acquisition at all—of either linguistic or communicative competence. It does involve the hope that a semantic labeling and grouping of language-items will lead to greater attention to meaning in the classroom but it makes no hypotheses about what meaningfulness consists of or how such meaningfulness will promote the acquisition of language-structure. It seems to rely simply on the belief that language items should be taught in association with their meaning and with maximal contextualisation—a belief which long pre-dates the communicative teaching movement. Notional syllabuses, that is to say, tell us very little about teaching or learning and cannot therefore claim to be communicative, in any particular sense, in terms of classroom activity.

A second comment is that notional syllabuses skirt the issue of input-systematicity. The point here is not just that the semantic analysis being used is of questionable consistency and exhaustiveness; the more important point is that such a syllabus necessarily destroys what systematicity is possible in purely structural terms. Given that the relationship between linguistic and semantic units is far from being one-to-one, any attempt to organise a syllabus semantically must involve a sacrifice on linguistic systematicity. There are of course arguments possible (and put forward) on this issue in terms of purposeful selection and surrender value but there seem to be no pedagogic arguments at all—in terms of whether or not input-systematicity facilitates acquisition. If linguistic systematicity is a help in language-acquisition, then notional syllabuses make a large sacrifice on that front; and if such systematicity is claimed not to be of value for language-acquisition, surely that claim needs to be argued in terms of an acquisition-model?

A third and final comment on this is that notional syllabuses are not just syllabuses in semantic terms; they are bi-dimensional syllabuses in which each unit has a semantic label and one or more associated linguistic items. Now, syllabus-specification has an important impact on what language data are made available to the learner at each stage: the data at any given point are those defined and delimited by the item of the syllabus being taught. This delimitation of data—either in the materials or in the classroom—can be looked on as an aid to learning but it can also reach a point which makes it deprivation. The delimitation demanded by a bi-dimensional syllabus is clearly much greater that that required by a unidimensional syllabus (in whatever terms). Further, notional syllabuses seem, in practice, to have set the trend for greater elaboration in syllabus-statements by the addition of further dimensions. Syllabuses have, for instance, been constructed which specify, at each unit, a notion or function, one or more structures, a situation or a task, etc. Each of these multiple dimensions has the effect of imposing a restriction on what can go into a teaching unit—and the combined effect of several dimensions must reach the point of impoverishing the actual input to the learner, causing deprivation.

A fourth concept of communicative teaching is that it is a matter of basing course-construction on needs analyses. The claims involved are, first, that there are material differences between the language (or discourse) typical of one situation and that typical of another; and, second, that it is desirable to equip learners directly with the particular language or discourse features which are typical of the target situations. The specification of typical features can be in structural, sociolinguistic, semantic or discoursal terms—or a complex combination of all these, as in Munby (1978)—and most effort on this approach seems in fact to have been confined to arriving at such specifications. The second claim—about the desirability of equipping learners directly with the relevant items of language or features of discourse—has hardly been argued in pedagogic terms, as pointed out forcefully by Widdowson (1984). And yet there are crucial issues here for a model of language-acquisition—issues involving the notion of equipping learners as against enabling them, the notion of "system" as an analyst's construct as against that of "system" as an operational ability, and the difference in kind between the rules of language and the rules of use. A specification of learners' communicative needs does not make the classroom teaching communicative in any particular sense—and may in fact tend to make it less communicative by putting a premium on equipping activities at the expense of enabling ones.

The fifth and final concept I want to discuss is that communicative teaching consists of meaning-focused activity in the classroom, unrestrained by any pre-selection or prediction of language. Two claims are being made: first, that meaning-focused activity, involving what I have referred to as non-deliberate deployment, is the best condition for the acquisition of language structure; and, second, that a linguistic syllabus, involving a planned progression in structural terms and a pre-selection of language items for particular activities, will undermine the quality and value of such meaning-focused activity. The stand taken on input-systematicity is that it is unhelpful to acquisition since "system" as an analyst's construct cannot be taken to be isomorphic with the system hypothesised to lie behind an ability to operate in language; and, moreover, the order of inputs is unlikely to correspond to a process of acquisition through interlanguage development. It is also thought that form-focused activity will promote a kind of knowledge which does not represent acquisition and that an ability to deploy language non-deliberately can only be acquired through experience of non-deliberate deployment. Whatever delimitation of input is demanded by this process is brought about, it is claimed, automatically by the pedagogic procedure—of selecting and conducting appropriate meaning-focused activities and of a natural simplification of language to facilitate comprehension, similar to what has been called "caretaker talk".

This concept is thus concerned directly with methodology and is based on a model of what may be called acquisition through deployment, in contrast to a model of regulated input-assimilation. A sustained attempt to develop and try out classroom activities in conformity with this concept has been made in the form of a teaching experiment in southern India in the past five years, as reported in a paper I gave at this seminar last year (Prabhu, 1984).

I have pointed out five different senses in which the term "communicative" has been used in the profession. They may not all be mutually exclusive in practice (and there are those who look on eclecticism as an absolute virtue) but I think it is important to be aware, in discussion, of which sense one is using the term in and what its implications are for one or another aspect of language pedagogy. This is especially necessary at a time, as now, when "communicative" has become very much a laudatory term.

I now wish to conclude this paper with a general observation on the five concepts. A central problem in language-teaching is: how can we ensure that the language experience provided in the classroom leads to an ability for language use outside the classroom? Different answers are possible to this question, depending on different perceptions of the difference between classroom phenomena and real-life phenomena; and I think the different senses of the term "communicative" can all be related to such different perceptions. Thus, if one saw the difference in terms of form-focused and meaning-focused activity but did not consider the two to be irreconcilable, one would seek to supplement form-focused work with communicative exercises. If, alternatively, one saw the difference in terms of rules of language and rules of use, one would propose post-initial teaching which can extend or convert usage into use. If, instead, one saw the difference mainly in terms of motivation and learners' perception of relevance, one might propose syllabus-statements which permit a modular organisation and surrender values or are conspicuously based on needs analyses. Finally, if one saw the difference in terms of form-focused and meaning-focused activity and considered the two to be irreconcilable, one would propose teaching which is based entirely on meaning-focused activity. It will be seen from this that the first and the last concepts in my list are closely related—and perhaps throw up the most crucial issues.

References

Brumfit, C. J. (1984). The limits of the language syllabus. In John A. S. Read (Ed.), *Trends in language syllabus design* (pp. 261–71). Singapore: Singapore University Press.

Johnson, Keith. (1982). *Communicative syllabus design and methodology*. Oxford: Pergamon Press.

Munby, J. (1978). *Communicative syllabus design*. Cambridge: Cambridge University Press.

Prabhu, N. S. (1984). Procedural syllabuses. In John A. S. Read (Ed.), *Trends in language syllabus design* (pp. 272–80). Singapore: Singapore University Press.

Widdowson, H. G. (1984). *Learning purpose and language use*. Oxford: Oxford University Press.

Wilkins, D. A. (1981). Notional syllabuses revisited. *Applied Linguistics*, II(1), 83–89.

Wilkins, D. A. (1981). Notional syllabuses revisited: A further reply. *Applied Linguistics*, II(1), 96–100.

6

Coping with the Unknown in Language Pedagogy

I want in this paper to identify a particular sense of the term "learner-centred methodology" and then to explore the implications of that view for language pedagogy.

It is perhaps useful to begin by making a distinction between "learner-centred" and "learning-centred". One can say that "learner-centred" approaches are those which justify themselves essentially in terms of a concern for the learner—a concern which reflects the teacher's (or specialist's) sense of social, ideological or educational responsibility for his client. One form in which this is often expressed is the educator's responsibility to give the learner the best value for his money or effort. Careful analyses of learners' needs prior to course-design, matching the objectives or content of courses to learners' stated preferences or real-life needs (or couching syllabus statements in terms suggestive of real-life language-behaviour), designing courses to graded objectives so as to ensure a surrender value to each level of attainment, an emphasis on the use of realistic samples of language or authentic texts in the classroom can all be seen as expressions of this concern. It would be wrong to imply that this contrasts with an earlier lack of social or educational concern for the learner but the particular form in which the concern has been expressed in the past decade—viz. the ESP movement in

---

This essay was first published in 1985. *Source*: Prabhu, N. S. (1985). Coping with the unknown in language pedagogy. In Randolph Quirk and H. G. Widdowson (Eds.), *English in the world* (pp. 164–173). Cambridge: Cambridge University Press.

general—and the primacy given to it in the theory or practice of language-teaching are certainly new and largely responsible for the new term "learner-centred".

This is not to say that ESP has been motivated solely by a social responsibility for the learner—some of the motivation has, for instance, been the teacher's own need to persuade the learner of the relevance of what is offered—but the educational argument for ESP has generally been in terms of economy and direct usefulness to the learner.

A different expression of this social concern for the learner is an argument for accommodating and protecting the learner's rights—an argument for a democratic sharing of control in pedagogy. Methodologies are thus proposed which allow (or train) learners to select their learning modes, use one another as learning resources, negotiate learning content with the teacher and generally take responsibility for the management of their own learning. The teacher is seen as only one of the resources available to the learner and the teacher's job is making the learner aware of other possible resources and encouraging his freedom in deciding which to use and in what manner. The ultimate goal is the autonomous learner and individualisation, while group work in the classroom is an important first step in the direction. There is an interesting contrast between this concept of learner-centredness and the concept behind ESP. ESP can be said to increase the teacher's responsibility and control in deciding what is learnt and how, while a recognition of the learner's rights leads to a transfer of responsibility and control from the teacher to the learner.

What I am calling learning-centred methodologies, in contrast, are those based on particular perceptions of the nature of learning. Some of these—referred to generally as the "humanistic approaches"—are concerned with learning in general and seek to create psychological (and physical) conditions in which memory is strengthened, personalities are engaged, mental and emotional needs are caused and met, attitudes considered favourable to learning are developed, strong associations are formed between the known and the new to help the retention of the new, and so on. What are involved here are hypotheses about the human mind as a learning device and the pedagogic procedures concerned are almost like an extension to human beings of the explorations made of the nature of learning in an earlier age by using animals.

A different form of learning-centredness—and the one I am concerned with in this paper—is that based on perceptions of the nature of language and, in particular, of language-learning as a distinct form of learning. Language can be viewed as a unique phenomenon—a defining characteristic of the species—and language-learning as being distinguishable in kind from other forms of learning. It would, in passing, be interesting to trace, in the history of language pedagogy, a recurrent tension between perceptions based on the uniqueness of language-learning and those concerned with learning in general—between language as "skill" and language as "knowledge", in one of their manifestations.

The uniqueness of language-learning was noted, some sixty years ago, by H. E. Palmer (1922), who said: "We are endowed by nature with capacities for assimilating speech...These capacities are not limited to the acquiring of our mother tongue but are also available for one or more languages in addition" (p. 127). Palmer thus made a sharp distinction between our "natural, spontaneous and universal capacities" for learning languages and our "studial capacities" which operate in the learning of other subjects (including such "skill" subjects as shorthand, piano-playing, typewriting and carpentry). Using a language, he said, involves "unconscious obedience to some rules unknown to us" (p. 5) and in learning a language "we learn without knowing what we are learning" (p. 44). Palmer therefore suggested that we "design forms of work in which the student's attention shall be directed towards the subject-matter and away from the form in which it is expressed" (p. 51) and argued that "the utilisation of his [that is, the adult learner's] conscious and focused attention [on language] militates against the proper functioning of the natural capacities of assimilation". Speculating on what processes might be involved in such unconscious acquisition, he suggested that the student had "capacities for retaining unconsciously what he may happen to hear (or read)" (p. 56) and that these retained "compounds" gave him the "working units" of language and the ability to engage in "ergonic construction" (in contrast to the more conscious process of "grammatical construction").

Palmer's further observation that the system of rules we obey unconsciously in using a language is "so complex and so vast that the learned world has not yet succeeded in unraveling it or sounding its depths" has since been brought home to us abundantly by developments in grammatical analysis. It is easy to look on Transformational-Generative Grammar as being limited in scope to "linguistic competence". The fact is that even such sophisticated instruments of analysis have not been able to provide anything like a full account of linguistic competence, while every successful instance of language acquisition in the world represents an unconscious mastery of it. Perhaps the most valuable lesson for language pedagogy from Chomskyan linguistics is a realisation of how much more complex language structure is than we had thought in the past, how little we consciously know about it still—and, by the same token, how much more than we thought is known unconsciously to every language user. The exercise of what Palmer called "studial" capacities is therefore not only an inefficient way of learning a language; it is inherently inadequate for the purpose since we still do not know consciously what we expect to be acquired unconsciously.

Palmer saw explicit grammar in the classroom as having been the main defect in earlier language pedagogy, since "grammatical construction" was totally unlike language use or natural language acquisition (pp. 119–20). He saw value in training the learner's capacity to "memorise without effort" so that "he may memorise a hundred or so real living sentences" and by so doing "acquire a hundred or so new habits or automatic actions" (p. 49). Palmer was, however, very aware of the generative character of language structure and went on to add that "certain forms of *synthetic* work exist which will enable us to form correctly an almost unlimited number of foreign sentences; we shall see that the utilisation of these *studial* forms of work will carry us very far on our way to acquire the language" (p. 48, emphases mine). The synthetic work was what he called "ergonic construction", which formed the basis of the substitution table and other forms of structure-manipulation. Among the other principles which Palmer enunciated were those of gradation ("passing from the known to the unknown") and accuracy ("Do not allow the student to have opportunities for inaccurate work"), and, together, they formed the basis of the Structural Approach which came to dominate second language pedagogy so much for so long.

The flux and ferment we are faced with in language pedagogy today is the result of a general disillusionment with the Structural Approach, but the new directions being explored are, to my mind, characterised by an avoidance of the issue of structure-acquisition instead of seeking alternative ways of bringing it about. Thus, notional-functional syllabuses aim at a more purposeful selection of grammatical material, thereby abandoning what value there was to Palmer's principle of "gradation"—that is, grammatical organisation. They also hope to bring about a stronger form–meaning association in the classroom but take no stand on the issue of conscious versus unconscious learning. ESP courses aim to equip the learner most directly with the language most relevant to his needs—and can almost be related to Palmer's emphasis on the memorisation of tokens, except that they don't seem to share Palmer's perception of the value of such tokens as "working units" for "automatic actions"—that is, for an internal generative system. Communicative methodologies seek to create opportunities for the learner to engage in naturalistic language use so that he can bring into free, fluent play what language he already knows—or learn to cope with communication despite his language deficiency—but they make few claims about the acquisition of the structural base of language. Finally, pedagogic approaches based on a perception of language as discourse seek to highlight abilities of language use which lie beyond a mastery of language structure and, in so doing, play down the importance of language structure itself. Explorations of the nature of interactional capacity (as in Widdowson, 1983) are valuable but do not justify a brushing aside of grammatical competence as being merely a set of conventions or a system of rules too rigid to permit creativity in a certain sense. If one wished to challenge the centrality of grammar for language use, one would have to show either:

i. that grammar does not matter, that is, communicative competence in some sense which does not involve grammatical conformity can be an acceptable educational goal, or
ii. that grammar is not a system, that is, grammatical conformity follows from communicational appropriacy and grammatical deviance can be explained in terms of communicational inadequacy, or
iii. that grammar is not a problem in pedagogy, that is, it generally gets acquired easily, unlike communicative ability.

In general, those pedagogic proposals which base themselves on the argument that grammatical competence is not enough are providing justification for a widening of the scope of what is to be taught and learnt but are being ambivalent in their implications for the promotion of grammatical competence itself. The implication cannot be that we already know how to promote grammatical competence and most language learners do in fact acquire that competence sufficiently: Newmark's example of asking for a light in perfectly grammatical but inappropriate language is a synthetic one (and such examples are generally hard-found, anecdotal ones) while examples of grammatical deficiency abound in the language-teaching (and second-language-using) world; and nearly all courses produced for communicative language teaching have in practice felt the need to make provision for the teaching (or remedying) of language structure. The only other possible implication is that we have done all we can about the acquisition of language structure and that language structure is therefore to be taught, to the extent possible, by the procedures of the Structural Approach, though the Communicative Approach claims to be an alternative to that approach.

There is a further point to be made about grammatical competence. When statements are made of the form "when grammar is taught, grammar alone is learnt", the word "grammar" is being employed with unhelpful ambiguity. If the grammar learnt is being equated with the grammar taught, then that knowledge of grammar cannot represent grammatical competence in the sense of an internally constructed and unconsciously deployed system—and one is ignoring Palmer's insightful distinction between "grammatical construction" and "obedience to rules unknown to us". If, on the other hand, an internalised competence is in fact what one has in mind in saying "grammar is learnt", then that grammar can hardly be equated with the grammar taught—or even assumed to be caused by the teaching of it. Moreover, there is at least a possibility that grammatical competence—in the sense of an unconsciously internalised system—leads not only to greater conformity to the system itself, when such conformity is not being attempted consciously, but to a readier deployment of the system in communication. The point I am making therefore is that arguments on the lines of "grammar is not enough" may be taking too restricted a view of what grammatical competence involves and that the achievement of grammatical competence in a truer (more deployable) form may by itself mitigate the problem of communicative ability. If we agree with Brumfit that accuracy activity in the classroom leads to an ability which is not readily available for fluent use, the conclusion is not necessarily that fluency activity should supplement accuracy activity to make that ability more deployable: it is quite possible that a more deployable form of ability can in fact be promoted by means other than accuracy activity.

Palmer, as we have noted, suggested the use of "ergonic construction"; as an alternative to "grammatical construction" (although he was aware that ergonic construction—that is, sentence construction based on "working units" of syntax—was a form of "synthetic work" which engaged "studial" capacities) and added "gradation" (of ergons—hence a structural progression) and "accuracy" (error-prevention) as further principles of language pedagogy. I think it is these principles that we need to re-examine, in the light of our current perspective on language acquisition, in order to understand our disappointment with the Structural Approach.

Ergonic construction implies the belief that the "working units" identified by the teacher (or borrowed by him from the linguist) are in fact units of the system which the language learner is hypothesised to construct unconsciously in his mind—the belief that we, as teachers, have conscious knowledge of the rules to which language-users show "unconscious obedience". It is a claim of isomorphism between the grammars constructed by linguists and the internal grammars of language-users—an attribution of psychological reality to linguistic models, which is more than any linguist has wished to claim. The fact that a successful model of linguistic analysis and success in learning a language are both subject to the same evidence (viz. conformity of their outputs to that of the language-using community) is not a relevant basis for this belief—even if we assumed that some model of linguistic analysis has in fact proved fully successful in those terms. What ergonic construction—or structural practice—implies is an identity of form between the analyst's construct and the unobservable reality; and one is justified in asking, in the light of results, if pedagogic procedures based on this unjustified assumption might not have acted detrimentally to language acquisition.

One of the most powerful current perspectives on language acquisition is the hypothesis of interlanguage development (Corder, 1981) which directly challenges the relevance of both deliberate linguistic grading and the principle of accuracy/error-prevention in language pedagogy. Grading implies that learning takes place part-by-part, in an additive sequence, while the notion of interlanguage implies that language development is holistic—a continual revision/elaboration of a transitional competence, prompted by new, conflicting language data. Further, since transitional competence is by its very nature not stable, not observable at any particular stage and not likely to be uniform to a group of learners, it is not possible to determine what piece of language data is relevant to it at what stage. It is of course important to make language data available all the time—that is to say, exposure to the language being learnt is necessary—but there can be no planning of an input-sequence; nor can input be equated with intake for any given learner at any given stage. Also, since the output of a transitional competence is bound to differ from that of a fully formed competence, errors are a natural manifestation of language development and the principle of accuracy (in Palmer's sense of preventing errors—hence providing language practice) is misconceived.

Given the strong plausibility of the interlanguage hypothesis (in the sense that language-learning takes place through a series of approximative systems—whether or not one sees equal plausibility to the associated hypothesis of a discoverable in-built sequence), one can no longer expect language pedagogy to benefit from a planned linguistic progression, pre-selection of language for particular activities or language practice as such. The only important requirement is that language data be made available continually; and one can then go on to ask whether there are any conditions which are likely to make the data more effective—that is, likely to increase the pace of interlanguage revision or, to put it differently, increase the chances of input becoming intake. Corder identifies motivation as the most important condition ("*given motivation,* it is inevitable that a human being will learn a second language if he is exposed to the language data" [p. 8]) while one of the suggestions Palmer made was focusing the learner's mind on the subject-matter ("The pupil must not be allowed to focus his attention on the structure of the language; he must keep his attention on the subject-matter" [p. 51]). What this suggests is classroom activity which brings about in the learner a preoccupation with meaning (or the message or content), since success in understanding things and success in saying what one wishes to say are both pleasurable activities for people—hence motivating, at least in the immediate context.

If meaning-focused activity is in fact the most important condition for the process of internal grammar-construction, we then have to regard structural progression and language practice as being not only not helpful to that process but as possible impediments to it. They promote what may be called form-focused work in the classroom, distinguishable from meaning-focused work in its having to fulfill predictions of particular language. Whenever classroom activity is based on pre-selected language (however well-disguised that fact may be from the learner), a criterion for the success of that activity must be the fulfillment of that prediction; and the teacher's own awareness of that criterion is likely to lead to an attempt to ensure success in those terms—that is, to an attempt to monitor language forms in a way that is unnatural in natural language use and certain to render the activity itself less meaning-focused. The nature of language is such that we cannot be engaged in genuine language use and simultaneously be scanning the language forms which emerge; and pedagogic attempts to set up classroom activity which constitutes both language practice (from the teacher's point of view) and meaning-focused use (from the learner's) seem to me a form of compromise likely to lose on both fronts.

What emerges from this discussion is that there are a number of things about language acquisition which we do not know and should not assume we do in language pedagogy. We do not know the form of the internal grammar we hypothesise and should not assume that it is the same as the linguist's grammar. We do not know the process of internal grammar-construction and should not assume that it is a linear one. We cannot say what any learner will learn at any given stage and should not assume that what is learnt is what we teach. We do not, that is to say, know enough about acquisition to seek to influence that process directly, and our best hypotheses at this time—viz. that the internal grammar develops as unconsciously as it gets deployed in language use and that the process involved is a holistic one—indicate a very indirect form of teaching, confined to ensuring availability of language data and attempting to bring about a preoccupation with meaning. Attempts in the past to do more than this—to control and regulate acquisition to a plan—turn out to have been based on unjustified assumptions of knowledge as well as disappointing in their results. If language is a genetic inheritance and language development an organic process (Palmer himself compared the process to learning to walk, in contrast to learning to cycle), it is indeed to be expected that attempts to influence that process indirectly will prove more beneficial than a more direct intervention. From a different point of view, there is a choice in language pedagogy between making minimal or maximal assumptions and, given the perception of language acquisition outlined in this paper, minimal assumptions seem the more promising.

I do not think there is any serious problem of feasibility with a methodology based on such minimal assumptions. Meaning-focused activity in the classroom can be attempted in a number of ways. One particular attempt—employing problem-solving tasks and without any language syllabus, pre-selection of language for particular activities or form-focused work—has been experimented with in southern India over the past five years (Prabhu, 1984), with tentative results which indicate that unconscious grammar construction does take place from such teaching and that the resultant ability is more deployable than the result of more form-focused teaching. Teaching a subject (such as science) through the language to be taught—thus regulating teaching in terms of the subject instead of in linguistic terms—is another possibility which has been suggested more than once in the past. Given the fact that subject-matter itself defines and regulates the language that comes into play in dealing with it, and the further fact that there are natural processes of simplification and negotiation which operate in any situation where communication is attempted between persons of different linguistic attainments, meaning-focused work in the language classroom is entirely practicable—and in fact simpler, in terms of the demands it makes on teachers and learners, than teaching which attempts to combine linguistic regulation with meaningful activity.

Where problems arise for such teaching—speaking from my own experience of the south India experiment—is in persuading teachers and administrators that an indirect attempt to promote acquisition is all we can usefully make in language pedagogy and that, given the nature of language and its acquisition, such indirectness is likely to be more beneficial than direct manipulation. There is a sense of insecurity arising from not knowing—for example, being unable to say what piece of language one is teaching at a given time and accepting the notion that what gets learnt may be quite different from what one attempts to teach—and a resultant preference for security even when it is suspected of being based on unjustified assumptions. Perhaps teaching, like many other activities, seeks to define and justify itself in its own terms, submitting only to criteria of success which it can (or thinks it can) directly produce or control; and perhaps the uniqueness of language-learning, as compared to the learning of other school subjects or to the notion of learning in general, is specially in conflict with that propensity.

There is another point at which the concept of language development as organic growth conflicts with what educational administration (and perhaps applied linguistics too) seeks. Educational planning (especially the planning of language education in the modern world) finds the need to regulate (often reduce) the time given to language instruction—and finds it convenient to work on the assumption that language-teaching specialism can find ways of speeding up the learning process through more effective methods. And more effective methods are generally seen to be those that seek to influence the learning process more directly—and define criteria of success which suit such methods. Palmer noted this phenomenon and commented: “If we are to obtain concrete and definite results in a limited space of time...we shall reluctantly be compelled to sacrifice a certain measure of soundness to the requirements of speed" (p. 26).

Finally, not only do we not have specific knowledge about language acquisition, we do not know what sources might be dependable for such knowledge. Does one trust a successful learner's introspection when he says (for instance) that he always learnt languages by studiously memorising lists of words—or a learner's rational view that if he is learning a language, he ought to know exactly what rules he should conform to? (How would we interpret the introspection of someone who is certain that he learnt to walk as a child by using a certain kind of push cart?) Does one treat theoretical constructs of language structure or language use as if they represented reality and could be used as operational models? Does one rely on empirical studies of first- or second-language acquisition, which too can make their perceptions only in terms of theoretical constructs? Or does one seek "scientific" evidence from language-teaching experiments themselves, in spite of the severe limitations of an experimental design when applied to a variable-ridden human enterprise such as teaching? Perhaps one can do worse than to look to an evolving sense of plausibility in the profession, informed by what evidence and theory are available but shared and sharpened through professional debate. From the point of view of a particular sense of plausibility felt by Palmer and strengthened by subsequent experience, learning-centred methodology is perhaps largely a matter of coping with the unknown in language pedagogy.

References

Corder, S. Pit. (1981). *Error analysis and interlanguage.* Oxford: Oxford University Press.

Newmark, Leonard. (1979). How not to interfere with language learning. In C. J. Brumfit and K. Johnson (Eds.), *The communicative approach to language teaching* (pp. 160–66). Oxford: Oxford University Press.

Palmer, H. E. ([1922] 1964). *The principles of language-study*. Oxford: Oxford University Press.

Prabhu, N. S. (1984). Procedural syllabuses. In John A. S. Read (Ed.), *Trends in language syllabus design* (pp. 272–80). Singapore: Singapore University Press.

Widdowson, H. G. (1983). *Learning purpose and language use*. Oxford: Oxford University Press.

GD: *In this article, you have critiqued ESP courses; I was hoping you would be able to tell us whether there was any way of making them enabling courses, for I felt that from what you have said, we need to either abandon ESP or find a way of making it move towards empowerment.*

NSP: Why not reserve specific-purpose courses for fulfilling only specific, limited needs and go for more general, enabling courses elsewhere?

7

Language Education: Equipping or Enabling?

This paper attempts to define a general distinction between two perspectives on language education and then to explore the significance of that distinction for both language teaching and the training of language teachers.

One view of education is that it provides young people with the knowledge and skill necessary for functioning in later years as useful and productive members of the society. The view implies that education should be based on an identification of society's future needs, and that what is taught in schools and universities should be what is relevant to those needs. There may, in practice, be difficulties in determining all the specific needs or in deriving curricular content directly from them, but the general aim is to overcome those difficulties maximally and to make education as direct a preparation as possible for the fulfillment of predicted functions. Educational effort, on this view, should be directed to defining expected outcomes more and more accurately and to relating means to ends more and more directly. I am calling this an "equipping" procedure in education—a procedure by which the learner gets equipped with the knowledge, skill or pattern of behaviour envisaged as educational ends.

A different view of education is that it provides young people with opportunity and support in realising their potential, in the form

---

This essay was first published in 1987. *Source*: Prabhu, N. S. (1987). Language education: Equipping or enabling. In Bikram K. Das (Ed.), *Language development in human resource development*, Anthology Series 20 (pp. 190–201). Singapore: Singapore University Press.

of understanding or ability. This view recognises that the demands to be made in later years can be varied and unpredicted, and that individuals will need to meet those demands in varied ways, such that there is a measure of fulfillment to themselves as individuals. Curricular content is therefore to be based, not on a specification of future needs but on an understanding of learning processes and of learners' current stages. It may, in practice, be useful to relate some part of what is taught to what is likely to be serviceable in later years but a major aim is to broaden such serviceability maximally by concentrating on the more fundamental abilities. I will refer to this as an "enabling" procedure in education—a process of developing the learner's capacity to extend and adapt what is learnt in the face of varied and emerging demands. In contrast to the equipping procedure, the enabling procedure can be said to fall short as a form of specific preparation but, on the other hand, to provide a broader base for further learning in response to a wider range of specific functions. Further, an equipping procedure aims at conformity and assesses success in those terms. An enabling procedure, by contrast, provides for divergence and regards ongoing adjustment as a part of its achievement.

The distinction I have made is a conceptual one, whose justification lies in its usefulness in exploring operational consequences. Although I have made the distinction in terms that suit this particular enquiry into language teaching and teacher-training, similar distinctions have been made in the literature in the context of other enquiries. Widdowson (1983), for instance distinguishes between "training" and "education", regarding training as a procedure of providing learners with "a restricted competence to enable them to cope with certain clearly defined tasks", in contrast to education which provides learners with "a general capacity to enable them to cope with undefined eventualities in future" (p. 6). Widdowson thus makes a double contrast: between "restricted" and "general" (competence) on the one hand (which is close to the distinction between "equipping" and "enabling"), and between "competence" itself and "capacity", on the other (which relates to different dimensions of language use—grammatical and discoursal—and as such is independent of the equipping/enabling contrast). A distinction is also made in educational theory between "skill" and "understanding" which, as Widdowson points out, is not especially helpful in discussing language pedagogy. Perhaps the title of this seminar itself suggests the contrast I have tried to make: "human resource development" implies an enabling procedure while an expression like "manpower planning" would suggest an equipping procedure.

Debate in language pedagogy tends to draw recurrently on one of two sources for support: perceptions of the nature of language competence and language learning, on the one hand, and evidence of the needs and expectations of language use, on the other. If one takes communicative language teaching to be the dominant paradigm in second language pedagogy at the present time, one can see, in its discussion, some perceptions of the nature of language as communication and of processes of language learning through communication, but one can also see that these are largely overshadowed by arguments about needs, expectations and direct usefulness. Grammar as a construct for understanding language competence is not extended or reinterpreted as the basis of pedagogy, but reduced or rejected in order to make room for considerations of end behaviour. Curricular content is called on to justify itself in terms of direct communicative use; and pedagogic staging is subjected to an anticipation of "surrender values". A functional specification of teaching content is regarded as being more progressive than a structural or cognitive one, on the grounds that it reflects more directly a concern for real-life language use. Role-play is regarded as a more purposeful classroom activity than either sentence-construction or meaning-exchange, in the belief that it represents a more direct preparation for conformity to linguistic conventions. In general, the influential approaches to language teaching developed in the Council of Europe's work (for example, Wilkins, 1976; van Ek, 1975) on the one hand, and in the field of English for Specific Purposes (for example, Mackay and Mountford, 1978; Munby, 1978) on the other, constitute emphatic assertions of the equipping procedure in language education, to the detriment of the enabling procedure. The approaches base themselves on analyses of desired outcomes and advocate the shortest pedagogic routes to their realisation. In the process, they devalue notions of language competence as a complex system of abstract rules, of language behaviour as a manifestation of rule-governed creativity and of language learning as a process of system development. Parts of the system are to be selected and taught on the grounds of their external relevance, without regard to the necessary interdependence of those parts with others in the system; or, going a step further, actual forms of language are to be identified and taught as appropriate verbal formulae for particular contexts of communication, thus ignoring system-development as such and aiming only at what may be called linguistic table manners. While, therefore, communicative language teaching can be said to represent an enrichment (in the sense of a fuller recognition) of language teaching objectives, it can also be seen to represent on impoverishment (in the sense of a loss of sight) of the processes involved in achieving those objectives in non-trivial ways.

It is, however, not the case that viewing language competence as a system necessarily leads to an enabling procedure in pedagogy. Grammatically organised teaching—which communicative language teaching is a reaction against—is also a procedure of equipping in a less obvious form, in that it seeks to provide learners with different parts of the system directly, through presentation, explanation or practice, in some teacher-determined order. It thus assumes learning outcomes to follow directly from teaching intentions and assumes too that the system which the learners need to develop as language competence is a replication of the descriptive grammar which is used to organise the teaching. Much grammar-based language teaching does no doubt recognise the possibility that what is imparted to the learner might turn out to be a form of descriptive knowledge instead of a system operating as competence, and tries to guard against that danger by presenting language forms, rather than rules, and concentrating more on practice than on explanation. But there are other possibilities which it ignores, such as that the system might operate internally only to the extent that it develops internally, and that a teacher-determined order in presenting parts of the system might have very little to do with the order of development of the internal system. It also ignores the important perception (Corder, 1981, pp. 65–78) that the system of language as competence develops holistically and, consequently, that a part-by-part presentation of the system in teaching is likely to be irrelevant to that development. As a result, it equates linguistic systematicity in teaching with the development of the linguistic system in learners, and directs a great deal of pedagogic effort to input systematicity on the assumption that teaching input at each stage will constitute learning intake. Grammatically organised language teaching is thus an attempt to equip learners directly with different parts of the language system, in contrast to possible attempts to enable them to develop the system internally, holistically and in whatever order is inherent to the system itself.

An enabling procedure for promoting system development involves pedagogic effort which seeks to create conditions favourable to such development, not effort to plan and regulate the process directly, much less to present the system itself as a descriptive entity. Now, it is likely that an important condition favourable to internal system-development is effort by the learner to communicate, that is, to make sense of verbally stated cognitive content, to interact in some way with that content or to find verbal means of putting cognitive content across (Prabhu, 1984). This view leads to a form of teaching based on communication but there are significant differences between such communication-based teaching and what I referred to earlier as "communicative language teaching". The former employs communication as a pedagogic means to system-development, that is to say, as an indirect, enabling procedure; the latter uses communication to increase goal direction in pedagogy, that is to say, as justification for an equipping procedure. Analyses of communicative functions to serve as syllabuses, predictions of learners' specific needs in later life, ensuring real-life resemblance to classroom activity and increasing the "authenticity" of the language samples used in teaching are all of marginal significance to communication-based teaching as an enabling procedure, but they are of central relevance to communicative teaching as an equipping procedure. An enabling procedure demands that what is done in the classroom have an instrumental value, in promoting the process of learning; an equipping procedure demands that classroom behaviour have a face value, as replication of real-life behaviour.

We have now looked briefly at what I regard as three major approaches to language education, in the light of the conceptual distinction between equipping and enabling. Communicative language teaching, in the sense of teaching directed to specific communicative goals, constitutes an equipping procedure in that it neglects the implications of language competence as a system. Grammatically organised teaching, which does base itself on language as a system, nevertheless equates grammar as an internal system with grammar as a descriptive entity and attempts to equip the learner directly with different parts of the system. Teaching which recognises language competence as a system but does not attempt to regulate its development directly employs communication as a condition favourable to system-development, thus relying maximally on an enabling procedure. Three general points can now be made.

First, it is possible to regard equipping and enabling as merely two ends of a scale, on the grounds that any given pedagogic procedure is only more or less an equipping or enabling one and, as illustrated by our discussion of grammatically organised teaching, what is an enabling procedure from one point of view can be an equipping one from another. However, the concepts of equipping and enabling are still distinct and can contribute to pedagogic understanding as well as to pedagogic action. Teaching is an equipping procedure to the extent it seeks to link means and goals directly and relies on a prediction of specific uses for learning outcomes. It is, conversely, an enabling procedure to the extent it posits complex mediating processes between means and ends, such as the development of a system as competence, and conceives of learning outcomes as being able to meet unpredicted demands. While an equipping procedure treats learning as the obverse of teaching and expects teaching and learning to be coextensive, an enabling procedure regards teaching as merely a support to (or favourable condition for) learning, the two being neither coextensive nor necessarily similar in form. Less obviously perhaps, an equipping procedure permits the teaching operation to be defined and justified in its own terms, through a kind of logical deduction from teaching objectives to teaching activities: learning can be assumed to follow (or else to be prevented by non-pedagogic factors) as long as the logical deduction can be seen to be sound. An enabling procedure, by contrast, is necessarily open to challenge not only in the light of learning outcomes but on the hypotheses it makes about mediating processes; methodology is continually subject to theoretical challenge and to consequent re-evaluation.

Secondly, formal education by its very nature exerts pressures in favour of instruction as an equipping procedure. State syllabuses imply an expectation of uniform learning outcomes from large numbers of classes and, since learners in any large system vary largely in their initial state and learning pace, teachers are faced at various points with a choice between teaching as an enabling procedure and a covering of the syllabus as an equipping procedure. State syllabuses also act as public declarations of educational intentions and attempt to be persuasive by stating learning outcomes in terms of their specific uses, rather than as general ability. Syllabuses are translated into sets of teaching materials which are looked on as fixed quanta of texts and exercises to be gone through in each classroom, thus setting up a choice between catering to learning and completing the coursebook. Educational administration attempts to monitor, inspect or regulate progress in teaching in different, classrooms, interpreting progress as the portion of syllabus or coursebook covered and thus endorsing teachers' choices in favour of equipping procedures. Finally, public examinations powerfully reinforce the expectation of uniform outcomes, encouraging learners, teachers and parents alike to give preference to examination-preparation over learning—to ensure arrival with or without the experience of travel. It is easy enough to conclude from such facts that an enabling procedure is unrealistic in formal education but a more constructive view would be that such pressures on equipping procedures make it all the more important to try to maintain and strengthen an enabling perspective in pedagogic activity—and to explore possibilities of stating syllabuses and examinations less prescriptively.

Thirdly, language education is specially susceptible to being interpreted as an equipping procedure, because language is, from one point of view, easily observed and easily specified verbal behaviour, and, from another point of view, a highly complex cognitive system whose development is extremely difficult to predict and specify as a normal outcome. It is difficult to tell how much instruction can be expected to lead to a given degree of system-development, when learners can be expected to move from reception to genuine production, what types of error can be expected to disappear at what stage or, indeed, whether a given instance of learner behaviour represents evidence on the internal system or merely a piece of verbal imitation. As a result, language education as an enabling procedure involves coping to a large extent with the unknown and the unpredictable. This increases pressure on the adoption of a simpler view of language as directly transmitted verbal behaviour, justifying an equipping procedure in pedagogy, but, once again, it also makes it especially important to preserve an enabling perspective and to seek at least to reduce the role of an equipping perspective.

There is a great deal of concern in teacher-training—especially in in-service training—for purposefulness and practicality. Training is thought to be purposeful to the extent it is directly linked to how teachers should teach in their classrooms after training. A prior determination of teaching objectives, teaching content and teaching methods is considered an advantage to teacher-training because it makes it possible to provide teachers with the specific teaching skills and procedures needed to carry out the desired form of pedagogy. The prior determination of curricular content and strategy is no doubt to be done with great care, as a specialist-level operation, but for that very reason it is looked on as neither very accessible nor very relevant to the classroom teachers to be trained. If there is a large number of teachers to be trained before implementing a given curricular change, it becomes all the more important to concentrate training effort on relevant practical skills and procedures, as a form of minimal adequate preparation—a guide to appropriate teaching behaviour in predicted classroom situations. This is clearly an equipping procedure in teacher-training, comparable to communicative language teaching as discussed above. It relies on a prediction of classroom needs and the provision of specific techniques for meeting them. It looks on a teaching method as a kind of laboratory procedure, guaranteed to yield predicted outcomes as long as it is carried out as specified. What it ignores is the unpredictability of any classroom situation as a context of human interaction and the probability that any teaching procedure may depend for its value, not on how good it is in the trainer's view, but on how far it is supported by the teacher's own pedagogic understanding and decision. It ignores, that is to say, the role of teachers' perceptions about teaching and learning, and their interpretation of particular classroom situations, based on what may be called a general pedagogic competence and professional awareness. Teaching must surely be too complex an activity for training to be direct preparation for specific behavioural needs.

This argument may seem to indicate that teacher-training should provide teachers with pedagogic theory as much as with practical skills, so that the classroom procedures of a trained teacher may be adequately informed by relevant theory. Training would then include persuasion on the specialist rationale behind the curricular change being aimed at, and success in training would result in the trained teachers accepting firmly the pedagogic perceptions they are provided with. However, teacher-training in this form can also be regarded as an equipping procedure, in that (like grammatically organised language teaching) it involves the transmission of a pedagogic theory to the teacher, rather than the development of a theory by the teacher. It assumes that the trainer's perceptions about teaching can be replicated as teachers' perceptions, and fails to recognise that teachers' perceptions can at best be responses to the perceptions presented to them and that these responses are likely to be greatly influenced by varied interpretations of experience and by varied levels of pedagogic awareness. Further, such perceptions as teachers are able to develop in the course of training ought to be of value to them in developing further perceptions (perhaps quite different ones) in the light of ongoing experience, but training which is an exercise in persuasion, resulting in a firm acceptance of received perceptions, can only reduce teachers' openness to change and general professional growth.

Teacher-training viewed as support to teachers' professional growth will be concerned with creating conditions favourable to such growth, rather than with preparing teachers to teach in predetermined ways. Such training as an enabling procedure will no doubt include attention to both practical procedures and pedagogic theory but the value of those inputs is now seen to lie in developing teachers' ability to interact with them, not in ensuring teachers' compliance or acceptance. Further, teachers' own varied perceptions, experiences and their interpretations are now equally legitimate inputs to the training process, not some unfortunate constraints to be reckoned with. Success in training is accordingly to be assessed not by the approximation of teachers' behaviour or belief to those of the trainer but by the increase in teachers' ability to interpret experience, relate perceptions to practical procedures, articulate emerging perceptions and interact productively with other perceptions. Indeed teacher-training is no longer a matter of training in the normal sense but rather a process of promoting teachers' professional activism (Brumfit, 1984, pp. 19–20). This necessarily implies that a given theory of language teaching is not true or false in some absolute sense; it is only more or less successful in capturing and articulating a pedagogic intuition, invoking corroborative experience or inducing a reinterpretation of experience, and generally enabling the profession to continue to gain fresh perspectives on what is involved in language teaching and language learning. Any notion of absolute truth about pedagogic theories not only brings up the question of provability in a social science; it also encourages the questionable view of teaching methods as objective procedures carrying a guarantee of success, independently of the human interaction and human perceptions involved.

We have briefly considered three general approaches to the training of language teachers, from the point of view of equipping and enabling. Teacher-training viewed as preparation for specific classroom activities is an equipping procedure which overlooks the effect of teachers' perceptions on classroom activity and the role of a general pedagogic ability to relate theory and practice. Teacher-training viewed as persuasion on a particular pedagogic theory is also an equipping procedure at a different level, because it envisages teachers operating with "received" pedagogic perceptions, rather than being able to develop fresh and varied perceptions through a process of interaction between available perceptions and ongoing experience. From this point of view, teacher-training is an enabling procedure only when it is viewed as a process of furthering teachers' professional activism. As in the case of language teaching, large-scale, formal education exerts various pressures in favour of equipping procedures in teacher-training as well; specific objectives, prescriptive syllabuses and public examinations all favour a predetermination of classroom procedures and, moreover, each official implementation of a new method usually results in a tighter specification of what teachers are to do. But that precisely is part of the case for maintaining an enabling perspective and for exploring ways of increasing its role in teacher-training.

Language education, like all education, demands, as an organised activity, some prediction of expected outcomes and some specific preparation to ensure those outcomes, both involving equipping procedures. But it is equally important for education to provide for the unpredicted, by helping to develop a general, generative competence through enabling procedures. There is a kind of self-evident logic which justifies equipping procedures and there are forces in formal education, as we have seen, which support them. Enabling procedures, in contrast, are less easy to develop and justify because they draw on less tangible entities such as general competence, and involve an indirectness in linking means and goals. It is for this reason necessary to attempt constantly to limit the role of an equipping perspective and to enlarge that of an enabling perspective, in pedagogic discussion as well as in pedagogic action. This is necessary not just because real-life demands on the outcome of learning are not fully predictable; it is necessary because the effect of basing pedagogy on possible predictions is to reduce attention to general abilities and thereby to make learning less capable of meeting unpredicted demands. Education has to provide for the future not just by ensuring future conformity to current predictions or predilections; on a larger view, it needs to accommodate ongoing change and help to ease the process of future change. It was noted above that language education is specially susceptible to an equipping perspective; it can be added that an enabling perspective is specially important in language education because language is, in its most central role, a facilitator of thought, a facilitator of change.

References

Brumfit, C. J. (1984). *Communicative methodology in language teaching.* Cambridge: Cambridge University Press.

Corder, S. Pit. (1981). *Error analysis and interlanguage.* Oxford: Oxford University Press.

Mackay, R. and Mountford, A. (Eds.). (1978). *English for specific purposes.* London: Longman.

Munby, J. (1978). *Communicative syllabus design.* Cambridge: Cambridge University Press.

Prabhu, N. S. (1984). Procedural syllabuses. In John A. S. Read (Ed.), *Trends in language syllabus design* (pp. 272–80). Singapore: Singapore University Press.

van Ek, J. A. (1975). *The threshold level.* Strasbourg: The Council of Europe.

Widdowson, H. G. (1983). *Learning purpose and language use.* Oxford: Oxford University Press.

Wilkins, D. A. (1976). *Notional syllabuses.* Oxford: Oxford University Press.

8

A World Language in Education: Defining the Domain

This paper is an attempt to identify a particular role for English as a world language and to examine the implications of that view for language education in multilingual settings.

The terms "second language" and "foreign language" are currently used mainly to specify the conditions in which a non-native language is learnt. If the language being learnt is used to a significant extent in the society at large, and exposure to the language is available to the learner outside the language classroom, the situation is said to be a "second language" one. A relative absence of such exposure outside the classroom is seen to mark a "foreign language" situation. This contrast no doubt has its value, but there is another way of making the distinction which, while not being in conflict with the prevalent contrast, nevertheless draws attention to a different aspect of language situations. A second language can be said to be one which serves certain necessary functions in the life of an individual or society—functions which the first language does not normally serve, and can be thought to have yielded to the other language. There is then a functional complementarity between the first language and the second: the total set of functions which a first language might serve in a monolingual society are now shared by that language with a "second language". A "foreign" language,

---

This essay was first published in 1988. *Source*: Prabhu, N. S. (1988). A world language in education: Defining the domain. In Verner Bickley (Ed.) *Languages in education in a bi-lingual or multi-lingual setting*, (pp. 161–167). Hong Kong: Education Department.

on this view, is a language which is learnt, not because it has to serve some specific part of one's normal linguistic needs, but as an additional accomplishment (for example, scholastic or cultural) or perhaps as a substitute to the first language in certain special circumstances (for example, travel or stay abroad). A second language, that is to say, is one which completes one's linguistic equipment; a foreign language is one which extends it as a special case. There is a partnership between the first and second languages; a foreign language is a standby.

It seems fair to say that English is today a world language, necessary in non–English speaking countries, largely because it is the medium of modern knowledge—of science, technology, information, advanced institutional organisation, higher-level professional training, discussion or collaboration. Less advanced countries need it as a means of modernisation and development, and of meaningful participation in the world at large. English is accordingly a language needed in these countries in higher education, the learned professions, the higher levels of administration, industrialisation, technological research, socio-economic awareness or action, and much of the intellectual debate in these areas. English is also used, of course, for more personal, social or cultural purposes by various individuals or groups, but in these functions it tends to alternate with a first language (or with a local common language), rather than to operate as the necessary, accepted medium. I think it is reasonable to say, in broad terms, that English serves an essential function in higher-level professional activity, while it has only a standby role in social and cultural activities. There are no doubt large variations in this respect between one non–English speaking society and another, but I would like to suggest, all the same, that the use of English in the learned professions is more central and essential than its social use, and that the value of English as a world language lies in the long run in its role as a language of learning and rational inquiry. Seen in this light, English can be regarded as the 'second' language of the non–English speaking world, a language which is complementary to each of the different first languages, performing a particular set of functions while the first language performs the other functions.

This view of a distribution of functions between English and local languages is a rough assessment of the situation that has developed in large parts of the world, but, independently of the accuracy of that assessment, I would like to suggest that it is a desirable distribution of functions, to be recognised, preserved or promoted in educational planning. Objective knowledge and the learned professions are the areas which most need English and can most benefit from its use, while social communication, cultural conformity and artistic expression are best served by a first language. This is not necessarily a position which enhances the role of English; it is equally a position which delimits and restricts that role, regarding it as undesirable for the more personal, emotional and artistically expressive roles to be taken over by English as a second language. The position can be clarified further through an examination of its implications for language education as well as of some sociolinguistic aspects of bilingualism.

It is common experience that decisions on the objectives of second language instruction are difficult to make and difficult to state with any degree of specificity. Language proficiency can be interpreted in many different terms and at many different levels—from oral fluency to accuracy in writing, from acceptable pronunciation to sustained, coherent textualisation, from a conformity to social etiquette to an ability to perceive, interpret or construct ideas and patterns of meaning. The difficulty arises partly from an inadequate delimitation of what the language being taught needs to do, and partly also from unclear relationships between the analytic components of language proficiency and its operational manifestations. However, it does seem possible to make one broad demarcation—between the type of proficiency involved in highly literate activities (as in the learned professions) and that which operates in fluent oral interaction (as in sociocultural participation or vocational transaction). Cummins (1979), for instance, makes a distinction between CALP (cognitive/academic language proficiency) and BICS (basic interpersonal communicative skills) and suggests that the two are relatively independent of each other. Crabbe (1978) makes a similar distinction between 'conceptual performance' and 'communicative performance' in a second language, and describes qualitative differences between them. It is also possible to see such a distinction as having been implicit in at least one of the arguments that led to the present movement for communicative language teaching: students who learn a second language from artificially complete sentences and impersonal academic texts, it was argued, are likely to find themselves using the language with a formal accuracy and deliberation which are unnatural to ordinary, social communication and without the oral fluency and conformity to social conventions which do mark such communication. The assumption therefore was that there were in fact two independent types of proficiency. The general result of this perception, as we know, has been a redirection of ESL courses, in varying degrees at various places, to oral-interactional fluency and functional appropriacy, but my own argument above about the value of English as a world language suggests the opposite; it is cognitive/academic language proficiency—the ability to assimilate objective knowledge and to engage in rational enquiry—that most needs to be developed in English, enabling the intellectuals of non–English speaking countries to participate in the more fundamental processes which shape the modern world. Priority to a BICS objective on ESL courses may enable learners to integrate socially with a target-language community, to seek careers in multinational corporations (or, as experience tells us, to develop a social snobbery within their own communities), but it will also involve a sacrifice on the potential for English to operate as the medium of intellectual collaboration in the world, and consequently an impoverishment of the notion 'world language'. As pointed out by Brumfit (1985, p. 155), "the emphasis on language interaction, and particularly on language as communication, is ultimately materialistic in its concentration on the messages that pass to and fro…Whatever other weaknesses there were in the earlier emphases, they were not as inherently trivial as some of the games which are now so much encouraged, nor as flippant about serious issues as some of the current exercises". It is more important, given the argument of this paper, for non-native users of English to be able to employ that language as an instrument of thought and as a means of making contact with thinking minds elsewhere (for example, through international journals), than it is for them to avoid sounding strange, slow or bookish in conversing in English with native speakers.

What I have just said is not an argument against all that is referred to as communicative language teaching but only against one particular form of it—that which directs itself to oral fluency and social, interpersonal functions. There is at least one other form of communicative language teaching—that which directs itself to the interpretation and creation of extended discourse and the rhetorical or textual functions involved in those processes—which is very relevant to cognitive/academic proficiency and is therefore supported by the view I have taken of English as a world language. Rhetorical structuring, as a means of controlling, organising and conveying sustained thought in language, is central to the more literate professions and to intellectual exchange. Indeed, cognitive/academic proficiency is firmly linked to literate uses of language; it is likely to receive support, in the early stages of its development, from the linguistic awareness and explicitness that go with literacy (Howatt, 1984, p. 296) and to develop, in its later stages, as an ability to process and formulate cognitive content in the form of texts. Communication can therefore still be regarded as a central concept in language instruction, but it is communication in the sense of meaning-exchange and substantive discussion, not in the sense of easy speech and conformity to conversational convention.

Two further points should perhaps be made in the context of this discussion of language instruction. First, the fact that instruction is not directed to proficiency in oral, social interaction does not mean that there is no place for oral interaction as a pedagogic procedure in the language classroom. Oral interaction is an important means by which transfer of knowledge or training in thinking takes place in all classrooms (not just the language classroom) and it is therefore a necessary part of language instruction which attempts to develop the ability to understand, think out and state cognitive meaning. It is, however, oral interaction in the service of meaning-exchange, not oral interaction as an imitation of desired social behaviour. Secondly, the reference above to the linguistic awareness associated with literate language use does not imply that other forms of linguistic awareness (for example, that which results from a focus on language forms or rules) are necessarily desirable or useful. The role of the explicit knowledge represented by linguistic descriptions in promoting the implicit knowledge represented by proficiency can no doubt be debated in various ways, but that issue as such is independent of whether language instruction is directed to interpersonal, communicative skills or to cognitive/academic proficiency. There is a language awareness which increases with the degree of precision aimed at in the interpretation and expression of meaning, with the result that intensive reading and exploratory writing are more linguistically aware activities than ordinary conversation, but such awareness has little to do with a knowledge of linguistic descriptions. To think otherwise would be to claim that being good at linguistics is necessarily being good at writing.

In the context of formal education, the adoption of cognitive/academic proficiency as the objective of second language instruction has a clear advantage. There is, in formal education, an inherent emphasis on literacy (two of the three R's) and on knowledge and rational enquiry. Education is seen in general as preparation for scholarship and the learned professions. For this reason, instruction which aims directly at practical, operational skills tends not to fit into formal education, especially when the practical skills are defined in opposition to cognitive content ("skills, not knowledge"). There has therefore been a tension in the past between procedures in language instruction which de-emphasised or postponed literacy, or emphasised activities such as repetition drills, on the one hand, and the expectation of serious content and studial procedures in formal education, on the other. There is a similar tension today between such "communicative" procedures as role-play, language games or a simulation of social situations, and the implicit orientation of formal education to cognition. In contrast, language instruction which aims at cognitive/academic proficiency and is therefore linked to literate uses of language as well as to the handling of cognitive content at increasingly sophisticated levels, is more in harmony with the assumptions and expectations of formal education and can expect to receive support from them. As Howatt observes, "the exchange of ideational meaning is more amenable to the conditions of the typical classroom than interpersonal socialisation (particularly if it is role-played)" (p. 297). Teaching English as a world language is thus likely to be a more congenial, or at least less disruptive, task for formal educational systems, when the role of the world language is seen to be primarily to promote an exchange of knowledge and intellectual collaboration.

To move on now to some sociolinguistic considerations, it is a familiar phenomenon that the adoption of an alien language leads at some point to an awareness, or fear, of alienation from one's own culture. A first language everywhere is a vehicle of cultural continuity and a changeover to a second language can break that continuity, both in the form of a loss of contact with one's past culture and in the form of an invasion by the cultural associations carried by the second language. While it is possible to see this as an inevitable consequence of modernisation and of having to live in a changing world—the price to be paid for the benefits of being able to operate in a world language—it is nevertheless important that, where options are available, they are exercised in a way which minimises the threat to one's own language or identity. I would like to suggest that the threat to identity is greater when the alien language takes over the more personal, social and cultural functions of the first language, than when it serves the relatively impersonal areas of objective knowledge, science and technology, modern institutions and the newer professions—functions, that is to say, which largely came into being or into prominence, as a part of modernisation and can be said to be retained, rather than usurped, by the world language. Employing a second language at the work place, in exercise of the profession for which one trained in that language or in pursuit of the intellectual contacts which are made possible by that language is much less likely to create a feeling of cultural alienation or loss than employing that language at home, in social activity or for cultural needs. The functional demarcation I have outlined for a first language and a world language seems to me to protect the traditional and cultural roles of the first language to a large extent and therefore to reduce the danger of alienation. This means, however, that it is desirable to confine the use of the second language to the more formal settings of the school, the university, the office, the industry and the research centre; it is undesirable to seek to extend its use to the family, the shop, pastime and social or cultural events, even though such an extension may offer a good deal of additional support to the acquisition of the second language.

A different consequence of the adoption of an alien language is, of course, a gradual localisation of that language, leading to a more or less divergent variety of it. Again, it is possible to view this as a natural phenomenon, to be accepted, legitimised, applauded or simply subjected to scholarly study (as illustrated, for instance, by Kachru, 1983) but it also needs to be borne in mind that a world language is worth having only so long as it remains one language used across the world. Increasing diversity and divergence can in time lead to a situation where the divergent varieties operate decreasingly as a common language and become, instead, merely additions to the local linguistic scenes. Such a development will obviously depend on a variety of historical forces, but I wish to suggest that the functions which a world language is called upon to serve are likely to make some difference to the relative stability of that language. A second language is open to influence not just by local languages but by local cultures and this means that the more the second language is used for personal, social and cultural purposes, the more it is likely to be localised. In contrast, localisation is likely to be slower or less pervasive when the use of the language is confined to the less personal and less culture-bound areas of cognitive activity. Added to this is the fact that written language, especially in its higher-order literate functions, is more uniform geographically and more stable through time than spoken language, and the role I have suggested for English as a world language is, as noted already, closely linked to literate uses. Further, language use in oral, social interaction has to meet greater demands on fluency and adaptation than language use in the give-and-take of cognitive content, which involves greater deliberation and considered formulation: while fluency and quick adaptation are abilities one acquires and exercises easily in one's first language, the demands they make in a second language can constitute undue pressure on proficiency, resulting either in an overdependence of fixed phrases (which can be harmful to using the language as a tool of thought) or in linguistic improvisation which constitutes at least deviance and at most pidginisation. It is, that is to say, the BICS functions of a second language that are likely to promote a local variety of that language more than the CALP functions. It is true that the restriction of a second language to CALP functions can result in a degree of formality, deliberation or anachronism in the use of that language, but at least those features are not unnatural to CALP functions, and they are much less likely to result in linguistic divergence than are localisation and improvisation.

I have suggested that we should value highly the role of English as a world language in enabling the intellectuals and members of the learned professions in different countries to share knowledge and ideas, and to participate in those processes of rational enquiry which shape the present-day world. I have also suggested that the concept of a world language as primarily a means of facilitating social interaction and vocational transaction is not only a trivialisation of the role a world language can play but an undesirable encroachment on roles which are best played by a first language. I have examined some aspects of language education and some effects of language contact, in the light of those suggestions.

Perhaps I can conclude with a comment from a different, wider view of the matter. The elevation of a particular language to the status of a world language entails, in effect, the conferment of a linguistic privilege by birth on the native speakers of that language. Less advanced countries adopt that language in order to participate and achieve parity in the modern world but, in that process, they become linguistically less privileged in having to operate in a second language where others operate in their first. Perhaps this too should be viewed as the necessary price to pay for the benefits of using a world language, but the linguistic disparity is at least mitigated when language use becomes secondary to higher-order abilities and to purposes and functions of a higher intrinsic value. It seems to me both more equitable and more productive for differential competences in a world language to be subordinated to intellectual interplay than for them to be reflected as social sophistication.

References

Brumfit, C. J. (1985). Creativity and constraint in the language classroom. In Randolph Quirk and H. G. Widdowson (Eds.), *English in the world* (pp. 148–57). Cambridge: Cambridge University Press.

Crabbe, David. (1987). Developing conceptual performance in a foreign language. Paper presented at the SEAMEO Regional Language Centre, Annual Seminar, Singapore.

Cummins, Jim. (1979). Cognitive/academic language proficiency, linguistic interdependence, the optimal age question and some other matters. *Working Papers in Bilingualism*, 19, 198–205.

Howatt, A. P. R. (1984). *A history of English language teaching.* Oxford: Oxford University Press.

Kachru, Braj B. (Ed.). (1983). *The other tongue.* London: Pergamon Press.

9

Materials as Support; Materials as Constraint

I am concerned in this paper with the general role of materials in language pedagogy. I wish to argue, in particular, that while materials are an important form of support to classroom activities, they also constitute a constraint which can undermine the value of those activities for the processes of learning.

The role of materials as support to teaching is clear enough. Teaching is a translation of syllabus intentions into classroom events, and the operation involved can be thought to consist of two stages. The selection of appropriate language samples and cognitive content, the designing and construction of useful activities or exercises for learners to attempt, and the sequencing or cyclic arrangement of such activities so as to fit them into lesson units, on the one hand, and facilitate cumulative learning on the other, constitute materials development as the first stage, while the planning and carrying out of actual classroom procedures which enable learners to benefit from those materials is classroom teaching as the second stage.

If teachers themselves try to perform both stages of the work, thus developing their own materials in the course of their classroom teaching, they are likely to find it too much work to do and be forced to make sacrifices on the quality of one or both stages. It is therefore desirable to divide the labour and promote specialisation.

This essay was first published in 1989. *Source*: Prabhu, N. S. (1989). Materials as support: Materials as constraint. *Guidelines: A periodical for classroom language teachers*, 11(1), 66–74.

Since the second stage of classroom teaching has necessarily to be done by teachers individually in each classroom, the first stage of materials construction can conveniently be separated and centralised, so that one effort at materials construction can be of use in many classrooms, many times over. This not only leaves teachers free to concentrate on classroom procedures; it also enables a highly skilled few to provide well-constructed materials to a large number of teachers, thus ensuring a certain uniform quality to classroom activities despite varying teacher qualities. Materials construction has thus come to be regarded as a specialist job, whose quality has a beneficial influence on the quality of classroom activities and, as a result, on the quality of learning. On this view, therefore, the more centrally materials are produced, the greater the chance of employing high-level expertise on the work; and the more widely such centrally produced materials are used, the larger the benefit to the population of learners.

There is, however, another side to the picture. Learning depends not just on what inputs are made available to the learner in the form of materials, but, equally, on what the learner brings to bear on those inputs, which can perhaps be called the learner's "investment". I am not referring here particularly to learners' attitudes, personalities or motivation, though these are obviously a part of the investment. I am referring, rather, to learners' current knowledge of the world and their current language abilities—that is to say, the same sorts of things as are considered in the construction of materials. Materials represent a selection of certain cognitive and cultural content, as well as a demand for linguistic effort at a certain level, as input; learners bring with them a certain state of cognitive and cultural knowledge, and a certain level of language ability, as investment. Learning can be said to result from an interaction between input and investment, the amount of learning being proportionate to the amount of interaction. The amount of interaction, in turn, depends on the relationship between input and investment, which we can think of in terms of their relative closeness and distance.

If the level of input is very close to the level of investment, the amount of interaction called for is small and the gain in terms of learning is also small. If, on the other hand, input and investment are too distant from each other, interaction can become too difficult or impossible, with little learning resulting. What is needed is an appropriate distance between the two, such that interaction can be maximal and successful. One can recall Vygotsky's view that "learning which is oriented toward developmental stages that have already been reached is ineffective—the only 'good learning' is that which is in advance of development". Vygotsky also posits a "zone of proximal development", which is the distance between the learner's actual development stage, at a given time, and the level of development attainable, at that time, through a learning experience (Vygotsky, 1978, p. 86, p. 91).

Learning, then, is dependent not on materials themselves, however sophisticated they are in their design and construction, but rather on an optimal approximation between materials and learners' current states. Now, learners' states (in terms of their world knowledge and language abilities, for our purpose) are necessarily varied, the variation increasing generally with geographical, cultural or linguistic spread, among others. The wider the area to be served by a given set of materials, the more varied the learners' states are likely to be, making optimal approximation between input and investment that much more difficult.

This points directly to a disadvantage of producing materials centrally. The idea behind central production is necessarily that of wide use, and the justification for central production, as noted earlier, is that it ensures quality. Quality is generally understood to mean things like a careful and detailed determination of inputs and their arrangement in a well-considered order—that is to say, a high degree of refinement, internal structuring and specificity to the input. Quality in this sense is preserved when different teachers use the materials in the form in which they are provided, and destroyed or diluted when they alter their content or form. If, however, we see plausibility to the concept of learning arising from an interaction between teaching input and learners' investment, we have a different concept of quality of materials. Quality now is a matter of optimal approximation between learners' current states and teaching inputs and, given that learners' states vary between different classrooms, inputs can achieve quality only by being altered or adjusted by teachers in the light of their perception of learners' states. From this point of view, therefore, centrally produced materials can achieve quality not by being highly specific in their content and arrangement, but by being maximally flexible and adjustable, not by being highly structured but by being loosely structured, not by guarding against alteration by teachers but by providing for and encouraging alteration or substitution in different ways.

Quality in the other sense of a high degree of pre-determination and specificity acts as a constraint on classroom activity, discouraging alteration and reducing the chances of optimal approximation to varied learner states. Also, the more centrally materials are produced (that is to say, the more widely they are to be used), the greater the need for flexibility and looseness, and the larger the task of teachers in altering and adjusting them. It is less centralised production of materials that is likely to make the degree of flexibility needed in them more manageable, and an optimal approximation to learners' states more attainable.

It is of course possible to point out, in reply, that all or most materials do in fact envisage being mediated by teachers before they reach learners, that few writers of materials forbid teachers to adjust or alter what is offered to suit their classrooms, and that many centrally produced coursebooks specifically ask teachers to exercise their pedagogic judgment in using them. After all, the production of materials is only the first stage in translating teaching intentions into classroom activities and there is a necessary second stage for teachers to carry out, which includes reducing or increasing the "distance" between learners and materials. However, such allowances for teachers' alteration are generally made (and viewed) as the declaration of a pedagogic stance, or the recognition of an unfortunate necessity of the situation, or a broad-minded concession from the specialist to the practitioner, if not as a protective measure against potential criticism or simply as an expression of authorial modesty.

What is needed, instead, is an exploration of ways in which provision for change and choice can be built into the materials themselves and, more fundamentally, a revision of the values attached to centralised production and teacher-level alteration. If value for learning lies in the match achieved between learners and materials, rather than in any inherent features of materials themselves, centrally produced materials ought to facilitate and enlarge the scope for teachers' decisions, choices and changes in what is provided. Indeed, centralisation of materials production is itself a move which increases the burden on teachers' decisions and choices; when some responsibility is removed from the level of the classroom and exercised away from it, that fact makes the remaining responsibility at the classroom level all the more crucial for the process of learning. It is centralised production that is an unfortunate necessity, not classroom alteration.

There is, no doubt, some recognition already of the gaps created between learners' states and teaching inputs when materials are produced for global use. Internationally produced materials are sometimes adapted or culturally localised for use in particular countries, and international publishers themselves often put out different versions of materials for different parts of the world—or bring out a set of materials specially for one country or region. Education systems in particular countries or states develop their own materials, in preference to using more global materials, on the grounds of local suitability. All of this is an attempt to reduce centralisation in order to reduce the distance between learners and inputs. However, this is only one level of approximation to learners' states—in terms of cultural and cognitive content, perhaps some aspects of local language norms, and a very broad categorisation of language abilities and learning conditions. There is another, I think more important, form of approximation to learners' states which demands, not just a decentralisation of materials production, but a fundamental change in the design of materials.

If learning is the result of interaction between learners' states and teaching inputs, then each experience of such interaction has the potential to yield some learning, and that piece of learning has the effect of changing the learners' state. What the learners invest in their next experience of interaction is therefore slightly different from what they invested in the last, and the input that can achieve optimal approximation to learners' investment is also different for the two occasions. There is, that is to say, ongoing change in learners' states, and teaching inputs can be optimal only by being continually responsive to that change.

Further, there is no assurance that any given teaching input on any given occasion will in fact lead to the intended learning: the process of learning being an internal mental phenomenon, all judgments about learners' states, optimal inputs and learning outcomes are in the area of probability, not certainty. But teaching is crucially a matter of making those judgments and adjusting inputs accordingly. Any inputs that are pre-determined for a relatively large span of teaching are pre-emptive in nature, not responsive to ongoing change in learners' states. All pre-constructed materials therefore constitute pre-emptive inputs and an important part of teaching is to change them as necessary in order to make them less pre-emptive and more responsive. Materials therefore need to be flexible and changeable, even when they are produced for use with just one class or just one learner.

The concept of ongoing change in learners' states is, of course, the rationale of grading in the construction of materials: inputs are so ordered that successive inputs assume the learning intended from previous units to have taken place. But this only represents a further dimension in the pre-determination of inputs. Not only are inputs presumed to be optimally related to learners' states at particular points; they are also presumed to have brought about the intended interactions and learning outcomes. If teachers judge the input provided for some lesson unit not to be optimal, they will need to adjust or alter it. But that alteration has an effect on what learning outcome can be expected from that lesson unit, which is now at variance with what is presumed by the next input provided, thus creating a need for further alterations in further inputs.

Added to this is the fact that optimal approximation itself is, as noted earlier, a matter of judgment, rather than determinable fact, and learning outcomes are very much a matter of probability, even when inputs are judged to be optimal. The writer of materials may have the advantage of professional expertise in making these judgments, but classroom teachers have the more important advantage of observing and assessing ongoing evidence from learners and being guided by trial-and-error. Given that learning outcomes are not predictable with any certainty, even in the best of circumstances, it is actual, ongoing evidence that should receive a higher value than prediction; and professional expertise should be employed in enhancing the chances of teachers acting on ongoing evidence, rather than on abridging those chances by increasing pre-determination.

Grading in materials constitutes a degree of detail in the pre-determination of inputs. The more detailed, and professionally sophisticated, the grading is, the greater the expectation that teachers will adhere to it, which makes the inputs so much more pre-emptive. What one needs, instead, is a recognition that detailed grading entails an increase in the probable need for teachers to re-grade the materials, and that the remedy to the situation might lie not in attempting more careful prediction and more detailed grading, but rather in trying to design materials which predict minimally and provide deliberately for grading or re-grading by teachers in different ways.

There is another aspect to the pre-emptiveness of materials. Our discussion so far has referred to teachers' judgments in regard to the relative distance between learners' states and teaching inputs. But there are also judgements involved in deciding on desirable forms of input, quite apart from their difficulty levels. Is input best provided in the form of texts and other samples of language use, in the form of controlled practice of structural or functional items, in the form of linguistic generalisations, in the form of simulated real-life activities, or in the form of a cognitive effort to make sense, think purposefully and get meaning across? These may be judgements about which form of input is likely to be productive at particular points in the teaching sequence—judgements, that is to say, about learner readiness for a form of work—or about the quantum of input likely to be optimal at those points. Equally (and inevitably), there are also judgements involved about which form of input is more productive of learning in a more general sense—that is to say, judgements concerned with a choice of method or "approach" in teaching. Now, pre-constructed materials not only represent predictive judgements about what input is to be made at what point in the teaching and in what quantity; they also represent judgements about what forms of input are generally preferable to others—that is to say, they incorporate a particular method or approach (or a particular combination of different methods, in preference to other possible combinations).

This must imply either that the teachers who are to use those materials do in fact share those judgements; or that they look on materials construction as being a specialist job, to be carried out by those with superior judgment—or it must imply that learning is better off when teachers act on the materials writer's judgement than when they act on their own. This latter assumption—that teachers are to follow the methodological judgements incorporated in the materials provided, ignoring or suppressing their own—seems to me to constitute the most serious aspect of the pre-emptiveness of materials, in that it denies or devalues the basis on which teachers (or anyone else) can engage in a human interactional activity in a meaningful way.

It reduces not only the role of teacher responsiveness to ongoing change in learners' states but, more importantly, the engagement in the classroom of teachers' pedagogic perceptions about what promotes learning, what constitutes evidence of learning, when learning may or may not be taking place, etc. A non-engagement of these perceptions is also a constraint on their growth: continual action based on someone else's judgement is unlikely to help one's own judgement to develop and change in the course of experience. Equally, if learning is the result of learners' investment and its interaction with optimal input, as we have proposed, a circumvention of teachers' perceptions and judgements can only lead to a reduction in responsive input-adjustment, and therefore to a reduction in learning.

In considering the consequences of these arguments for the design of materials, it is useful to make a distinction between "course" materials and "source" materials. Course materials are those which attempt to provide all and only the inputs to be presented to learners, in the order in which they are to be presented. They constitute both the teaching content and the teaching agenda, in the sense that their units are easily usable (and meant to be used) as lesson plans. They incorporate a number of decisions made by the materials writer on behalf of the teacher—on the desirable forms, difficulty levels, quantities and sequence of inputs. They also anticipate the pace of learning they will bring about, and grade themselves accordingly.

Source materials, in contrast, are those which provide a range of possible inputs, without envisaging that all of them will be used in any classroom or that all classrooms will use the same inputs. They may suggest different teaching agendas and lesson formats but are not themselves organised into lesson-units. They may provide inputs at different levels of difficulty and in different quantities, leaving it to the teacher to select from the range in both respects.

With course materials, the expectation is that teachers will use them in the form in which they are provided, accepting or respecting the judgements they incorporate, and being as faithful to their intentions as possible. With source materials, the expectation is, rather, that teachers will find it useful to draw on them in implementing the decisions they make as teachers, being as faithful as possible to their own perceptions of learner states and learning processes. Course materials represent a great deal of support, but also a large degree of constraint, in teaching; source materials represent those forms of support which are likely to act minimally as constraint.

One can recognise some forms of source materials already in the market. There are, for instance, books which contain activities of just one type, such as drama techniques, role-play, project-work, reading comprehension, listening activities, etc. These are not meant to be used as coursebooks but, rather, to be drawn on by teachers if and when they decide to use activities of those kinds. They provide possible teaching activities, without specifying a teaching agenda.

A further step in this direction is a loosely organised collection of varied samples of language use (or authentic texts), illustrated by Maley and Duff's *Words!* Inputs in this form call for teachers' decisions both on which of them to use, and on what form of classroom activity to use them for. They provide possible content (linguistic and cognitive), without specifying any particular method. A reversal of this makes yet another form of source material—that which provides detailed procedures for constructing particular forms of classroom activity (for example, composition, simulation), but leaves the teacher free to select appropriate texts or topics to base them on.

Such materials can perhaps be termed "semi-materials" (referring to those that provide single-type activities, or only language samples, without activities) and "meta-materials" (referring to those that provide only abstract formats for activities, without content). A third possibility, I think, is materials as a compendium of varied content, various forms of activity and various possibilities for arrangement. Thus one can put together a wide range of texts and information in non-textual forms, varied in cognitive content as well as in complexity. One can provide some activities of each kind, and procedures for constructing more. One can also suggest and illustrate ways of linking information-content and activities in different ways to make up lesson-units, and indicate possibilities of regulating the difficulty level of activities. Indeed, one would indicate ways of changing the compendium itself through additions, omissions, extensions in particular directions and reduction in others, so that different teachers can gradually evolve sets of materials which are most supportive of their teaching.

A compendium in this sense is a set of source materials from which teachers can develop their own course materials; equally, it is a possible means of promoting the process of teachers changing their course materials continually in the light of their classroom needs and judgments. Such a compendium can also enable teachers to pursue, explore and develop, in the process of recurrent pedagogic decision and action, their own pedagogic perceptions of desirable teaching methods—including, I think, the possibility of sharing classroom decisions with learners, thus using source materials as an instrument of "learner-training" (in the sense of Allwright, 1981).

I have tried to show that our current concept of centrally produced materials for use in many classrooms involves a pre-emption of several decisions which are best left to teachers in the interests of learning. Such materials are commonly thought to support teaching by reducing the need for teachers' decisions, and to ensure a higher quality to classroom work than can be expected from teachers' decisions. I have argued in reply that what is regarded as support is also an undesirable form of constraint, and that the quality achieved through a pre-determination of inputs has less value for learning than that which is achieved through responsive inputs. I have also suggested a broad direction in which materials design can move in order to promote more responsive classroom inputs. Perhaps I can conclude by making two further points, in anticipation of objections.

First, I am not arguing against central production of materials as such, much less against all pre-construction of materials for teaching. Some pre-construction of materials is a necessary part of planning a teaching programme, and central production is probably an essential need of large educational systems. I am, however, questioning current interpretations of the value of central production—seen as a pre-determination of classroom inputs—and suggesting that materials, whether more centralised or less, should attempt to limit input-determination and increase the chances of classroom inputs being responsive to varied learner states. I am therefore arguing for an effort to construct materials in a different form, which I have called "source" materials.

Secondly, I am not assuming that all or most teachers are good at judging learners' states or at making inputs responsive to them. Nor am I assuming that the professional expertise of materials writers is less than good. What I am suggesting is that teachers' judgements and decisions—by virtue of their being teachers' judgements and decisions, open to influence by ongoing classroom evidence—have a higher value for learning than judgements and decisions which are only predictive of learners' states and which, moreover, are pre-emptive of teachers' decisions. I am also suggesting that the professional expertise of materials writers is best employed, not in preventing decisions by teachers with low levels of judgement, and thus causing a continuance of those low levels of judgement, but instead, in finding ways of requiring and assisting the exercise of teachers' judgements, so that judgements at all levels can develop to higher levels, and teaching can become more productive of teachers' professional growth.

References

Allwright, R. L. (1981). What do we want teaching materials for? *English Language Teaching Journal*, 36(1), 5–18.

Maley, A. and Duff, A. (1976). *Words!* Cambridge: Cambridge University Press.

Vygotsky, L. S. (1978). *Mind in society: The development of higher psychological process.* Harvard: Harvard University Press.

10

Acquisition Through Comprehension: Three Procedures

This paper attempts to analyse in some detail a current concept in language pedagogy, namely, that input-comprehension by the learner is the most favourable condition for language acquisition. It also attempts an assessment and comparison of three general classroom procedures for their value in promoting desired forms of input-comprehension.

If we ask what we know with certainty about language learning, the answer is likely to be disappointingly small, namely, that there has to be exposure to the language to be learnt. About twenty years ago, in a paper which challenged most prevalent assumptions in language teaching, Corder (1981, p. 8) made the suggestion that "given motivation, it is inevitable that a human being will learn a second language if he is exposed to the language data". Corder thus identified two factors as being essential, namely, motivation and exposure, and put forward the view that language learning is a natural, automatic, indeed "inevitable", process. Of the two factors, motivation has always been something of a name for the unknown, not easy to identify and, even if identified, not open to prediction or control. It is exposure that language teaching has tried to do something with, both by way of understanding (that is, conceptualising ways in which exposure may lead to acquisition) and by way of action (that is, creating in the classroom conditions in which desired forms of exposure can occur). It has, for instance,

This essay was first published in 1989. *Source*: Prabhu, N. S. (1989). Acquisition through comprehension: Three procedures. *Focus on English*, 5/4, 1–12.

been thought that a desirable form of exposure is a conscious, analytic focus on language as language, similar to a grammarian's focus on it, though at a much less sophisticated level. This has led to the teaching of grammar as a way of teaching the language, getting learners to understand the analysis made by grammarians. Alternatively, exposure has been thought to consist of repeated contact with similar samples of language, its value lying in the frequency of contact rather than in any analytic focus. This has led to language teaching which aims at "practice", in the sense of a recurrent handling of pieces of language which all exemplify a given feature of language structure. Such repeated contact with similarly-structured pieces of language is thought to establish the structural feature involved as a "habit" in the learner's mind. A third interpretation of exposure is that it consists of comprehending the meaning (or message-content) of various samples of language. This has been the basis, in more or less explicit ways, of such forms of teaching in the past as the "Direct Method", the "Conversation Method" and the "Natural Method" (Howatt, 1984, pp. 192–208), and has, in the past few years, drawn a good deal of professional attention, as a result of the powerful concepts of a "natural order" of language learning and of interlanguage development. Krashen's input hypothesis, for instance, is a strong assertion of the centrality of comprehension to language acquisition:

> The Input Hypothesis claims that humans acquire language in only one way—by understanding messages, or by receiving "comprehensible input". We progress along the natural order by understanding input that contains structures at our next "stage"—structures which are a bit beyond our current level of competence. Speaking is the result of acquisition and not its cause. Speaking cannot be taught directly but "emerges" on its own as a result of building competence via comprehensible input (Krashen, 1985, p. 2).

We may note, in passing, that this view of language acquisition has a consequence for our perspective on the four language skills of listening, speaking, reading and writing. The four skills, as we know, have two dimensions to them: the skills of oracy versus 1–12 the skills of literacy, on the one hand, and the skills of comprehension versus the skills of production, on the other. Following the Reform Movement a hundred years ago, which criticised the earlier Grammar-Translation Method for its concentration on written language and made the emphatic assertion that language is primarily speech and only secondarily writing, it has been a widely accepted principle in language pedagogy that the oral skills of listening and speaking should be taught prior to the literate skills of reading and writing. If, however, comprehension is the primary process of language acquisition, with production being best left to emerge at a later stage, the two comprehension skills of listening and reading need to have high priority over the production skills of speaking and writing. Reading, that is to say, takes precedence over speaking, and, further, speaking and writing are both of much less relevance to the process of acquisition.

Let us consider a little more closely the view that comprehension is the basis of acquisition. What we are saying is not that comprehension results from acquisition—that we understand messages in a strange language when we have learnt that language. What we are saying is that acquisition results from comprehension—that we will acquire a strange language when we understand messages in it. What justifies this apparently un-commonsensical view? When something is translated for us from a strange language into a language which we know, we comprehend the message involved but are unlikely to be acquiring the strange language thereby. When we watch foreign films which are subtitled in our own language, we can be said to comprehend those films but are clearly not acquiring the foreign language. It therefore cannot be that comprehension as a product—the actual understanding of messages, by whatever means—is of value to acquisition. It must instead be the case that comprehension as a process—the effort to understand messages—is what brings about acquisition. When a message is translated for us from a strange language, we are not called upon to make any effort to work out the message from that language—we are in fact deprived of such effort and of the contingent opportunity to acquire a little of the strange language. For acquisition to take place, one needs to be engaged in an effort to work out meaning from language, that is to say, in the process of making sense from language with some difficulty. "Receiving comprehensible input", which is the way Krashen puts it, is a misleading statement of the matter, since it suggests that we can acquire a language by merely receiving input which has been made comprehensible for us by someone else. If input has already been made comprehensible for us, we need to make little effort to comprehend it and there is therefore little likelihood of language acquisition. Value for acquisition lies neither in the comprehensibility of the input itself nor in the actual comprehension we achieve of it, but rather in the effort we make to comprehend it—our struggle to understand the message. What is needed, strictly, is not "comprehensible" input, but rather the "comprehending" of input; and, moreover, the input needs to be less than readily comprehensible so that the act of comprehending may involve an effort.

But how does an effort to comprehend result in acquisition? We are talking here of a complex and inaccessible psychological phenomenon, and can only hope for a concept which has plausibility, not a fact which has certainty. Any sample of a language is a piece of meaning (or "message") formulated according to the structure of that language. It is therefore an entity which represents some meaning as well as some (parts of) language structure, and there is a close integration of the two, in that at least some of the meaning is embodied in the structure: a sample of language has meaning by virtue of the fact that it is linguistically structured (Prabhu, 1987, pp. 69–70). Therefore, any comprehension of the language sample must involve a perception of the relationship between meaning and structure—an understanding (perhaps at some subconscious level) of how that piece of language is structured so as to embody that piece of meaning. This will clearly include an "unravelling" of various syntactic relations and functions (for example, those which linguists describe as "subject", "object", "adverb", "modifier"—or "actor", "agent", "patient", "goal"), as well as some discernment of how those relations are signified in that sample of language. Such discernment may, in addition to being largely subconscious, be vague, imperfect, incomplete or even misconstrued, but, to the extent it is successful, comprehension of the sample of language concerned can be said to have been achieved. Further, the effort that goes into achieving comprehension is in fact effort at discerning and unravelling the linguistic structure of the sample. Effort at comprehension can thus be thought to cause a form of intensive exposure to language structure—the greater the effort, the more intensive the exposure. Furthermore, although on any single occasion, such intensive exposure can bring about only a momentary discernment of the language structure involved, subsequent occasions of similarly intensive exposure to other samples of the language are likely to have the cumulative effect of leaving in the comprehender's mind a relatively stable impression of the language structure concerned—something of a cognitive formation which constitutes a recreation of (a piece of) language structure (Chomsky, 1976, p. 23). It is this process of cognitive formation which we refer to as "acquisition", the ultimate result of the process being an internal representation of the structure of the language, referred to as "competence".

While this outline of the process of acquisition is only a plausible conceptualisation of the phenomenon, it nevertheless helps to give content to a linguistic and pedagogic intuition which has been voiced repeatedly in the history of language teaching—the intuition which has supported all the "natural approaches", to use Howatt's (1984, pp. 295–97) cover term, as distinct from "rational approaches", however different the actual terms used in stating it. Harold Palmer, for instance, seems to have used the term "memorizing" to refer to what we call "acquisition" today, and the terms "catenizing" and "semanticizing" to refer to the processes of discerning structure and meaning in a sample of language. In a book published in 1921, he said:

> The memorizing of speech material consists of two processes: catenizing and semanticizing. Catenizing means: learning to

> recognize or to produce a chain of sounds or syllables as an integral whole, irrespective of all considerations of meaning. Semanticizing means: forming a perfect association between a word (or word-group) and that for which it stands...The perfect combination of these two processes results in a perfectly memorized unit. (p. 21)

Palmer is talking here of a "perfect combination" of "catenizing" and "semanticizing" a given unit of language (that is to say, a simultaneous perception of structure and meaning in a given sample of language) as constituting successful acquisition—a concept which is very similar to the one I have outlined above.

It needs to be emphasised that the perception of structure brought about by an effort at comprehension can only be a fleeting one, and any cognitive formation of structure resulting from it is likely to be slight, weak, and unstable: acquisition, that is to say, is not envisaged as a one-step phenomenon, attaining a firm or final form on the basis of a single instance of comprehension. Nevertheless, any slight cognitive formation which results from one act of comprehension is likely to be brought to bear on the next (or a subsequent) act of comprehension, and to get either firmed up a little (if supported by the perception of structure on that occasion) or revised or replaced (if contradicted by that perception). Successive effort at comprehension thus leads to a relatively firm cognitive formation, through a process of repeated revision and confirmation. Now, this account of acquisition not only shows why comprehension needs to have first priority in language instruction; it also points to the reason why production needs to be left to emerge much later. Language production demands cognitive structures which are relatively firmly formed, and can be engaged in only when recurrent effort at comprehension has led to such firmly formed structures. I am of course referring to genuine production here, not to reproduction (in whatever form) which involves no more than a repetition of contact with language, and does not provide even the intensive exposure which effort at comprehension provides. Genuine production, when it does emerge, brings into operation the cognitive structures which are sufficiently firmly formed and can, as a result of the operation, increase their firmness. The initial emergence of genuine production, however, can be helped only through successive effort at comprehension, not through reproduction.

Given this view of acquisition through comprehension, we can try to identify some general criteria by which comprehension activity in the classroom can be considered to be good or bad, that is, more or less helpful to acquisition. I think there are three such criteria which we can use.

First, comprehension activity needs to be such that learners are called upon to make the maximal effort they can at comprehension, and any assistance which the teacher provides is in response to learners' effort, not in lieu of it. As we noted above, value for acquisition lies in the process of trying to comprehend, not in the amount of comprehension gained as a product. It is true that the maximal effort which learners can make is limited in various ways and may well fall short of the effort needed to comprehend a given sample of language; and it is also true that an essential part of the teacher's role is to ease, support or regulate learners' effort, so that the comprehension achieved may be in the desired direction and there may be enough success in comprehension to maintain learners' morale. But, if the teacher aims at learners' success so much that he/she provides assistance which pre-empts learners' effort (or renders it less than the maximum possible), the activity will lose its value for acquisition to that extent. Any assistance the teacher provides needs to be an addition to learners' effort, not a substitution for it. Further, since the amount of effort which learners can make at any time is neither predictable with any precision nor likely to be uniform to a group, the principle of addition, rather than substitution, means, in practice, that learners should first make the most effort they can and the teacher's assistance should be made available only in the light of actual evidence of such effort and its measure of success. More importantly for our discussion, the form of classroom activity should be such that it is likely to bring about an effort by learners in the first place, and to occasion the teacher's assistance only (or largely) as a response to such effort.

Secondly, comprehension activity should be such that there is an immediate purpose to comprehending and, equally, there is a criterion of adequacy which can be applied to the comprehension achieved. It is natural for learners to achieve limited degrees of comprehension, and it is, in fact, only by achieving relatively low degrees of comprehension on some occasions that they can be expected to achieve higher degrees of comprehension on later occasions. There is therefore a legitimate place for rough (or partial or imperfect) comprehension, and there are purposes for which such rough comprehension is adequate. Indeed the notion of full or perfect comprehension is something of an illusion, not just for learners but for all language users: no one can be said to have comprehended a sample of language fully, such that no higher level of comprehension is possible. Or, to put it differently, no sample of language can be said to be comprehensible or incomprehensible by itself to any of us: it can only be comprehensible enough (or not comprehensible enough) for a given purpose, with a given criterion of adequacy. This means, in pedagogic terms, that classroom activity should allow the teacher to set levels of adequacy differently on different occasions and to permit learners to work to those limited levels.

Thirdly, classroom activity should allow different learners to make different amounts of effort at comprehension, whether on the same occasion or on different occasions. A learner making an effort at comprehension brings to bear on the task, as we have noted, such cognitive structures as he/she has formed so far, and can hope to enlarge (or elaborate or revise or firm up) those structures as a result of the current effort. The pace and progress of language acquisition are bound to vary from one learner to another (as do most other forms of learning), and there is, in principle, no way of knowing which learner has formed what cognitive structures, or what effort at comprehension will yield what enlargement of those structures. This means that, to maximise the scope for acquisition by different learners (or even by a single learner), the samples of language acting as inputs should be rich—that is to say, structurally varied and composite, and integral to the meaning-content. Inputs, that is to say, should be "texts", in a broad sense of the term—not sentences selected or constructed to exemplify features of language structure, but chunks of meaning which select their own, varied structural features in order to make themselves communicable. Language will no doubt need to be simplified often, but only as a form of assistance to comprehension (in the way it gets simplified in real-world communication with persons who have limited levels of linguistic competence), not as a form of planned linguistic delimitation. Further, what provides assistance to comprehension is not just linguistic simplification; equally important is a sustained context of communication, where comprehension at one point has consequences for comprehension at other points, and where inference of meaning is aided by the interdependence of different parts of the message-content. Such sustained contexts to communication also demand language which is structurally composite.

These, then are three criteria by which classroom activity can be assessed for its value in promoting acquisition through comprehension:

i. whether the teacher's assistance is likely to be responsive to learners' effort, rather than pre-emptive of it;
ii. whether the activity demands purposeful comprehension with an adjustable level of adequacy; and
iii. whether the samples of language employed in the activity are likely to be structurally composite and supported by sustained contexts.

I will now go on to examine three general types of classroom activity in the light of these criteria.

The most obvious classroom procedure for promoting learners' comprehension of language samples is what is referred to as "situational presentation". This has been in vogue for over fifty years now, and is perhaps the most widely used (at any rate, the most widely recommended) procedure for ensuring that learners understand the language being taught to them. Situational presentation, as we know, consists of the teacher creating or exploiting classroom situations—often with the help of pictures, gestures or realia—in order to enable learners to infer the meaning of the language being used. It is thought that, when this procedure is employed, learners will comprehend the samples of language concerned easily and "directly", that is, without the intervention of some other language known to them. A good deal of training for language teachers consists of providing varied ways of presenting language situationally, and a good deal of lesson planning by teachers is taken up with selecting or preparing suitable classroom situations. Indeed the procedure has been seen as a central principle of language teaching, as denoted by the term "Situational Approach" (Hornby, 1959, pp. 150–56) to refer to a methodology.

Notice, however, that successful situational presentation depends crucially on the teacher's anticipation of learners' inference of meaning. The teacher has to anticipate, in advance of the lesson, what difficulties learners will have in comprehending language, what situations will lead them to what inference of meaning, and how far the inferencing will go. The teacher's assistance is accordingly prepared and provided on the strength of a prediction of learners' effort, not in the light of actual evidence of such effort. The more assistance is provided in this way, the less effort learners need to make, and it is in fact thought to be the teacher's aim to make comprehension as easy as possible for the learners—that is to say, to minimise the need for learners' effort. The most successful situational presentation of language makes the meaning so clear that learners need to make little effort—or are likely to make little error. This therefore is teacher's assistance as a substitute for learner effort, pre-emptive rather than responsive. Further, even if the teacher should wish to ensure an effort at comprehension by learners, the activity offers little scope for doing so because situational presentation does not demand comprehension by learners for a perceived purpose by which it can be considered adequate or inadequate. The aim of situational presentation can only be full comprehension (in some vague sense) by learners—or as full as possible, with no basis for operating with limited levels or with "rough" comprehension which is adequate for a purpose on hand. In the absence of an immediate purpose and a criterion of adequacy, the teacher can get no actual evidence of learners' effort and of its success or failure; he/she has to assume that learners' comprehension will be proportionate to his/her own effort at situationalising the language—that is to say, that learning is proportionate to the teacher's effort, not the learner's. Also, situational presentation is linked to a pre-selection of the language to be presented: it is normally a presentation of some specific piece of language, such as a structural, lexical or functional item. This results in a deliberate delimitation of language, on the one hand, and a matching abridgement of situations, on the other: if similar samples of language are to be made to recur, one needs to use a series of different but parallel situations, as anyone who has attempted situational presentation over a stretch of time will have realised. Situational presentation thus fails to meet any of the three requirements we have identified for the promotion of acquisition through comprehension.

As we know, situational presentation is thought to have the advantage of avoiding the use of the learner's mother-tongue in the classroom. It developed in the context of a rejection of the Grammar-Translation Method, which included teachers' translation of new language in order to make it comprehensible to learners. But the Grammar-Translation Method also involved a good deal of translation by learners, and translation by learners is not the same thing as translation by teachers. When teachers translate, they provide assistance to learners' comprehension, in a way which is highly pre-emptive; when learners translate, however, they make an effort at comprehension, aiming at a relatively high degree of precision. Translation by learners can thus be of value as effort at comprehension, and there is a case for re-examining the Grammar-Translation Method, which used learners' translation as one of its main procedures. As we know from Howatt's informative account (pp. 131–46), the Grammar-Translation Method did not introduce either the use of grammar or the use of translation in language teaching; it merely continued the use of grammar and translation (as well as a concentration on written language) from an earlier tradition. What it did introduce was the principle of grammatical grading in the presentation of language, and the principle of practice by learners—both principles preserved by later traditions. In its later stages, it also brought in a great deal of grammatical information for learners to memorise, in an unfortunate attempt to compete with the prestige of classical languages. What is of interest for us here is its earlier form and, in particular, its use of translation as the main means of providing practice to learners. As Howatt points out, learners translated samples of language both from the target language into their mother-tongue and in the other direction, usually in that order. It is possible to see translation into the mother-tongue as an exercise in comprehension, and translation into the target language as one in production. We can then see that comprehension was given precedence over production in the Grammar-Translation Method. It is translation as an exercise in comprehension that is of interest to our discussion.

Since translation demands a relatively high degree of precision in understanding the meaning of language samples, it brings about a correspondingly large amount of effort at comprehension—effort, in particular, at perceiving syntactic relations and their semantic readings—"catenizing" and "semanticizing", in Palmer's words—which has special value for acquisition. Moreover, this effort has necessarily to be made by the translator, that is, the learner. Any anticipatory assistance by the teacher can only be limited to the provision of lexical equivalents and some demonstration of translation, which are unlikely to be a substitute for the learner's main effort. All other assistance by the teacher, as evaluation or feedback on the result of the learner's effort, is responsive, not pre-emptive. By the first of our three criteria, therefore, translation by learners into the mother-tongue is a very good form of comprehension activity.

It does not, however, meet the second criterion so well. The immediate purpose of translation is generally seen to be the product of the activity itself, namely, a sample of language in the other language; and it is not clear how purposes beyond the activity can be set in a way integral to the activity. More seriously, translation does not permit varied levels of adequacy for its success. As a result, translation can no doubt be more or less successful, but it is not easy to see how a less-than-successful result can nevertheless be seen as being successful enough for a given need. It is, that is to say, difficult to work with "rough" comprehension as being adequate for a purpose on hand. Our third criterion can be met quite well by translation, in that the samples of language set for translation can be extended texts rather than sets of sentences, with such overall simplification as may be necessary but without any planned delimitation of language to suit specific teaching items. However, the Grammar-Translation Method itself was attempting grammatical grading as another principle of teaching, and seems to have used sets of sentences, illustrative of particular grammatical features, rather than larger texts in larger contexts.

On the whole, translation by learners fulfills the requirements of acquisition by comprehension better than situational presentation does, and I think it deserves more of our consideration than it has received in recent decades. Translation used to be objected to strongly on the grounds that it would increase the risk of mother-tongue interference, but our notion of mother-tongue interference has since undergone considerable change, to the point of our regarding the phenomenon as possibly beneficial language-transfer, or the legitimate use of an existing communicative resource in trying to develop another. Besides, as Kandiah (1978) argues, an insistence on monolingual classrooms implies the ideal of developing a monolingual competence in learners, whereas most second-language learners expect to operate as bilinguals, rather than monolinguals. This is not just a question of learning objectives; a conceptual model of bilingual competence can be of great relevance in exploring possible learning processes and re-assessing teaching procedures such as translation.

Translation does, however, have the disadvantage of not permitting a regulation of levels of adequacy, and we noted earlier how situational presentation too suffers from this disadvantage. We therefore need to look for a possible classroom procedure in which comprehension can have an immediate purpose variable in its demands, in which the teacher's assistance to comprehension is likely to be responsive to learner's effort, and in which the language needs to be delimited only for communicative success. This suggests an activity which consists of setting learners a problem to solve—a problem which calls for an understanding of information relevant to it, involves some "working out" in the mind in order to relate the information to the problem and to arrive at a possible solution, and allows a process of trial and error in testing the solution arrived at and making a fresh effort if necessary. Such problem-solving, which I have referred to elsewhere (Prabhu, 1987) as "task-based" activity, meets our three criteria for acquisition through comprehension particularly well. Problem-solving necessarily involves the provision of some information which is relevant, as well as a statement of what may be called "the rules of the game", largely or at least partly in language; and the learner has to attempt to comprehend those inputs in order to engage in the activity. Indeed, learners are likely to want to comprehend the inputs concerned, since human beings have a natural desire to solve a problem which they confront, if only to feel pleased with themselves that they can do so. Any assistance which the teacher provides in learners' comprehension of inputs is likely to be subsequent to it being guided by some evidence of learners' success or failure in comprehending them on their own—hence responsive to learners' effort, not pre-emptive of it. There is, moreover, likely to be plenty of opportunity for such responsive assistance, since the activity allows a trial-and-error procedure in solving problems, and each error followed by a fresh effort is an opportunity for further assistance from the teacher. Problems can of course be at varied levels of complexity or sophistication, according to what may be called the "distance" between information and solution (that is, the amount of "working out" involved), the quantity or variety of information to be processed, the number and variety of the rules or constraints to be observed, etc. In general, relatively simple problems can be solved with a relatively "vague" comprehension of information, while more sophisticated problems will demand a more precise comprehension. A criterion of adequacy for the comprehension achieved is provided readily by the adequacy of the solution to the problem (as specified by the "rules set for the game"), and this can clearly be controlled and regulated by the teacher on the basis of his/her assessment of learners' abilities as evidenced in the ongoing activity. Finally, problem-solving, by its very nature, involves a relatively large and sustained context—perhaps each problem occupying the length of a lesson or half a lesson—and the language used can well be (indeed, needs to be) structurally composite, though it may be simplified for general accessibility to learners. It may look surprising that the goal of solving problems through language makes all other requirements natural and easy to achieve, but such experience as we have of using problem-solving as the main (in fact, the only) classroom activity (Prabhu, 1987) indicates that the procedure does, indeed, have the advantages I have pointed out.

Let me conclude with a very brief summary. It is an important current concept in language pedagogy, as well as an interpretation of the intuition behind "natural approaches" to language teaching in the past, that language acquisition, conceived of as a process of cognitive-structure formation, is occasioned by an effort to comprehend samples of the language being learnt. Given this concept, we can formulate at least three desirable conditions which classroom activity should meet—namely, maximal effort at comprehension by learners, adjustable levels of adequacy for the comprehension achieved, and the availability of structurally composite language samples as a part of sustained contexts of communication. Of the possible forms of classroom activity which are thought to promote comprehension, situational presentation of language is least successful in creating the desirable conditions, translation by learners creates those conditions more successfully, and problem-solving (or task-based activity) is more successful than both.

References

Chomsky, N. (1976). *Reflections on language*. London: Temple Smith.

Corder, S. Pit. (1981). *Error analysis and interlanguage*. Oxford: Oxford University Press.

Hornby, A. S. (1950). The situational approach to language teaching. *ELT*, IV(4), 98–103.

Howatt, A. P. R. (1984). *A history of English language teaching*. Oxford: Oxford University Press.

Kandiah, Thiru. (1978). The notion of interference and the universalist hypothesis: Theory feeds into practice. Paper presented at Central Institute of Indian Languages, Mysore.

Krashen, S. D. (1985). *The input hypothesis*. London: Longman.

Palmer, H. E. (1921). *The oral method of language teaching*. Cambridge: Heffer.

Prabhu, N. S. (1987). *Second language pedagogy*. Oxford: Oxford University Press.

GD: *In this article, you have made a case for translation as an exercise in comprehension, rather than production, because it fulfils two of the requirements of enabling acquisition through comprehension; your 'problem' with translation is that it does not permit varied levels of adequacy for it to be termed successful. If we were to focus on the process of translation as language enabling, and consider that such an activity might lead to beneficial language transfer, what are the kinds of translation-tasks that would trigger such acquisition? Could you elaborate on this?*

NSP: I can't understand 'translation as language enabling'. Enabling in which language? 'Enabling' in what sense? Nor can I see what 'beneficial language transfer' can mean. Beneficial in what way? To which language?

I don't in any case now think translation is anywhere as good as problem-solving; translation can only give evidence on the comprehension achieved, not push up the comprehension ability in the process. Task-based teaching can push the learner's ability slightly up with each successful effort, thus providing both enhancement and evidence.

11

Three Models in Second Language Pedagogy

The teaching of second and foreign languages is at present a field full of old and new ideas, established and emerging concepts, conflicting theories, and mutually incompatible proposals. While this can be a favourable situation for promoting fruitful debate and stimulating progress in the profession, it can also be a situation which scatters professional attention, obscures essential issues and renders much of the debate superficial or tangential. In this paper, I attempt to bring together a range of the concepts and proposals prevalent at this time under three pedagogic models, in the hope that this will provide an overall picture of the current scene and help to direct discussion to the more fundamental issues. Broadly, two of my three pedagogic models involve psycholinguistic issues while one reflects sociolinguistic concerns.

Model 1: Guided Grammar-Construction

I would like to refer to the first model as guided grammar-construction. This implies two basic notions: first, that learners, in learning a language, need to construct a grammar of that language in their own minds; and, secondly, that the process of grammar-construction can beneficially be guided, part by part, by teachers. Each notion can be commented on briefly.

The notion that language is structured, and that language use is a form of rule-governed behaviour, has been dominant in twentieth-

---

This essay was first published in 1989. *Source*: Prabhu, N. S. (1989). Three models in second language pedagogy. *Journal of English and Foreign Languages*, 3, 1–14.

century linguistics; and linguists' attempts to describe languages have shown that the structure is a complex and abstract one. An obvious implication of this for language pedagogy is that learners need to acquire the abstract structure of the language being learnt, in order to be able to conform to it in their linguistic behaviour. This was seen, early in this century, as both a challenge and an opportunity for second language teaching—challenge because of the complexity of language structure, and opportunity because it offered a plausible way of defining and systematising the concept of language instruction. Possible alternatives to such a perception are that language learning is a matter of storing in memory a large body of actual sentences or expressions, or that language use involves continual structural improvisation, instead of conformity to given rules—both notions clearly implausible. Harold Palmer, one of the makers of what we are calling the guided grammar-construction model, observed in 1917: "Were the number of sentences in a given language limited to a few hundreds, or even a few thousands, a student might reasonably be expected to learn them off by heart, and by so doing to become master of the language. The number of sentences, however, being infinite, recourse must be had to the study of their mechanisms in order that from the relatively limited number of lesser ergons an infinite number of sentences may be composed at will" (p. 22). Learning a language, that is to say, is mastering the principles of sentence construction in that language—a process which we are calling "grammar-construction".

The view that grammar-construction in the learner's mind is what language teaching should aim at leads naturally to pedagogic effort at guiding the process of grammar-construction in helpful ways; and an obviously helpful way is to regulate the construction one part at a time. Palmer used the term "ergon" to refer to the optimal unit of the grammar to be constructed but the terms that have gained currency since are "structure", "structural item" and "pattern". Palmer also referred to the learner's internalisation of a given ergon as a "habit"—that is, a particular part of the grammar successfully constructed and able thereafter to support conformity in language behaviour. Teaching structural items (or patterns), one by one, with the aim of promoting corresponding "habits" in learners thus became central to language pedagogy.

It will now be clear that I am identifying guided grammar-construction as the conceptual model which underlies a range of pedagogic procedures variously referred to as "the structural approach", "the structural-oral-situational approach", "the audio-lingual method", "pattern-practice", "the cognitive code approach" etc. They are procedures developed, in very persuasive forms, in the first half of this century and implemented, with great professional zeal, in large parts of the world. They are also procedures which prevail, at the present time, in most contexts of ESL/EFL instruction, a recent shift of theoretical attention to other conceptual models notwithstanding. The actual forms in which the procedures are stated or carried out in different places may seem to vary in different ways, but it is possible to point to certain features of the underlying model which are common to the varying forms.

I think there are four such features: planned progression, pre-selection, form-focused activity and contextualisation. Let me comment briefly on each.

Planned progression is a sequencing of the different units of grammar, prior to teaching, such that (i) the sequence as a whole is exhaustive (at some level of generality) of what the learner has to internalise, and (ii) the relative positions of different units in the sequence reflect general educational principles such as simple-to-complex, known-to-unknown, central-to-peripheral movements. This is what a structural syllabus represents, whether it is stated "tightly" or "loosely", in more specific terms or less. It crucially involves the assumption that the order in which grammar-construction takes place in the learner's mind is open to prior determination (and direct regulation) by the syllabus-maker. The second feature, pre-selection, is a consequence of this assumption. Pre-selection refers to particular teaching units being geared to particular units of the syllabus—a lesson with a structural item as its teaching content. It implies an equation between what is taught and what is learnt—an assumption that a unit of grammar is internalised by the learner at the point at which the teacher chooses to teach it. Form-focused activity, the third feature, is the means by which that equation is to be ensured. It consists of what is generally called "practice", that is, an encounter for the learner with many examples of the structural item being taught, the encounter being brought about in any of a number of ways. It is practice that is seen to make sure of internalisation—to make sure that the ergon or pattern being taught is established as a "habit" in the learner's mind. The fourth feature, contextualisation, is a corrective to the possible ill-effects of form-focused activity. It refers to activities in which some of the examples of the pattern being taught are encountered by the learner in appropriate semantic contexts, so that the pattern is learnt in association with its meaning and can thereafter support appropriate meaning-exchange. Contextualisation is also seen to reduce the learner's focus on forms, thus reducing the danger that the patterns being taught are received merely as pieces of linguistic knowledge, instead of being internalised as habits.

Planned progression, pre-selection, form-focused activity and contextualisation thus constitute what I have called the guided grammar-construction model in language pedagogy. It is primarily a psycholinguistic model in that it bases itself on specific assumptions about the psychological process of language learning—the assumptions, for instance, that language learning involves internal grammar-construction, that the sequence of internal construction is open to direct external regulation and that repeated encounter with examples ensures internalisation of a structural pattern as habit. It is also a powerfully persuasive model as shown by its widespread adoption in large parts of the world and by the skepticism or hostility which its adherents tend to show to models different from it. Indeed, features of the guided grammar-construction model tend to influence or persist in models which claim to be its rivals, as we shall see in the discussion of our next model.

Model 2: Simulated Communication

The second model, which may be called "simulated communication", bases itself on aspects of language learning other than grammar-construction, directing attention to language performance, rather than to language competence. It involves a broadening of the scope of teaching, on the grounds that it is not enough to enable learners to conform to language structure in their language behaviour, it is necessary to teach them socially appropriate language behaviour as well. Leonard Newmark, whose influential paper twenty years ago provided some of the initial stimulus to the model, drew pointed attention to the fact "that a person, even an intelligent one, who knows perfectly the structures that the linguist teaches, cannot know that the way to get his cigarette lit by a stranger when he has no matches is to walk up to him and say one of the utterances, "Do you have a light?" or "Got a match?" (not one of the equally well-formed questions, "Do you have fire?" or "Do you have illumination?" or "Are you a match's owner?")" (Newmark, 1966). Hymes argued, at about the same time, that dimensions of social appropriacy are systematic in their own way and that "there are rules of use without which the rules of grammar would be useless" (Hymes, 1970). Widdowson's contrast between "usage" and "use" (Widdowson, 1978) represents a pedagogic exploration of what needs to be taught and learnt, in the light of a social perspective on language. Learners should, on this view, not only internalise the grammar of the language being learnt but, in doing so, be able to perceive and put to use the communicative values of the expressions being employed.

An enlargement of language teaching content, however, is only one feature of the simulated communication model; and, if that were all that was being proposed, we would simply have an extended version of the guided grammar-construction model, rather than an alternative to it. What makes it an alternative is a second feature, which relates to principles of organisation in teaching. Work done in the Council of Europe has led to the radical proposal that language teaching should be organised not as a planned progression of grammatical units but, instead, as a configuration of different units of meaning or use, called "notions" and "functions" (Wilkins, 1976). The use of notional/functional syllabuses involves a reversal of pedagogic priorities between grammatical competence and socially appropriate use: social appropriacy now receives central attention in teaching, leaving grammatical conformity as a secondary consideration or incidental issue. Since there is no one-to-one correspondence between grammatical units and functional units, the adoption of a functional organisation necessarily results in an abandonment of grammatically systematic progression—an abandonment which is held to be justified (Wilkins, 1981). Pre-selection of teaching content for particular lessons is primarily in terms of functional units, though there is frequently a secondary pre-selection of the grammatical or lexical units relevant to particular functions. The chief consideration in designing classroom activity is that it should exemplify and focus attention on socially appropriate language use, by involving learners in a simulation of the typical roles of real-life communication (hence the label "simulated communication" to this model of pedagogy). The classroom, that is to say, is a place for imitating the language use of the world outside, and language learning is a matter of rehearsing real-life language behaviour.

Real-life language use, however, is too varied and vast a phenomenon to be replicated in the classroom and some criterion is therefore required for identifying relevant parts of it. This points to a third feature of the simulated communication model, namely, purpose-orientation. It is held that any exercise in language teaching should begin by identifying learners' specific purposes in learning the language in question and that those purposes should be constantly borne in mind both in selecting the functions to be focused on and in designing particular classroom simulations. Where learners are within sight of their chosen occupations—in what are called ESP situations—it is a relatively straightforward matter to survey and select the functional needs of those occupations, and the resultant classroom replications of typical occupational situations can arguably have the added value of increasing learners' motivation. Language teaching in such situations becomes a form of occupational training and it is therefore not surprising that functional syllabuses have most readily been adopted by tertiary-level ESP institutions around the world. Purpose-orientation, however, is not confined to tertiary-level ESP instruction. It is held to have relevance at lower levels of education as well, such as primary and secondary schools. At these early levels, it takes the form of what are called "graded objectives"—that is, a specification of possible real-life uses for the limited amounts of language that can be taught in each school year (or school term). Such specification of limited real-life uses at interim points of language instruction is thought not only to support pedagogy based on simulated communication but to ensure a "surrender value" to the learning done by those who drop out of foreign language courses at various points. Purpose-orientation is therefore a general feature of the simulated communication model, with relevance to all levels of language instruction.

An extension of the scope of instruction beyond grammar-construction to include aspects of appropriate use, primacy to the functions of language as an organising principle, and purpose-orientation in the selection and replication of functions—these three are the main features of the pedagogic model which I have called "simulated communication". The actual forms in which the model is implemented, formulated or labeled vary according to which of the features is given priority: an extension of teaching objectives to appropriate use leads to what is commonly referred to as "communicative language teaching"; an abstraction of aspects of use to be treated as teaching units results in "notion/functional syllabuses" or "functional language courses"; and an overriding priority to learners' real-life needs marks "ESP" (or "LSP") courses. The model as a whole differs from guided grammar-construction in that it addresses itself to learning objectives rather than to learning processes, and it also operates with the concept that classroom learning is generally a matter of rehearing real-life behaviour—that acting out is a good preparation for actual action. It is primarily a sociolinguistic model, both in the sense that it draws on the results of sociolinguistic studies and in the sense that it gives central importance to the social objectives of language education.

One further comment can be made on the simulated communication model. In directing attention to aspects of language use which lie beyond grammar-construction, it seems to say very little about the process of grammar-construction itself or how it is to be brought about. The explanation cannot be that grammatical conformity is unimportant as an educational objective or as an aspect of language use: stray remarks such as that "some occasions call for being appropriately ungrammatical" (Hymes, 1972) or that "good communicators" with a poor command of English may be better able to cope with communication problems in English than fluent speakers who are poor communicators" (Allwright, 1976, p. 10) are only points scored in a debate, rather than substantive proposals. The actual explanation consists of one of two positions on the issue, the two being mutually incompatible. One position is that grammar-construction takes place in the way it is envisaged to do under the guided grammar-construction model. Functional syllabuses generally have a linguistic dimension to them and most language courses labelled "communicative", "functional" or "ESP" make provision for form-focused language practice, within an overall framework of simulated communication (and, as a result, without much systematic progression). The other position is that grammar-construction takes place, at least in large measure, as a natural outcome of communicative activity, without any need for specific grammatical practice. This position is reflected, for instance, in Widdowson's remark that participants in communication do not just employ their knowledge of pre-existing rules; they "commonly bring new rules into existence by so doing" (p. 69) or in Allwright's remark that "we would be well-advised to focus on communicative skills, in the knowledge that this will necessarily involve developing most areas of language competence as an essential part of the product" (p. 3). This leads directly to our third model.

Model 3: Autonomous Grammar-Development

I am calling the third model "autonomous grammar-development", a name which immediately invites comparison with "guided grammar-construction". What is common to the first model and this third model is that both are focused on the nature of linguistic competence and possible processes by which it comes about. Both regard grammatical conformity as being central to language ability and regard such conformity as arising from an internal system of great complexity and abstractness. The difference between the two models is signalled by the words "guided construction" as against "autonomous development". The first model views the learner's internal system as something that can be constructed part by part, according to a plan made by the teacher. The third model, in contrast, sees the internal system as something which develops by itself, according to an inherent plan, with pedagogic activity providing only a stimulus, and favourable conditions, for that process. A rough analogy for the first model is building construction, which is planned and caused by the builder; a rough analogy for the third model is plant growth, which is a natural, organic process, though it can be influenced in various ways by the farmer or gardener. From another point of view, the first model posits a major, qualitative difference between the development of first language ability and the learning of second or foreign languages, while the third model perceives the acquisition of all languages—first, second or foreign—as involving the same processes, with only quantitative differences in outcomes resulting from different learning conditions. There are, in particular, three concepts which form the basis of the autonomous grammar-development model.

First, knowledge of a language is taken to consist of an internal system of rules which operates at a subconscious level of the mind, ensuring grammatical conformity to the language being employed while the conscious mind is occupied with decisions about the meaning or message being exchanged. It is a distinctive characteristic of language use that it involves operations at least at two different levels—a subconscious level at which conformity to grammatical rules (or social conventions) is determined, and a more conscious level at which matters of semantic content are decided. There is of course a similarity here to the notion of grammatical patterns operating as "habits" in our first model but there are also important differences in the rest of the concept. The internal system is thought, in the autonomous development model, not only to operate subconsciously but to develop subconsciously as well. It is also claimed that deliberate inputs of grammatical units from the teacher lead to a form of knowledge which fails to operate subconsciously and which therefore does not constitute a truly internal system. The knowledge which form-focused activity promotes in learners is more explicit than implicit—able to operate when the focus is on form but much less operative when the conscious mind is occupied with genuine meaning-exchange. We all have experience, as language teachers, of how students appear to have learnt a grammatical unit when it has been taught in the classroom and are able to do the relevant exercises or grammar tests reasonably well, but nevertheless give frustratingly negative evidence when they later speak spontaneously or write an essay or use the language outside the classroom. Krashen has used the terms "learning" and "acquisition" to refer to explicit and implicit forms of knowledge, and claimed that they constitute two different systems arising and operating independently of each other. It is "acquisition" which language teaching ought to promote but guided grammar-construction procedures tend to promote "learning" instead.

Secondly, there is a categorical difference between grammar as a linguistic description and grammar as a hypothesised internal system. The descriptive entity is only a construct put together by the linguist or grammarian—and, as we all know, can vary greatly in its form between one linguist and another. It is true that all descriptive grammars are attempts to provide accounts of the internal system, but none of them can (or does) claim to be isomorphic with the internal system as a psychological entity. There is, as I have argued elsewhere (Prabhu, 1987, pp. 72–75), no basis for regarding the specific units, rules or patterns of a descriptive grammar as corresponding directly to the way the internal system is organised. Yet guided grammar-construction attempts to regulate the development of the internal system—unit by unit, pattern by pattern—in terms of the units and patterns of some descriptive grammar. Further, linguists' attempts to account for grammatical competence have shown clearly that the internal system is far more complex than any grammar yet constructed, however complex and sophisticated. A pedagogic grammar, such as a structural syllabus, is necessarily a simplification of the linguist's grammar and consequently even less likely to correspond to the internal system. In view of these probabilities, language teaching which is directed to the units of a descriptive grammar can be largely irrelevant to the development of the internal system—or even an unhelpful interference with it. We do not know the design of the internal grammar sufficiently to be able to regulate its development directly.

Thirdly, guided grammar-construction involves teaching the different parts of grammar one at a time and it therefore implies that the internal system is constructed linearly, one part after another. It is, however, likely that the internal system actually develops holistically, not linearly. Studies of second language acquisition and interlanguage powerfully suggest not only that there may be an inherent, built-in order of grammar-development but that the development probably takes place as a series of system-revisions or system-elaborations, rather than as a sequence of individual parts. The concept is that learners acquire, not one unit of grammar followed by another, but rather a system or grammar as a whole from the beginning, in however simple or imperfect a form. This imperfect system is then revised and elaborated successively as a system, the different stages in the process forming a sequence of transitional systems, as discussed, for instance, by Corder (1981). The development of language competence is thus seen as an organic process and, like all other processes of organic development, a holistic one. This once again shows a serious mismatch between the assumptions of guided grammar-construction and the probable process of actual competence development. Linear teaching is in conflict with holistic learning.

The pedagogic model of autonomous grammar-development is thus based on (i) the psycholinguistic concept of a subconsciously operating system which also develops subconsciously; a non-equation between the internal system and descriptive grammar; and (ii) the further psycholinguistic notion that the development of language competence is an organic, holistic process. Procedures of teaching which result from these concepts are those which employ meaning-focused activity in the classroom, avoiding planned progression, pre-selection and form-focused activity, but ensuring that learners are constantly engaged in making sense of what is heard or read, or getting some meaning-content across. It is thus a pedagogy which concentrates on causing and regulating learners' effort at communication, and on ensuring that learners succeed in such effort at each stage sufficiently to make a further effort at the next stage. Krashen and Terrell have used the name "natural approach" for one such form of teaching; and I have used the term "task-based teaching" to describe another. Brumfit provides another account of such teaching under the label "fluency activity". In general, the autonomous grammar-construction model regards classroom activity as a matter of creating conditions favourable to language acquisition, not as a direct causing of acquisition. Such a perception of language teaching and learning may appear at first sight to be new or radical, but there is in fact a tradition of similar perceptions and proposals in the history of language teaching, as Howatt's historical account of English language teaching shows. Corder draws attention to a clear statement in the last century—that of the German linguist, von Humboldt, who said that we cannot really teach language, we can only create conditions in which it will develop spontaneously in the mind in its own way (Corder, 1981, p. 12).

AN ECLECTIC MODEL

I have outlined three general models in language pedagogy, bringing together under each a group of related concepts and procedures, and trying to highlight differences between one model and another. The question naturally arises: which of the three is right or superior to the others? There can be no objective answer to this question. Guided grammar-construction held the field for a few decades, but gradually led to different forms of dissatisfaction, one of them motivating the simulated communication model and another prompting the autonomous grammar-development model. It can perhaps be claimed that the second and third models are more representative of recent and current concerns than the first which is somewhat dated. But current issues in professional discussion do not necessarily reflect prevalent pedagogic practice and the first model, as we have noted, is probably the most widely in use still. In any case, the question, "Which model is most talked about or followed?" can only yield objective measures of popularity, not objective evaluations of merit. It would be good to believe that objective evaluations of merit can be made through scientifically designed experiments in teaching, but the history of such designed experiments makes that belief difficult to sustain. As Brumfit has forcefully argued, language teaching is too complex and too human an activity to be treated as a set of replicable procedures with pre-determinable results and, therefore, "it makes little sense to treat language teaching, or any teaching, as if it can be prescribed as a result of experimentation or predictive hypothesising at a specific level" (p. 21). Pedagogic activity involves not just objective procedures but the perceptions, interpretations and responses of its participants, all of which directly affect the value of the procedures. It is common to hear that a good method failed at a certain place because it was carried out by teachers "mechanically". Mechanical teaching is almost inevitable when the procedures being followed are not in harmony with the perceptions of at least one of the participants in pedagogy—the teacher.

The fact that no model can be shown objectively to be superior to the others seems to suggest that educational systems should make up their own eclectic models, combining features from different available models. I think such eclecticism is reasonable and sound, but not in the form in which it frequently operates.

What frequently happens is that a small group of people (perhaps forming a committee) put together an eclectic model which is then presented for implementation to a large number of teachers. But this procedure directly undermines the value of eclecticism. We need an eclectic model because pedagogic perceptions vary between different teachers, and available models are unlikely to match any given teacher's own perceptions. A desirable eclectic model is therefore one which is in sufficient harmony with a given teacher's perceptions to be able to avoid or reduce the risk of mechanical procedures. Any model put together by a small group of specialists for use by a large number of teachers will fail to ensure such harmony, in the same way that other available models do. Since no model can be said to be objectively superior to others, no eclectic model can claim to be objectively superior to available models, either. The only value which an eclectic model can have is in terms of its relative closeness to individual teachers' perceptions, and that value is sacrificed when a small group of people decides what model a large number of teachers should adopt for their teaching. I think therefore that eclecticism should operate at the level of the individual teacher and that educational systems should seek to encourage and facilitate its operation at that level. It can be professionally valuable for teachers to interact with available models, thus letting their own perceptions be influenced in different ways; and it can be beneficial to learning when teachers adopt teaching procedures which are in accord with their changing perceptions. Pedagogic models, on this view, are not prescriptions for institutional or individual action; rather, they are constructs which teachers can usefully interact with and perhaps be influenced by, in the interests of both their own professional growth and their students' learning.

References

Allwright, Richard L. (1976). Language learning through communicative practice. *ELT Documents*, 76/3, 3–15.

Brumfit, C. J. (1984). *Communicative methodology in language teaching: The roles of fluency and accuracy*. Cambridge: Cambridge University Press.

Corder, S. Pit. (1981). *Error analysis and interlanguage.* Oxford: Oxford University Press.

Howatt, A. P. R. (1984). *A history of English language teaching.* Oxford: Oxford University Press.

Hymes, D. H. (1972). On communicative competence. In J. B. Pride and J. Holmes (Eds.), *Sociolinguistics* (pp. 269–94). New York: Penguin Books.

Krashen, Stephen. D. (1981). *Second language acquisition and second language learning.* Oxford: Pergamon Press.

Krashen, S. and Terrell, T. (1983). *The natural approach.* London: Pergamon Press.

Newmark, Leonard. (1966). How not to interfere with language learning. In C. J. Brumfit and K. Johnson (Eds.), *The communicative approach to language teaching* (pp. 160–66). Oxford: Oxford University Press.

Palmer, Harold E. ([1917] 1968). *The scientific study and teaching of languages.* Ed. George G. Harrap. Oxford: Oxford University Press.

Prabhu, N. S. (1987). *Second language pedagogy.* Oxford: Oxford University Press.

Widdowson, H. G. (1978). *Teaching language as communication.* Oxford: Oxford University Press.

Wilkins, D. A. (1976). *Notional syllabuses.* Oxford: Oxford University Press.

Wilkins, D. A. (1981). Notional syllabuses revisited: A further reply. *Applied Linguistics,* II(1), 96–100.

12

There is No Best Method—Why?

It is uncommon these days to have a sustained discussion on language teaching without someone at some point declaring that there is no best method, or words to that effect. Such a declaration usually occurs at a late stage in an indecisive debate about different methods, and has the general effect of altering the orientation of the debate itself, somewhat abruptly. It also carries the ring of an incontrovertible statement—or a statement so tolerant and reconciliatory in spirit that to dispute it would be professionally churlish. As a result, one rarely sees a detailed examination of what it might mean to say that there is no best method.

I think it helpful to see the statement as having an illocutionary as well as a propositional meaning. As an illocutionary act, it seeks to terminate a debate without reaching any substantive conclusion, and it does so not by admitting defeat in the effort to reach a conclusion, but by appearing to raise the debate itself to a higher level, thus helping to save professional face all round. It suggests not just that proponents of different methods agree to disagree, but that they give up their pursuit of agreement and disagreement as being unproductive. It manages to reconcile conflicting views by defining a position to which all can honourably subscribe, and by striking a philosophical note on which enlightened discussion can properly end. It is thus a convenient device for legitimising non-resolution of methodological issues.

The propositional content of the statement, on the other hand, calls for a great deal of clarification and substantiation, in

---

This essay was first published in 1990. *Source*: Prabhu, N. S. (1990). There is no best method—Why? *TESOL Quarterly*, 24(2), 161–76.

terms of the sense in which a method can be considered good, the reason why no method can be thought or shown to be better than others, the consequence of that position for the theory and practice of pedagogy, the revaluation it demands of the assumptions currently underlying conflict and debate between methods, and the forms in which debate or discussion may still be of use from the new perspective. What is involved is not just the termination of a discussion, but the beginning of a new one—or rather the beginning of a new phase in the discussion, as a positive outcome of the earlier phase. It is this propositional content of the statement that is the concern of this paper; I hope to clarify the sense in which there can be said to be no best method of language teaching.

First, however, a word about the term *method.* I use the term inclusively, to refer both to a set of activities to be carried out in the classroom and to the theory, belief, or plausible concept that informs those activities. The reader will thus find one or both of these aspects the focus of particular parts of the discussion. I consider this "global" interpretation of the term appropriate to analysing a statement that is equally global in spirit.

There are, I think, three general lines of argument that can be advanced in support of the statement to be discussed. These are examined in turn.

IT ALL DEPENDS ON THE TEACHING CONTEXT

If those who declare that there is no best method are asked why, the most immediate and frequent answer is likely to be "Because it all depends," meaning that what is best depends on whom the method is for, in what circumstances, for what purpose, and so on. That there is no best method therefore means that no single method is best for everyone, as there are important variations in the teaching context that influence what is best. The variations are of several kinds, relating to social situation (language policy, language environment, linguistic and cultural attitudes, economic and ideological factors, etc.), educational organisation (instructional objectives, constraints of time and resources, administrative efficiency, class-size, classroom ethos, etc.), teacher-related factors (status, training, belief, autonomy, skill, etc.) and learner-related factors (age, aspirations, previous learning experience, attitudes to learning etc.). There have been several attempts to categorise such variables systematically and comprehensively (see Brumfit, 1984), but even the brief and random listing above shows that they are at different levels of generality, as well as of discreteness and tangibility. Moreover, recent and current work in the field seems to be adding new factors and categories to the inventory, in the form of varied learning styles, communication strategies, personality factors and psychological processes. Together with slightly earlier work on variations in learners' needs and purposes, this seems to suggest that variability on such dimensions is infinite, thus strongly challenging the notion that any given method can be good for everyone. "It all depends," and what it depends on is a vast number of things.

Notice, however, that to say that no single method is best for everyone is also to say that different methods are best for different people—or for different teaching contexts. This implies that, for any single teaching context, there is in fact a method that is best and, further, we are able to determine what it is. If we are unclear or in disagreement about what method is best for a specific context, there is need for discussion, debate, and interaction between differing perceptions; we should be seeking to further pedagogic debate rather than to terminate it with a face-saving formula. It is perhaps not without significance that statements like "There is no best method" are made most often as defensive postures—as ways of saying not only that one does not agree with what is being argued, but that one refuses to engage any further in the argument. Such statements succeed in preserving the conversational peace, but cause a loss to the productive potential of professional debate. For such statements to act as a contribution to debate, we will need to interpret them as proposing only a narrowing of the scope to some single teaching context, so that dependencies between contextual variables and methodological options might be explored, and a search for the best method might be continued with greater focus. The statement that there is no best method would then be an assertion, not of the futility of looking for the best method, but of the desirability of asking what method is best for some specific context; contextual variability would serve not as a means of avoiding methodological issues, but as a possible new approach to resolving them.

I think it is important to realise how complex it can be to determine dependencies between contextual factors and instructional methods. To begin with, many of the factors that are discussed are neither easy to identify nor simple to assess: they tend suspiciously to fit different slots in different taxonomies. *Formal environment,* for instance, may refer to classroom learning, as against learning through social exposure, or to the formal school system, as against private language instruction, or to relative formality in teacher–learner relations, as against informal relations, or even to teacher-fronted activities, as against group work among learners. *Motivation* may mean anything from future career ambitions, to a desire for group approval, to a passing interest in a particular classroom activity. What are identified as attitudes are seldom clear-cut or unmixed or even stable. When we come to factors like preferred learning styles, sociocultural influences, or personality factors, we are faced with unclear and overlapping distinctions, and are therefore forced to simplify and stereotype, often in preconceived ways. Further, even when some contextual factors are clearly identifiable, their consequence for instructional procedures can be far from clear. Do older learners need a different method of teaching from younger ones, and if so, how fundamentally different? Is a change in method more likely to succeed in the hands of experienced teachers, or less? If there is a mismatch between official language policy and learners' personal goals, which should have what weight in the choice of an instructional method? If we identify certain learning strategies that learners naturally tend to employ, do we conclude, for that reason, that they are good learning strategies? If not, are learners likely to learn more by following their own strategies, which may be less than good in our view, or by adopting strategies we consider more conductive to learning, though they may go against such natural tendencies? If earlier experience has conditioned learners or teachers to certain perceptions of learning and teaching, does that constitute an argument against change, or indicate a greater need for change?

The point I am making is not just that our knowledge is uncertain at this time; the more important point is that it is only when we can show a relationship between a contextual factor and a methodological decision that the contextual factor becomes significant for pedagogy. What we need is not just an identification and projection of variation but, equally, some way of determining which form of variation matters to instruction and how, and which does not. If we look for variation merely on the assumption that the teaching context matters for teaching methodology, we are sure to find indefinite variation on many dimensions, thus making it impossible to justify any instructional method for any single group of learners. If all physiological variation among individuals (including fingerprints) were assumed to call for matching differentiation in medical treatment, no medical practice would be justifiable.

It is, of course, possible to obviate the problem of relating contextual factors to instructional methods by giving contextual factors a central role in pedagogy and treating instructional methods as a kind of logical derivation from them. This is the move often advocated: from a preoccupation with teaching methods to an effort at "curriculum development" or "course design". The assumption is that, with such a move, decisions concerning methods will either be rendered unnecessary or play only a small part in the enterprise. As one applied linguist puts it, "The important issues are not which method to adopt but how to develop procedures and instructional activities that will enable program objectives to be attained"

(Richards, 1985, p. 42). The procedures envisaged are those of situational analysis, needs analysis, analysis of "authentic" samples of target language use, surveys of opinions and attitudes, estimates of resources, etc.—that is to say, compilations of different kinds of information about learners, teachers, the school, and the society, with a view to determining instructional objectives. Instructional procedures are seen to follow, or be easily determinable, from the profile of contextual factors and the statement of objectives. This is, in effect, a kind of discovery procedure for methods: that method is best, it seems to say, which results from a careful implementation of the procedure, the soundness of the method being guaranteed by the soundness of the procedure leading to it.

There is, however, a price to pay for this simplification of pedagogy. The instructional procedures most directly derivable from a specification of needs, wants and objectives are those of supplying to learners the relevant tokens of language, or getting them to rehearse target language behaviour in simulated target situations. Any concept of developing in learners a more basic capacity for generating tokens of language when needed, or for adapting to unforeseen target language behaviour as necessary, leads one toward ideas about the nature of language ability and the process of language acquisition—complex methodological issues that the discovery procedure seeks to avoid. Besides, a more elaborate analysis of contextual factors results in a correspondingly larger set of criteria to be met by instructional content or procedure, and the larger the set of criteria to be met, the fewer the choices available in meeting them. Language instruction that attempts to cater directly to social objectives, learning needs, target needs, learners' wants, teachers' preferences, learning styles, teaching constraints, and attitudes all round can end up as a mere assemblage of hard-found pieces of content and procedure—a formula that manages, with difficulty, to satisfy multiple criteria and therefore cannot afford to let itself be tampered with. What sets out to be a widening of attention to varied educational considerations can thus end up as an abridgement of choice and flexibility in the practice of pedagogy.

In avoiding adherence to a single method, one will have arrived instead at a single, fixed, teaching package.

Avoiding adherence to a single method has a certain ideological aura to it. It suggests liberation from a monolithic mould, a refusal to be doctrinaire, an espousal of plurality. It is, however, also a denial of the role of understanding in language pedagogy, which is necessarily a matter of ideation: we understand something when we have a set of ideas or principles that cohere to make up a conceptual model, or theory. Although theory is only an abstraction, it is about the only instrument we have (at any rate, the most accessible instrument) for making sense of complex phenomena and conveying that sense to one another. Theory, as we know, arises not from a cataloguing of diversity, but from a perception of unity in diverse phenomena—a single principle, or a single system of principles, in terms of which diversity can be maximally accounted for. If the theories of language teaching (that is to say, methods) that we have at present fail to account sufficiently for the diversity in teaching contexts, we ought to try to develop a more general or comprehensive (and probably more abstract) theory to account for more of the diversity, not reject the notion of a single system of ideas and seek to be guided instead by diversity itself. Pointing to a bewildering variety of contextual factors as a means of denying the possibility of a single theory can only be a contribution to bewilderment, not to understanding.

There is also the fact that a concentration on dissimilarities between teaching contexts is likely to obscure similarities between them; in the case of language learning, we are dealing with a human ability that constitutes a defining characteristic of the species. It is true that variations in social situation, institutional organisation, individuals' histories, attitudes, or intentions can all have the effect of limiting or extending opportunities for desired forms of pedagogic action. However, to imply that they call for a matching differentiation in pedagogic theories is to make the very large claim that the process of language acquisition—a basic human attribute—itself varies according to contextual factors.

THERE IS SOME TRUTH TO EVERY METHOD

I have discussed in some detail one form of substantiation of the statement that there is no best method, namely, that different methods are best for different teaching contexts. A different form of substantiation is also heard fairly frequently, namely, that there is some truth (or value or validity) to every method—or, at any rate to several different methods—even though the methods may be conceptually incompatible. This, as we know, is an argument for eclecticism in language pedagogy—not an argument that different contexts should use different methods, but an argument that the same context should use a number of different methods, or perhaps parts of different methods. There is an immediate appeal to common sense in this stance: if every method is a partial truth, then it seems clear that none represents the whole truth; to adopt any single method is to settle for much less than one can get by adopting all or several of them.

As a comment on our state of knowledge at this time (or indeed at any time), the suggestion that no method contains more than a partial truth is clearly unexceptionable. We continue to engage in the professional activity of research, concept development, discussion, and debate because all of our understanding of language learning and teaching is at best partial, and for any of us operating with a theory, which can represent only a partial truth, it remains entirely possible that other theories represent partial truths as well. However, this philosophical perception of imperfect knowledge does not help us to see which theory represents which part of the truth—or which part of a given theory represents the truth. Were we able to see that, we would no longer be operating with a theory of which only a part is known to represent the truth, and missing those parts of other theories that are known to represent other parts of the truth. Our knowledge would make a leap toward the whole truth—whatever that might mean. The fact, however, is that the understanding one has of a phenomenon at a given time—the theory one is operating with—represents for one the whole truth. Other theories are true to the extent they share the understanding represented by one's own theory. In this sense, each theory can claim to represent the partial truths of other theories: if there is an overlap of understanding between it and certain parts of other theories, then it can be said to contain those parts of other theories that constitute partial truths.

But the statement that there is some truth to every method needs to be seen not just as an epistemological observation, but as a plea for an eclectic blending of all or several methods. Now, any such blending of different methods is either done with a perception of what is true about each method, or it is done without any such discrimination. If there is a perception of which part of what method is a partial truth, then that perception constitutes a theory, which happens to have an overlap of understanding with various other theories. It therefore represents a method, which is like any other method, with an overlap of understanding with others. There is no reason to think, on the strength of its being a blend, that it has any more of the truth than any other method. It is simply one of the methods that share some of their concepts or procedures with other methods; how much of the truth it represents is a matter not of how much blending it does, but of what particular perception makes the blending possible. What we have, therefore, is not an eclectic blend, but a different method—or else, all methods which happen to have partial overlaps with others are equally eclectic.

If, on the other hand, an eclectic blending of different methods is done not with any particular perception of what parts of those methods represent the truth, but rather in the hope that whatever is true about them will be captured in the blending, then the eclectic blend does not constitute a method, but instead an act of gambling or a hedging of bets: it can only have treated all parts of different methods as being equally likely to be true or untrue, and, as a result, there is as strong a possibility of its being a blend of the untruthful parts of different methods as there is of its representing the truthful parts (whatever notion of truth and untruth we may care to employ). Further, such indiscriminate blending of methods adds nothing to our pedagogic understanding, since it offers no perception of what may be true about which method. It simply plays it safe—as safe from truth as from untruth. An eclectic blending that constitutes a form of pedagogic understanding at least offers us an additional method, though it makes an unjustified claim to being more than an additional method; an eclectic blending that does not constitute an additional method in that sense leads us away from any furtherance of understanding, while offering us a chance at what may be called "truth by accident".

WE NEED TO RETHINK WHAT "BEST" MIGHT MEAN

Let me now turn to a third possible way of substantiating the statement that there is no best method. This is that we have no adequate notion of what "best" might mean—or that the notion of good and bad needs to be re-examined and clarified.

A prevalent notion of the best method is that it is the method that yields the best results in terms of learning outcomes. Since the aim of all teaching is to bring about as much learning as possible as quickly as possible, it seems self-evident that teaching methods should be judged by the amounts of learning they can lead to, in a given period of time. This appears to call for a comparison of methods and a quantification of learning outcomes, through well-designed, controlled experiments, in keeping with the spirit of objective, scientific enquiry. It is true that such objective evaluation is so difficult to implement that all attempts at it in the past have resulted in a wider agreement on the difficulties of doing an evaluation than on the resulting judgement on methods. It is also true that arguments have been put forward for a possible alternative to the experimental design. Nevertheless, we generally continue to assume, more or less consciously, that there is a method that is objectively the best, that it is in principle possible to demonstrate that fact, and that once demonstrated, the superiority of the best method will lead to its widespread acceptance in the profession. That is to say, we generally see ourselves as working to that ideal, on the tacit premise that what is unrealised is not necessarily unrealisable, and that all our professional endeavour is a form of progress towards it. Alternatives such as trying to construct comprehensive descriptions of methods—as "illuminative" evaluation (Parlett and Hamilton, 1977)—involve an abandonment of that ideal, thus threatening to disorient our professional thought. We prefer to retain the ideal as the basis of all our professional effort.

Seen in this context, the statement that there is no best method is a questioning of the current concept of the best method—an argument that the ideal of objective and conclusive demonstration is not only an unrealised one, but an inherently unrealisable one, and that working with such an ideal is unproductive for the pedagogic profession. Brumfit, for instance, has strongly questioned the notion that teaching methods, which are essentially concerned with human interaction, can usefully be subjected to the processes of objective testing and prediction, which are part of the scientific method. He argues, in summary, (a) that a teaching method in operation is necessarily an embodiment of certain general pedagogic principles into a variety of specific contextual features (including participants' psychological states); (b) that predictive testing of a method demands manipulation and control of the manifold contextual features; (c) that many of the contextual features are either difficult or impossible to control; and, most important, (d) that any success actually achieved in controlling contextual features will have only the effect of disembodying the method, as it were, of its actual, operational form, thus rendering the outcome of the testing inapplicable to the operation of the method in any specific context. Brumfit comments:

> A claim that we can predict closely what will happen in a situation as complex as [the classroom] can only be based on either the view that human beings are more mechanical in their learning responses than any recent discussion would allow, or the notion that we can measure and predict the quantities and qualities of all these factors. Neither of these seems to be a sensible point of view to take. (1984, pp. 18–19)

While Brumfit's argument is based largely on the complexity of the pedagogic operation, it is also possible to point to the complexity of assessing language attainment as such. Examining aspects of this latter complexity further underscores the futility of attempts to objectify method evaluation. To begin with, an important consideration for language teaching methods is the quality of learning to be promoted, as distinct from the quantity. The question of quality has been a recurrent concern for the profession through the ages, being conceptualised and verbalised variously as grammar in contrast to practice, knowledge in contrast to skill, explicit knowledge in contrast to implicit knowledge, accuracy in contrast to fluency, learning in contrast to acquisition, ability to display in contrast to ability to deploy, etc. There may be disagreements about how the different kinds of knowledge or ability are related to each other, but it is remarkable how, whenever a distinction is made between different forms of knowledge of a language, it is the less conscious, less observable, and less quantifiable form that is seen to be of greater value or validity. Objective evaluation of methods, however, necessarily relies on a quantification of learning outcomes, and therefore tends to measure the more quantifiable form of knowledge. This means that the more objective the evaluation is, the less likely it is to assess learning of the desired quality, and vice versa.

Second, a perception of language ability as an implicit form of knowledge is linked to a perception of its development as an internal, unobservable process that is organic rather than additive, and continuous rather than itemisable. This means that at any stage of the growth process, there is not only the growth achieved so far, but a potential for further growth achieved as a part of it—a potential that can be thought of in terms of inchoation or incubation. Our most ambitious effort at language testing can only hope to give us evidence on the actual growth achieved at the stage of testing, not on the potential generated for further growth, since knowledge in an inchoative state is even less accessible to elicitation and quantification than implicit knowledge as such. Again, not everyone in the profession may regard knowledge of a language as being equally implicit in nature or organic in its development, but the point is that an objective evaluation of methods is unlikely to be able to cope with concepts of implicitness and inchoation and, as a result, unlikely to provide widely acceptable decisions.

Third, an objective evaluation of methods is not just an assessment of learners' language attainments; it also involves an objective attribution of the learning that has taken place to the teaching that has been done. However, the relationship between language teaching and language learning becomes less and less direct as one perceives language as being an implicit ability and an internal development: what is less conscious and less observable is also less directly teachable. The more indirect the relationship is between teaching and learning, the more difficult it is to attribute any specific piece of learning to any specific piece of teaching. It is, ultimately, difficult to tell what learning has taken place as intended by the teaching, and what has taken place independent of it (or, indeed, what in spite of it). We have problems enough maintaining a subjective perception of general causation between teaching and learning in the development and discussion of particular methods. An evaluative comparison of different methods calls for a degree of objectivity and specificity in cause–effect relations that may well be unreasonable to expect in the field of language pedagogy.

More generally, the notion behind an objective evaluation of methods is that there is something in a method that is by itself—independently of anyone's subjective perception of it—superior or inferior to what there is in another method. If some method were shown by such evaluation to be superior to all others, then that method would be expected to benefit all (or a large number of) classrooms, regardless of how it is subjectively perceived by the different teachers involved. A method, in this view, is a set of procedures that carries a prediction of results; the fulfillment of the prediction depends only (or mainly) on an accurate replication of the procedures, not on any perceptions of those who do the replication—rather in the way the replication of a procedure in chemistry yields the predicted result, regardless of the chemist's thoughts or feelings about it. No doubt the idea looks fairly absurd when put in this form: it reduces teaching to a faithful following of highly specified routines—something of a pedagogic ritual. I am, however, unable to see how a serious pursuit of objective method evaluation can be sustained without some such idea. The only alternative to it is to maintain that the method that is shown to be objectively superior will somehow carry with it the subjective perception that lay behind its development and, equally, that the perception concerned will then replace the differing perceptions of all the teachers who may be led to adopt that method on the strength of the objective evaluation. This implies, among other things, that teachers' pedagogic perceptions are as easily replaceable as classroom procedures, an idea that could hardly be less absurd.

It is useful to ask why it looks absurd to suggest that a good teaching method can be carried out, without loss, as merely a routine. We find it necessary to think of good teaching as an activity in which there is a sense of involvement by the teacher. When we encounter an instance of really bad teaching it is most often not a case of the teacher following a method with which we disagree, but rather of the teacher merely going through the motions of teaching, with no sense of involvement. When a method considered to be good has been implemented on a large scale and later thought not to have "worked", an important part of the reason identified has been that teachers followed the method "mechanically," with no sense of understanding or identification. Indeed, the more "efficiently" a method is implemented (that is to say, with all procedures envisaged), the more likely it is that mechanical teaching will turn out to be the main impediment to success.

Perhaps, then, there is a factor more basic than the choice between methods, namely, teachers' subjective understanding of the teaching they do. Teachers need to operate with some personal conceptualisation of how their teaching leads to desired learning—with a notion of causation that has a measure of credibility for them. The conceptualisation may arise from a number of different sources, including a teacher's experience in the past as a learner (with interpretations of how the teaching received at that time did or did not support one's learning), a teacher's earlier experience of teaching (with similar interpretations from the teaching end), exposure to one or more methods while training as a teacher (with some subjective evaluation of the methods concerned and perhaps a degree of identification with one or another of them), what a teacher knows or thinks of other teachers' actions or opinions, and perhaps a teacher's experience as a parent or caretaker. Different sources may influence different teachers to different extents, and what looks like the same experience or exposure may influence different teachers differently.

The resulting concept (or theory, or, in a more dormant state, pedagogic intuition) of how learning takes place and how teaching causes or supports it is what may be called a teacher's *sense of plausibility* about teaching. This personal sense of plausibility may not only vary in its content from one teacher to another, but may be more or less firmly or fully formed, more or less consciously considered or articulated, between different teachers. It is when a teacher's sense of plausibility is engaged in the teaching operation that the teacher can be said to be involved, and the teaching not to be mechanical. Further, when the sense of plausibility is engaged, the activity of teaching is productive: there is then a basis for the teacher to be satisfied or dissatisfied about the activity, and each instance of such satisfaction or dissatisfaction is itself a further influence on the sense of plausibility, confirming or disconfirming or revising it in some small measure, and generally contributing to its growth or change. I also think that the greater the teacher's involvement in teaching in this sense, the more likely it is that the sense of involvement will convey itself to learners, getting them involved as well and helping to create that elusive but highly regarded condition in the classroom: teacher–learner rapport. It is of course possible that other factors have a role, too, in the creation of rapport, such as learners' own perceptions of learning and their interpretations of the teaching activity (Allwright,

1984). My point is that an engagement of the teacher's sense of plausibility is a major condition for classroom rapport, whether or not it is the only condition. It is common to hear that learning is enhanced when learners enjoy classroom activity, but enjoyment is a broad notion and is often equated with some form of light entertainment interspersed with more serious activity. I think there is a form of enjoyment arising from teacher–learner rapport that is less conspicuous but more integral to classroom activity, and more truly productive of learning.

The picture of classroom activity that engages the teacher's sense of plausibility is no doubt closer to an ideal than to a factual description of much of the teaching that actually goes on. But that does not detract from the suggestion I am making, namely, that that ideal is more worth our while to pursue than the notion of an objectively best method. The question to ask about a teacher's sense of plausibility is not whether it implies a good or bad method but, more basically, whether it is active, alive or operational enough to create a sense of involvement for both the teacher and the student. Mechanical teaching results from an over-routinisation of teaching activity, and teaching is subject to great pressures of routinisation. It is, after all, a recurrent pattern of procedures on regularly recurrent occasions. It is also a form of recurrent social encounter between teachers and learners, with self-images to protect, personalities to cope with, etc. And, like all recurrent social encounters, teaching requires a certain degree of routine to make it sustainable or even endurable. There are, in addition, varied feelings of adequacy or confidence among teachers, varied degrees of concern for maintaining status, stress of overwork, threat of peer comparisons or of expectations from superiors, etc., all of which can use the protection offered by role-defining routines. More fundamentally, there is the fact that learning by learners is essentially unpredictable and, consequently, it is an unacceptably high risk for teaching to have to justify itself in direct relation to learning: there is need for a way to claim that the teaching expected has been performed, though the learning expected may still not have occurred; and teaching defined as a routine precisely meets that need.

An active sense of plausibility is very difficult to maintain among such pressures on routinisation, and can easily become frozen, ossified, or inaccessibly submerged, leaving only a schedule of routines. When teachers profess to believe in some method they have been following—perhaps to the point of swearing by it—they may well be merely demonstrating how frozen their sense of plausibility is and, as a result, how insecure they feel against a threat to their teaching routines. When a teacher's sense of plausibility is active and engaged in the teaching, it is necessarily open to change, however slowly or imperceptibly, in the process of the ongoing activity of teaching. Such teaching can perhaps be regarded as being "real", in contrast to teaching that is mechanical. We can then say that a distinction between "real" and mechanical teaching is more significant for pedagogy than any distinction between good and bad methods. The enemy of good teaching is not a bad method, but over-routinisation.

If it is important for a teacher's sense of plausibility to remain alive and therefore open to change—not frozen but fluid in some degree—then an important goal for the pedagogic profession is to seek ways in which the sense of plausibility in as many teachers as possible can be helped to remain as alive as possible, though necessarily in varied forms. It is true that the ongoing activity of teaching is itself a source of continual influence on a teacher's sense of plausibility, thus helping to keep it alive, but we have noted how the ongoing activity of teaching is, at the same time, subject to varied pressures of routinisation, which can have a deadening effect on the sense of plausibility. A second source of influence on the sense of plausibility—perhaps the most important one outside the classroom—is interaction between different senses of plausibility. This interaction can arise from an articulation and discussion among teachers of one another's pedagogic perceptions, from professional reading or writing, and in other, more or less formal, ways.

A specialist-level debate between different methods is, in fact, an interaction between different senses of plausibility, seeking to exert an influence on all those who participate in it (more or less overtly) through a process of sharing, sharpening, strengthening, weakening, changing, or helping to develop further the different forms of understanding involved. A specialist who advocates a method is on the same footing as a teacher who operates with a sense of plausibility, except that the specialist can be said to have achieved fuller and more communicable articulation of a particular sense of plausibility, perhaps in the course of wider (or longer or more intensive) interaction with other similarly well-articulated perceptions. If ossification is less likely to occur at the specialist's level, it is only to the extent that the specialist has more of a commitment to professional interaction and is more continually engaged in exploring and articulating some sense of plausibility. The resulting well-developed and well-articulated senses of plausibility (that is to say, methods) have value not as desirable replacements for many teachers' senses of plausibility but for what may be called their power to influence—to invoke, activate, interact with, alter in some way, and generally keep alive—different teachers' differing senses of plausibility, thus helping to promote and enlarge the occurrence of "real" teaching. A method, from this point of view, is not good or bad in any objective sense, but has more or less pedagogic power to influence teachers' subjective understanding of teaching; and debates between different methods are important for the profession because they help to give expression and opportunity to the pedagogic power of different methods.

Conclusion

To summarise, if we regard our professional effort as a search for the best method which, when found, will replace all other methods, we may not only be working toward an unrealisable goal but, in the process, be misconstruing the nature of teaching as a set of procedures that can by themselves carry a guarantee of learning outcomes. To say that the best method, in this sense, varies from one teaching context to another does not help because it still leaves us with a search for the best method for any specific teaching context. To say that there is some truth to every method does not help either, because it still does not tell us which part of which method is true. Objective method evaluation has either to assume that methods have value for learning independent of teachers' and students' subjective understanding of them, thus perpetuating an unrealisable goal and reinforcing the misconstruction of pedagogy, or to try to take into account teachers' subjective understanding of teaching, thus ceasing to be objectively evaluative. If, on the other hand, we view teaching as an activity whose value depends centrally on whether it is informed or uninformed by the teacher's subjective sense of plausibility—on the degree to which it is "real" or mechanical—it becomes a worthwhile goal for our professional effort to help activate and develop teachers' varied senses of plausibility. A method is seen simply as a highly developed and highly articulated sense of plausibility, with a certain power to influence other specialists' or teachers' perceptions. Perhaps the best method varies from one teacher to another, but only in the sense that it is best for each teacher to operate with his or her own sense of plausibility at any given time. There may be some truth to each method, but only in so far as each method may operate as one or another teacher's sense of plausibility, promoting the most learning that can be promoted by that teacher. The search for an inherently best method should perhaps give way to a search for ways in which teachers' and specialists' pedagogic perceptions can most widely interact with one another, so that teaching can become most widely and maximally real.

References

Allwright, Richard L. (1984). The importance of interaction in classroom language learning. *Applied Linguistics*, 5(2), 156–71.

Brumfit, C. J. (1984). *Communicative methodology in language teaching.* Cambridge: Cambridge University Press.

Parlett, M. and Hamilton, D. (1977). Evaluation as illumination: A new approach to the study of innovatory programmes. In D. Hamilton, D. Jenkins, C. King, B. Macdonald, and M. Parlett (Eds.), *Beyond the numbers game: A reader in educational evaluation* (pp. 6–22). Basingstoke: Macmillan.

Richards, Jack C. (1985). *The context of language teaching*. New York: Cambridge University Press.

13

The Learner's Effort in the Language Classroom

It is normal in the discussion of language pedagogy to focus attention either on teaching activities or on learning theories. In discussing teaching activities, we are concerned with what the teacher does or gets done by learners in the classroom and, at a remove, with what supports, demands or constrains the teacher's work, in the form of syllabuses and materials. In the discussion of learning theories, we are concerned with what might happen to the learner's language ability as a result of such teaching activities or, more widely, as a result of encounter with the language anywhere. These two areas of pedagogic discussion can be said to constitute two dimensions of the notion of a "method"; a method is, on one dimension, a set of classroom procedures for the teacher to carry out and, on another dimension, a concept or theory of language learning which informs or justifies those teaching procedures. Accordingly, we classify different views or formulations of language pedagogy as different methods, that is, different combinations of teaching procedure and learning theory.

There is, however, one other aspect of language pedagogy which can usefully be brought under focus and, when examined, can reveal a meaningful basis for linking teaching activities and learning theories. This has to do with the nature of the learner's

---

This essay was first published in 1991. *Source*: Prabhu, N. S. (1991). The learner's effort in the language classroom. In Eugenius Sadtono (Ed.), *Language acquisition and the second/foreign language classroom.* Anthology Series 28 (pp. 49–58). Singapore: SEAMEO Regional Language Centre.

effort in carrying out classroom activities—not with the teacher's effort or intention in setting the activities, nor with the hypothesised psychological impact of those activities, but simply with what the learner has to do to perform them successfully. The form of an activity set by the teacher does not always indicate correctly the nature of the effort demanded of the learner in its performance, and the teacher's intentions about the learner's effort may often be at variance with the actual effort the learner has to make. Any impact that a teaching activity has on the learner's language development, however, has to be the result of what the learner does, rather than of what the teacher does or intends the learner to do. An examination of the learner's effort is thus of some importance in relating teaching activities to learning theories.

The purpose of this paper is to identify different forms of effort by the learner in the language classroom, and to suggest what may be called a broad typology of learner effort. I will also try to point out the possible benefits of bringing such a typology to bear on the discussion of teaching activities and learning theories.

Imitation versus Cerebration

Let me begin with a very general distinction between two types of effort by the learner, which I will call "imitation" and "cerebration". Imitation is a matter of the learner attempting to do, as accurately as possible, what the teacher does in an exemplary role—such as producing a sound or pattern of sounds as exemplified, repeating words or sentences, altering sequences of words as demonstrated, copying strings of words or sentences from the textbook or blackboard into a notebook, or conforming to a given format of writing (such as the format of a letter or job application). The effort is to achieve a close resemblance to the model provided—to conform to it as completely as possible. The language learner imitates the behaviour of the language knower in order to become a language knower himself/herself, in due course. Cerebration, in contrast, involves the learner thinking things out—finding ways of distinguishing between sounds or sound sequences, looking for workable rules for putting together word sequences, puzzling out reasons why sentences are right or wrong, applying given rules to make choices between alternatives, guessing the meaning of a word, making the most sense of what is heard or read, performing a piece of reasoning on the strength of what is known or can be inferred, or putting meaning across as well as can be done with available resources of language. Cerebration is essentially effort to cope with problems—to make sense, to work things out, and to put solutions to a test. The language learner attempts to become a language knower, not by copying the latter's language behaviour, but by constructing the knowledge-system that underlies that behaviour.

There have, as we know, been pedagogic approaches which aimed primarily, or exclusively, at the effort of imitation by the learner. The audio-lingual method was, at one stage, more frankly labelled as the mimicry–memorisation ("mim–mem") method, and the term "language drill" clearly refers to an activity in which the learner is called on to imitate repeatedly and quickly. Dialogues have been used to get learners to imitate longer stretches of language, and there are modernised versions of the same basic activity today, in the form of role-play activities. There have also been pedagogic activities aiming mainly or entirely at the effort of cerebration by the learner. The Grammar-Translation method of the past century, and the classical-scholastic procedures that preceded them, both involved getting learners to puzzle out parts of the language system, as did later teaching procedures which were labeled "cognitive-code". These approaches too have their modernised versions, in the form of "grammatical consciousness-raising", "focused learning", "instructed language acquisition" and task-based teaching. Indeed, one way of understanding the periodical pendulum swings in the history of language pedagogy is to see the profession as moving its bets, as it were, between the effort of imitation and the effort of cerebration (or hedging its bets between the two in some way).

While imitation and cerebration can be related relatively easily to different teaching approaches, it is less straightforward to relate them to different learning theories. On the face of it, imitation implies the theory that language learning is a matter of copying the language knower—with some effort to begin with, but with less and less effort as recurrent attempts are made, leading eventually to an effortless, automatic copying of the behaviour involved. This is the familiar notion of habit-forming as a process of language learning. Similarly, cerebration seems to imply the theory that language learning is a conscious process of rule-discovery and rule-application, the rules discovered at different stages eventually forming a less conscious knowledge-system able to support language behaviour. This is the notion of learning a language by internalising its grammar. However, this is only an obvious interpretation. It is equally possible to see imitation as a facilitator of internal grammar construction: repeated copying of a piece of language, it can be argued, brings about a subconscious abstraction of its structural features, leading to rule-formation. The fact that the learner's effort consists of imitation need not mean that language-learning itself, or later language-use, is a matter of mere imitation. Indeed, if one looks at the early ideas of language drills and habit-formation, developed by such thinkers as Harold Palmer in the early part of this century, one can see the notion that a "habit" is in fact a principle of sentence-construction, or pattern, abstracted subconsciously from the set of sentences imitated, and employed thereafter to construct new sentences (Palmer, 1921). Imitation, therefore, may well be thought of as a favourable condition for internal system-development, far from being a denial of it. Similarly, cerebration need not imply the theory that language-learning is a process of conscious grammar-construction which then becomes a subconscious knowledge-system. There can be forms of cerebration which do not focus at all on the language as such; and even forms of cerebration which do focus on language can be viewed as merely favourable circumstances, or useful triggers, to a process of subconscious grammar-development, as done in arguments for grammatical conscious-raising (Rutherford, 1987).

There is, in passing, one area of language pedagogy where imitation points clearly to the theory that learning is a matter of copying behaviour. I am referring to the teaching of language for specific purposes, that is to say, the teaching of specific, and limited, language for specific, and limited, use. If limiting the learner to specific forms, samples or uses of language is seen as creating favourable circumstances for internal system development, there would in effect be a claim about the possibility of limited internal systems, de-limitable by pedagogic decision—a claim larger than has been made in the discussion of specific-purpose language teaching. Therefore, teaching language for specific purposes must mean getting the learner to copy the typical behaviour of language-users in specific situations, with imitation as the most relevant learner-effort. The teaching of limited language thus implies what may be called a limited theory of language learning—one which regards copying as the learning process.

Reproduction versus Simulation

Let me now go on to a further distinction in learner effort, within the category which I have called imitation. I would like to distinguish between imitation of the language form itself, which I will call "reproduction", and imitation of language behaviour with attention to its context, which I will call "simulation". Reproduction thus aims at linguistic accuracy or approximation in the act of copying, while simulation aims at a match between language form and its context, that is, at appropriacy. The kinds of activity that are normally called language-practice, or perhaps un-contextualised language practice—such as a repetition drill, the use of a substitution table, memorisation and recall of language samples, sentence construction on a given model, some forms of heavily guided composition (which make copying look like composing)—are all a matter of reproduction, in the way I am using the term. Many kinds of activity which are referred to as communicative practice, or "structural practice with functional honesty", to use Johnson's term (1982, p. 109)– such as role-playing a given dialogue, making choices between given expressions in the light of such requirements as politeness and formality, writing a letter, report or job application by imitating a given model—are all a matter of simulation. In reproduction, learners are occupied with linguistic forms; in simulation, they are occupied with what may be regarded as an indexing of linguistic forms with their communicative values or functions. Reproduction can be said to lead to the ability, as Newmark (1966) saw it, to ask a stranger for a light with "Do you have a light?", "Do you have fire?" or "Are you a match's owner?", while simulation is meant to lead to a choice of "Do you have a light?" or "Got a match?" in preference to the other expressions.

Reproduction has clearly been a central part of the Structural Approach to language pedagogy, though it has had a stricter adherence in the Audio-lingual Method, arising from the work of Fries and Lado, than in the Situational Method advocated by Hornby, which represented some attempt at simulation. Arguments for a central place for simulation have been advanced, and accepted fairly widely, in the last twenty years, under the label Communicative Approach. Following normal rhetorical tactics, the Communicative Approach has been presented as a challenge to the Structural Approach and as a radical replacement for it. It is therefore, important to realise that replacing the Structural Approach with the Communicative Approach is, in terms of learner effort, replacing reproduction with simulation. The general nature of the learner's effort is still imitation—a matter of copying language behaviour. Further, although simulation represents, from one point of view, a widening of pedagogic intentions based on a less restricted view of language ability, it also represents, from another point of view, a more restricted view of language and a more limited theory of learning. Learners' imitation of language forms can, as we have noted, be seen as a favorable condition for internal system development, the system so developed forming the basis of subsequent language behaviour. Reproduction, that is to say, permits the view that language learning is a matter of internalising a system of rules, not just a matter of copying the language knower's behaviour. It is difficult to see how such a view of learning can be reconciled with simulation, since the situational appropriacy of language forms is at best a matter of established convention in a language community, falling far short of being a productive system. When learners are able to say to a stranger, "Do you have fire?", "Have you got illumination?", "Are you a match's owner?" etc. they are giving evidence of an internalised grammatical system, since they are producing well-formed linguistic expressions which they could not have merely copied from a language knower. When, on the other hand, learners are able to choose the situationally appropriate expressions "Do you have a light?" or "Got a match?", they can only be copying a language knower's behaviour in a similar situation, simply because it is impossible to see what system of rules could lead to a choice of appropriate expressions over inappropriate ones, without any copying of behaviour as such. One can perhaps point to the possibility of a rule system of pragmatics underlying some aspects of apppropriacy in language behaviour, but it is still fair to say that a very large part of situational appropriacy is a matter of ad hoc convention, rather than rule-governed behaviour. In any case, pedagogic arguments in support of simulation have consistently appealed to conventional appropriacy, rather than to any rule system underlying appropriacy—indeed, they have laid stress on the fact that appropriacy is not a matter of rule systems and therefore needs to be acquired through simulation. If this is so, the claims that can be made for simulation in preference to reproduction are not very large. Simulation is preferable to reproduction only in terms of pedagogic intentions. In terms of learner effort, it is as much a matter of imitation as reproduction and, in terms of learning theory, it is much more limited than reproduction, since it regards learning itself as no more than a copying of behaviour.

Construction versus Deployment

I now wish to make one further distinction in learner effort, this time within the category of cerebration. We can, once again, distinguish between cerebration focused on language itself, which I call "construction", and cerebration focused on a knowledge of the world handled through language, which I will call "deployment". "Construction" refers both to an effort by the learner to understand some part of the language system—a matter of construing the system—and to any effort to put together linguistic expressions on the strength of that understanding. The term "exercise", in contrast to the term "practice", generally refers to the effort of construction—an activity in which the learner is challenged to understand and demonstrate that understanding. An exercise is like a test, in that it presents the learner with risks of going wrong, unlike practice which aims to avoid or minimise such risks. All grammatical exercises, in this sense of the term "exercise", call for the learner's effort at construction, as do various forms of vocabulary or pronunciation exercises, and indeed exercises calling for an assessment or explanation of appropriacy, though these are rarely employed. In contrast, what I am calling "deployment" involves learners handling information and developing knowledge about the world, by drawing on what information and knowledge of the world they already have, what cognitive abilities of inferring, reasoning, relating, etc., they possess, and what linguistic resources they command. Reading, in the sense of interpreting texts, involves the effort of deployment, as does free composition, in the sense of learners finding ways of saying what they have to say. The "immersion" classroom—learners studying a curricular subject in the medium of the target language—calls for the effort of deployment, in that it makes learners acquire new knowledge through the language. Task-based activity, in the sense the term was used on the Bangalore Project (Prabhu, 1987) is a means of getting beginner-level learners to make the effort of deployment in the language classroom. Deployment is typically the effort called for in problem-solving activities. Reading, writing, acquiring new knowledge can all be regarded as processes of problem-solving in a very general sense; task-based teaching can then be seen as a more deliberate, more focused and more manipulated form of problem-solving, as a language teaching device. It is true that what I have called the effort of construction is also a form of focused problem-solving, except that it involves solving problems of language as such, unlike deployment which involves the use of language as a resource in solving problems of world knowledge.

I pointed out earlier that cerebration in regard to the language being learnt—what we are now calling construction—has been a part of language pedagogy for a long time, in such approaches as the Grammar-Translation Method and the Cognitive-Code method. I also pointed out how the language teaching profession has, at various times, upheld or denied the value of such effort of construction for the learning of a language. It is perhaps worth asking, for a moment, what follows when the effort of construction is rejected as a pedagogic procedure. One may, in rejecting construction, reject all cerebration, as happened more than once when grammar-teaching was rejected as a means of language teaching. Such rejection of all cerebration leaves one with only imitation as desirable learner effort, whether in the form of reproduction or simulation. Alternatively, one may deny the value of construction but still see value to cerebration. This leads to the adoption of deployment as a desirable form of learner effort. To put it differently, the learner grappling with the rules of grammar is making a cerebral effort focused on language. If, in rejecting this, one rejects both the cerebral effort and the focus on language, one is only left with relatively mindless activity, with the focus at best on a faithful copying of behaviour. If, on the other hand, one rejects only the focus on language but not cerebral effort, one has the option of setting up activity involving cerebration on things other than language—that is to say, deployment.

The effort of construction can, as we noted earlier, be related to one of two theories of learning: it can be seen either to lead the learner to a conscious knowledge of the linguistic system, which then gradually descends to a subconscious level, or merely to serve to trigger a separate, subconscious process of system development. In contrast to this, the effort of deployment is relatable only to the latter theory—that a subconscious process of system development is triggered and promoted when language is employed as a resource in an effort to understand the world.

FOUR TYPES OF LEARNER EFFORT

I have now identified four types of learner effort in the language classroom—reproduction, simulation, construction and deployment. Reproduction and simulation both involve imitation—of the forms of language in one case, and of the social role of the language-user in the other. We can perhaps call classroom activities involving these two types of effort "form-focused" and "role-focused", respectively. The other two types of effort—construction and deployment—involve cerebration, cerebration on the rules of language in one case, and on knowledge of the world in the other. Activities involving these two forms of effort can therefore be called rule-focused and meaning-focused, respectively. From a different point of view, we can group together the effort of reproduction and that of construction, both being focused on language as an autonomous phenomenon. They differ between them in that one involves a copying of the phenomenon while the other involves trying to make sense of it. Terms such as "grammar-teaching" or "the teaching of structure" are often used ambivalently—to refer to reproduction and/or construction—thus obscuring a major difference in terms of learner effort, namely, that between imitation and cerebration. Similarly, simulation and deployment can be grouped together, as forms of effort focused on things outside language as a formal entity. The focus, in one case, is on the performance of a social role, and in the other on an understanding of the world. The term "communicative" is often used ambivalently to refer to either or both of them, thus blurring the distinction, once again, between imitation and cerebration.

USEFULNESS OF THE TYPOLOGY

What is the usefulness of this categorisation of learner effort? First, it enables us to see known forms of language pedagogy in a somewhat new light, or from a newer point of view. Looking at things from as many viewpoints as possible is one of the mental tools we have for increasing understanding. It is, for instance, common in the discussion of language pedagogy to contrast a formal, grammar-based approach with an apparently more comprehensive communicative approach directed to real-life language use. But this is a contrast based neither on teaching intentions, nor on learning theories. An examination of learner effort leads us to a different contrast, that between imitation and cerebration, which is likely to be more significant for the process of learning. We then begin to see that both a grammar-based approach and a communicative approach can involve no more than a copying of behaviour and that, between the two approaches it is the grammar-based approach which permits a non-behaviourist theory of learning even when it involves only the effort of imitation.

Secondly, a categorisation of learner effort provides us with an additional frame of reference to which we can usefully relate concepts and issues in pedagogy. Take, for instance, the concept of authenticity. The prevalent notion is that authenticity is a characteristic of the samples of language presented to the learner: the samples are authentic if they are taken from actual instances of language use. This notion has been challenged by Widdowson (1978, pp. 79–80) who regards authenticity, instead, as a characteristic of the learner's engagement with language samples: the learner's engagement is authentic if the learner responds, interacts or copes with language samples in the same way that language users do. Given our categories of learner effort, we can see that the first notion of authenticity makes sense when the learner's effort consists of simulation, while Widdowson's notion clearly envisages the effort of deployment. What is involved therefore is not just a terminological difference but a difference in theories of learning: simulation-based pedagogy cannot possibly adopt Widdowson's notion of authenticity simply because simulation cannot be claimed to be the central characteristic of real-life language use. Or take Widdowson's well-known distinction between "usage" and "use".

The distinction is clearly between language-focused and non–language-focused learner effort—between reproduction and construction on the one hand, and simulation and deployment on the other. However, the usage–use distinction leaves out the equally important contrast between imitation and cerebration, though Widdowson elsewhere takes a stand against simulation-based ESP, and in defence of grammatical problem-solving. The usage–use distinction, therefore, is only a distinction between reproduction and deployment, though it is presented as a more global one. Similarly, Krashen's (1981) distinction between "learning" and "acquisition" is only a distinction between construction and deployment, in our terms; it ignores reproduction and simulation, with the result that its proponent often finds himself recommending simulation procedures as if they were deployment procedures. We can also relate the issue of error-treatment in language pedagogy to our categorisation of learner effort. Imitation-based pedagogy (reproduction and simulation) is necessarily committed to error-prevention: if language learning takes place through an imitation of language behaviour, then it is crucial for the imitation to be accurate; any errors in imitation can, in principle, make the learner an erroneous language user. Cerebration-based pedagogy, on the other hand, has necessarily to permit errors by learners; problem-solving would be a mere pretense if it did not permit trial and error. Further, construction-based pedagogy has a commitment to dealing with errors when they occur—for example, setting further exercises or promoting a better understanding of the rules, in some way—while deployment-based pedagogy is necessarily error-tolerant, since dealing with errors as such will undermine the genuineness of deployment.

Finally, let me point out briefly a possible use of this typology of learner effort in the preparation of teaching materials. It is common to find, in textbooks for language teaching, an apparently varied pattern of activities for the learner, under such labels as comprehension, vocabulary, grammar or structure, pronunciation, and composition. In the more modernised textbooks, one also finds sections on such communicative activities as role-play, writing an office report, etc. A closer examination of such materials, however often reveals that most of the comprehension questions demand of the learner little more than a copying of relevant parts of the reading text (a question merely serving as a clue to which part of the text is to be copied), the vocabulary exercise calls mainly for a copying of words or an imitation of given sentences by incorporating given words in them, that the grammar or structure work involves a piece of intensive "practice" (that is to say, reproduction in some form), that the pronunciation work is understandably a matter of accurate imitation, that the communicative activity of role-play is a matter of learners (working in pairs in keeping with enlightened pedagogy) mouthing to each other their parts in a scripted dialogue, and that the writing of an office report is a matter of imitating faithfully all the essential parts of a model office report, making only some substitutions of content words to alter the information content. It is clearly the textbook writer's intention to employ a variety of teaching activities (and indeed, different teaching approaches—both linguistic and communicative), but, from the viewpoint of learner effort, what all or most of the activities call for is just imitation. Perhaps it would be useful for textbook writers to bear a typology of learner effort in mind and to ensure that the activities provided do involve the type of effort which they see the most value to—or, if they wished to be eclectic, to ensure that there are some activities which involve each type of learner effort. A typology of learner effort can thus serve both as a further dimension to pedagogic understanding and as a further aid to pedagogic practice.

References

Johnson, Keith. (1982). *Communicative syllabus design and methodology.* Oxford: Pergamon Press.

Krashen, Stephen D. (1981). *Second language acquisition and second language learning.* Oxford: Pergamon Press.

Newmark, Leonard. (1979). How not to interfere with language learning. In C. J. Brumfit and K. Johnson (Eds.), *The communicative approach to language teaching* (pp. 160–66). Oxford: Oxford University Press.

Palmer, H. E. ([1921] 1964). *The principles of language study*. Oxford: Oxford University Press.

Prabhu, N. S. (1987). *Second language pedagogy*. Oxford: Oxford University Press.

Rutherford, William E. (1987). *Second language grammar: Learning and teaching*. London: Longman.

Widdowson, H. G. (1978). *Teaching language as communication*. Oxford: Oxford University Press.

14

The Dynamics of the Language Lesson

This paper is an attempt to explore the nature of the language lesson—indeed, of any lesson—as an event in the classroom. It is speculative, in the sense that it represents an effort to make sense of a complex phenomenon by reflecting on experience and by perceiving a plausible pattern. In the first part of the paper, I try to show that the classroom lesson is indeed a very complex event, with several different dimensions to it. Here I take further a suggestion made by Richard Allwright (1989), namely, that the lesson is not just a pedagogic event, but a social event as well. I try to show that the lesson is at least four different types of event. In the second part of the paper, I examine the consequences of that perception of the classroom lesson to specialist effort at pedagogic reform. I argue that it is naïve to think that specialists can formulate a good teaching method and then get teachers to implement it in their classrooms. I suggest that classroom teaching can improve only to the extent that teachers themselves act as specialists.

The Lesson as a Curricular Unit

Let me begin with a familiar perspective on a lesson, namely, that it is a stage in the implementation of a course. The curriculum normally is organised as an incremental sequence of teaching units, the sequence as a whole meant to achieve a large objective, and

This essay was first published in 1992. *Source*: Prabhu, N. S. (1992). Dynamics of the language lesson. *TESOL Quarterly*, 26(2), 225–41.

each unit in it meant to achieve a small sub-objective. Classroom teaching is seen as a steady movement from the first unit to the last, and any given lesson is viewed as the completion of one small part of the journey. What happens in a lesson is, from this perspective, best understood by reference to earlier and later lessons and by seeing the logic of the overall sequence.

It is worthwhile noticing here the nature of the connection between curricular progression and the educative process. Education is centrally concerned with the mind: language education aims to promote one form of mental development in learners, whether we conceive of it as the development of cognitive structures or cognitive skills, the realisation of an inherent capacity, or the creation of a new capacity. In designing educational activity, this concept of psychological progress is translated into one of curricular progression, the metaphor of a journey being equally applicable to both. The completion of a lesson as a curricular unit is thus meant to represent the completion of a step in the learner's psycholinguistic development. If this is taken seriously, a given lesson has to be understood and assessed in relation to its match with the learner's developmental stage at that point, rather than in relation to preceding and following units. The reason why this is not done is that it is extremely difficult to perceive the learner's actual developmental stage at each point and that the day-to-day activity of classroom teaching needs to have a more accessible and stable source of guidance. The provision of a curricular sequence enables the teacher to assume, without having to ascertain, that each unit in the sequence matches a corresponding point in the learner's progress. A fundamental reason for constructing a curriculum, therefore, is to give the classroom teacher a workable alternative to the difficult task of following the learner's actual development. However, this workable alternative involves the belief that the curriculum represents a pre-determination of the learner's development, both at particular points and over a stretch of time (that is, the course); and this in turn implies that the curriculum developer has far better access than the teacher to the learner's mental development: the curriculum developer attempts to predict or decide in advance the process of development before it takes place, while the teacher has difficulty perceiving it as it happens. It may be that curricula are necessary, even indispensable, in educational activity, but it is nevertheless important to realise that they rest on a very large assumption and that the perception of a lesson as a curricular unit involves an appeal to that assumption.

The Lesson as Implementation of a Method

A second perspective on a lesson, which is also familiar, is that it represents the implementation of a method of teaching. A teaching method, in the sense I am using the term, has two aspects to it: a conceptual aspect and an operational one. While the conceptual aspect consists essentially of a theory of how learning takes place, or can best take place, the operational aspect consists of a specification of what should be done in the classroom, within each teaching unit. A method in operation is commonly seen as a pre-specified pattern of activity within a given lesson (or a sequence of related lessons), the pattern being recurrent from one stretch of teaching to another. Given a logical link (or at least a conventional association) between the conceptual and operational aspects of a method, it is possible to observe the pattern of activity in a single lesson and infer the theory of learning involved—to label the teaching, for instance, as structural, communicative, experiential, and so forth, or as a mix of two or more. A method is what lies behind a lesson plan—what guides the teacher in deciding what activities are to be undertaken, and in what order, in the course of a lesson.

Let us juxtapose briefly the two views of a lesson mentioned so far. The lesson as a curricular unit makes reference to the teaching content and to one stage in an incremental progression. The lesson as implementation of a method makes reference to the teaching procedure and to one cycle in a cyclic sequence. As a curricular unit, a lesson needs to be seen in relation to other curricular units; as a method in operation, it needs to be seen in relation to the theory of learning that corresponds to it. It was noted above that in following the curricular progression the teacher is assuming that that progression is a dependable indicator of the learner's psychological progress. In following a method as a pattern of activity, the teacher is assuming that the theory of learning that informs that pattern of activity is in fact a valid theory. I will have occasion to return to this point a little later in this discussion.

The Lesson as a Social Event

Seeing a lesson in relation to a curriculum or to a teaching method is seeing it as a pedagogic event; and this is how lessons are seen, most of the time, in specialist-level discussions of classroom teaching and learning. We can in fact regard this as the specialist's perspective on the language lesson, perhaps shared or trusted partially by the teacher in the classroom, but rarely shared by the learner. A different perspective on a lesson, shared by teachers and learners alike though seldom brought into professional discussion, is that it is a routinised social event, with roles and role relationships established by tradition and with a ritualistic aspect to the actions performed. There are roles assigned by custom to teachers and learners in the classroom, though these may vary from one culture to another, just as there are roles assigned to the priest and the worshippers at a temple, or to the judge, the lawyers, and the litigants in a court of law. There is also a certain agenda of events associated with a classroom lesson, though this may be very general in form, just as there are agendas associated with religious worship, the courtroom, communal decision-making, the annual shareholders' meeting, the company boardroom, or an academic seminar. The classroom lesson, that is to say, is a kind of social genre, stereotypic and to some extent ritualised, generally not noticed as such when it is conformed to but disturbing when it is violated. The ritualisation may or may not take the form of dress regulations, standing up to show respect, the use of honorifics, first names or last names, not speaking unless asked to, procedures for assignment and submission of work, procedures for punishment and reward, opening and closing moves for the lesson as a whole or for any phase of it, and so on; but there is at least a set of shared notions about the different phases of a lesson, legitimate and deviant behaviour, the extent of teacher's authority and learner's right, and duties and obligations on both sides. Further, these notions are prevalent not just among teachers and learners but among parents, educational administrators, and the general public. There is indeed a form of classroom ethic, just as there are forms of ethic associated with doctor–patient or lawyer–client transactions.

Although this view of the classroom lesson as a routinised social event may look largely irrelevant to professional discussion of pedagogy—or, at best, a possible hazard to beware of in curriculum construction and method determination—it would be a mistake not to see an essential function which it serves. The classroom lesson is a recurrent encounter between people and, like all recurrent encounters, needs the sense of security arising from shared expectations. Human encounters which are entirely unpredictable, with no foreknowledge or even an expectation of what is to happen, are inherently threatening and would be intolerable as regularly recurrent events in any social group or institution, including the family. One needs to be able to anticipate events, in some general form, take some things for granted, even tentatively, and have a frame of reference and roles with which to interpret and respond to what happens. The more recurrent the encounter, and the more numerous its participants, the greater the need for a shared routine and a shared set of expectations. It is only with some notion of where one belongs and where the others belong that one can engage in a repeated encounter with no great sense of threat. With classroom lessons, moreover, it is not just the participants in the encounter—teachers and learners—who need the security arising from shared expectations; parents need it too on behalf of their children, as do educational authorities and indeed the society as a whole. Social routinisation is therefore a necessary support in making the classroom lesson possible as a recurrent event.

The Lesson as an Arena of Human Interaction

Behind the conventionalised roles and routines of a lesson are a group of individuals—a teacher and many learners—with varied personalities, motives, self-images, fears and aspirations, levels of tolerance, and degrees of maturity. A teacher perceives different learners not just as being strong or weak in learning, but as being interested or indifferent, modest or presumptuous, accepting or rebellious, supportive or subversive, trusting, skeptical or mocking, accessible to empathy or inscrutable, and so on, in varying degrees. Conducting a lesson is, first and foremost, handling a collection of friendly and unfriendly people in a way that maximally protects or projects, and minimally hurts or diminishes, one's own self-image as a teacher. The learners in their turn perceive the teacher as being friendly or unfriendly, helpful or hostile, tolerant or vindictive, and so on, both to themselves and to different fellow learners, and try to act in a way that protects or enhances their own varied self-images. Such play of personalities takes place not just between the teacher on the one hand and learners on the other but, in a more fierce form, between learners themselves, in a highly complex and multilateral form. There are likes and dislikes, loyalties and rivalries, ambitions and desires to dominate, injured pride and harboured grudge, fellow feeling and jealousy, all creating a continual threat to security and self-image, and calling for protective or corrective action. Perhaps the most immediate and pervasive concern of teachers and learners alike in classrooms is to guard against a loss of face and, to the extent possible, to win approval, sympathy or loyalty from others as a safeguard against future hazards to "face".

A classroom lesson is thus an arena of human interactions—not the pedagogic interactions desired or elicited as a part of teaching strategy (which may or may not occur as expected) but the more elemental, inevitable interactions which occur simply because human beings, with all their complexity, are involved. They are interactions which occur equally on the playground, at a youth club, or in any other social group, though the modes of their expression may vary from one arena to another. One may therefore wish to ignore them as being nothing special to the classroom, much less to the language classroom, or try to control and manipulate them directly as in some humanistic approaches, by reducing and simplifying them to manageable proportions. My point here is simply that they constitute an important dimension of the classroom lesson and, although it may be naïve and unproductive to try to prescribe ways of handling them, it would be equally naïve not to be aware that they operate powerfully in the classroom and will have a large influence on whatever one does prescribe by way of a curriculum or method.

Conflict between Different Dimensions

I have now identified four dimensions of the classroom lesson: the lesson as a curricular unit and as a method in operation, which may both be regarded as pedagogic dimensions; and the lesson as a social genre and as a play of personalities, which may be considered social and personal dimensions. A part of the value of such an analysis, as I see it, is that it enables us to understand a range of problems that arise in the classroom as conflicts between different dimensions. Thus, the method being implemented may require the teacher to be maximally supportive of learners' efforts and achievements in the classroom and to highlight positive feedback rather than negative feedback. But learners as a social group often have the notion that it is opportunism or a form of surrender to be praised or favoured by the teacher and that there is bravery in defying the teacher's wishes and values. This notion of heroism, based on rejection and rebellion, can set up a source of approval and disapproval directly in conflict with the teacher's approval and disapproval, thus creating a dilemma for many learners and a threat to the teacher's sense of security. To take another instance, a recommended teaching procedure may incorporate the principle that learners' efforts should precede the teacher's input, such that much of the learning takes place as a form of discovery, by the learner, and the teacher's input is responsive to the learner's effort, rather than preemptive of it. But the classroom lesson as a social genre often includes the notion that it is a part of the teacher's role to provide the necessary inputs and that it is therefore unfair or incompetent of the teacher to demand effort by learners in the absence of such inputs.

Such conflict can arise in a more acute form when the pedagogic approach involves a principled refusal to provide a curriculum in advance and a demand, instead, that the classroom itself engage in evolving a curriculum through teacher–learner negotiation (Breen, 1984). Not surprisingly, proposals of this form have had to incorporate a component of "learner-training" (Allwright, 1984) partly in the hope of altering the expectations of a lesson as a social genre. A related area of conflict is group work. It is common these days to highlight the pedagogic benefits of small-group work by learners, peer support and peer correction, in place of teacher-fronted activity, and it is often argued that such small-group work provides a sense of security to learners. But there is, as we have noted, a complex play of personalities between learners, involving dominance, rivalry, rebellion, submission or withdrawal, and there isn't a socially established frame of roles and routines for small-group interaction as there is for teacher-fronted activity. It has also been common for some time now to give a high value to learner talk in the classroom and to require the teacher to make a special effort to draw out the silent learners by various means. But learners are, like all other people, varied in their personalities—some taciturn and others vociferous, some shy and others showy, some diffident and others adventurous, and so on, and being drawn out conspicuously can constitute for some a disconcerting exposure and a disorientation on the lesson.

My purpose in drawing attention to such conflicts is not to recommend any specific procedures for resolving them, but simply to suggest a way of perceiving and understanding them as the outcome of an interplay of different forces at work in the classroom.

I think, in fact, that it is unlikely to be fruitful for the language teaching specialism to take on board the social and personal dimensions of the classroom lesson, in addition to the pedagogic dimensions, and to try to provide general procedures for reconciling them. This is not only because the classroom lesson as a social genre varies across societies and cultures, and the mix of learners' personalities in any classroom is unpredictable and irreducible to simple patterns; it is equally because the teacher's own personality is a major factor in the interplay of forces, and conflict resolution will necessarily have to vary from one teacher to another.

Reconciliation of Conflicts

Conflict resolution, however, does take place in all classrooms, in varied forms and to varied extents—or else it would be impossible for the class to function. It takes place in the way it does in any other social group—by each participant arriving at a set of relationships which give him or her the maximum security, stability, or room to manoeuvre attainable in the circumstances. Opposing forces accommodate each other or hold each other at bay, and the different dimensions reinforce their common ground and limit their encroachment on one another. Personalities come to terms, as best they can, both with other personalities and with prevalent social and pedagogic frames. Perhaps the social and personal dimensions are so strong in some classrooms that they subordinate the pedagogic ones; and perhaps it is the reverse in other classrooms. Perhaps a concern with getting on with the curriculum (with a view to getting ready for an examination) is sufficiently dominant to absorb or suspend other concerns in some school systems; or perhaps there is a strong concern for the socially sanctioned roles and routines such that conflicting parts of other dimensions are subdued or suppressed. Perhaps the teacher has enough status or strength of personality to ensure priority to one dimension or another; or perhaps the teacher is sufficiently insecure to take the line of least resistance. As a result, the balance of different dimensions and forces arrived at is bound to differ from one classroom to another, in terms of its composition. It is also bound to differ in terms of its relative stability, some classrooms operating with a more precarious balance than others.

When language pedagogy is discussed in professional forums, it is the pedagogic dimensions that chiefly come under focus, rather than the social and personal dimensions. It is generally assumed that the central task is to arrive at the best possible curriculum and the most promising method and that, once arrived at, these pedagogic inputs can be carried into classrooms fairly easily, given an agreement to do so by those who have the authority to prescribe curricula and methods. It is true that a large effort is made to persuade authorities to adopt the putatively better curricula and methods, and to ensure that they understand the rationale of these new inputs as fully as possible. It is also true that various forms of teacher training are undertaken to make sure that teachers understand what is to be done, how, and why. But all these are measures meant to make certain that the intended inputs do in fact get to the classrooms, with minimal dilution or distortion on the way. They still assume that the inputs will work in the way envisaged once they get to the classrooms.

Perhaps it will be objected that professional discussion of language pedagogy does not restrict attention these days to what I have called pedagogic dimensions but pays increasing attention to such contextual and social factors as the local educational policy or expectation, various characteristics of learners and teachers, features of the school system, features of prevalent and favoured forms of classroom interaction, and so on, and that this more comprehensive view ensures a larger relevance or feasibility to specialist inputs than I have suggested above. The question, however, is not how much attention should be given to contextual and social factors in arriving at pedagogic recommendations but, at a more basic level, what any such attention can hope to achieve. Making a prior study of contextual and social factors and taking them into account in determining desirable pedagogic procedures is at best an attempt at anticipating and preempting difficulties arising from those factors in the classroom, not at resolving difficulties as they arise. Anticipation depends on generalisation: one needs to identify characteristics of sets of learners and sets of teachers in order to accommodate those characteristics while recommending methods. But several factors involved in the social and personal dimension of the classroom—in particular, in what I have referred to as the play of personalities—are characteristics of individuals rather than of sets, or of particular groupings of individuals in contrast to other groupings. Besides, taking account of a set of factors is not the same as taking account of the interplay between those factors. The latter is necessarily a process of ongoing change, which can only be managed responsively as different situations arise, not preemptively through an anticipation of those situations. Indeed any attempt to deal with it preemptively can by itself constitute a form of intervention which adds to the different forces at play, instead of easing them. It therefore does not seem very worthwhile for specialist inputs to try to take in more than the pedagogic dimensions in order to be less unsettling to the classroom. It may be more useful to reconsider the role of specialist inputs themselves and to ask how the teacher's own management of the forces at play in the classroom might become pedagogically more constructive.

An important concern for teachers and learners in the classroom, as noted already, is their sense of security and the protection of their self-images. In the course of conflict resolution, all participants are likely to give first priority to those options which will most safeguard their self-esteem and leave them to play their roles as teachers or learners in relative security. Teachers come to terms with learners in a way that least erodes their status, in their own eyes, in the learners' eyes, and perhaps in the eyes of fellow teachers and superiors. Learners too come to terms with the teacher and with fellow learners in a way that most protects their individual self-images and leaves them least vulnerable to a loss of face or façade. The different dimensions of the classroom lesson, both pedagogic and social, are all so interpreted and accommodated as to arrive at an overall balance which all or most participants can live with, though not necessarily in equal comfort (and some only by building shells around themselves, as independent protection). The availability of conventionalised roles, routines and agendas is a significant help in the process, roles acting as shields to personality. The availability of a curriculum to go through is also a help in that it provides a non-personal entity to focus on, thus de-emphasising personal tensions. Patterns of activities dictated by the teaching method act as a further form of routine which, being recurrent and predictable, affords a measure of security. For these reasons, the routines of a classroom lesson are not just routines but carriers of a more complex though less perceptible balance of the different forces at work. Consequently, the more well-established the routines are, the more settled the balance is. The reverse is also true: the more stable and comfortable the balance is to teachers and learners, the more quickly and firmly the routines get established, becoming less and less open to change.

Effect of Specialist Inputs

The picture of the classroom I have just outlined may strike some people as being an exaggeration of the non-pedagogic dimensions. I hope, however, that it will be recognised as being at least partially true, and reminiscent of some uneasy feeling we have all had about classroom lessons on some occasions. I would like to suggest that, because we deliberately focus on the pedagogic dimensions of the classroom in professional discussion, we tend to exaggerate the role of those pedagogic dimensions, at the expense of the non-pedagogic ones. I would also like to suggest that what I have said about classroom lessons—namely, that they go on largely as routinised events, the routines sustaining a workable arrangement of relations between the participants involved and making the recurrent encounter tolerable or comfortable to them—is generally true of other institutionalised groups in recurrent encounter, whether in public or in private life; so it would be surprising if classroom lessons did not share those characteristics. In any case, my purpose in highlighting the routinised nature of classroom lessons is to point out its implications for our professional discussion of language pedagogy—a matter which I now turn to.

If classroom lessons take place as routinised events, they can only provide the kinds of satisfaction that routinised events do—the satisfaction of having performed a routine enjoined on one (as with much religious worship) or of having gone through one more stage in a prescribed sequence (as with many committee meetings), at a cost not higher than necessary. Any learning that takes place, in the sense of cognitive development, is incidental to the process and generally independent of the specific routines engaged in. But professional discussion of pedagogy makes the fundamental assumption of a cause–effect relationship between the activities performed in the classroom and the learning that results. As specialists, we are concerned centrally with identifying those classroom activities which promise to be most productive of learning and with commending to teachers the outcome of our search. We decide, from time to time, that a structure drill, or a grammatical explanation, or a role-play, or a problem-solving task, or a discourse-processing task, or small-group interaction, and so on, are specially productive of language learning, and urge teachers as strongly as we can to carry out these activities in their classrooms. If what I have said about classroom lessons is even partly true, there is a need for us to pause to ask what effect the new procedures we recommend are likely to have on existing classroom routines.

Since existing routines in classrooms are a source of relative security and stability, any intrusion of new activities is a threat to that stability. It is therefore understandable that teachers tend to be reluctant to alter their teaching procedures despite recommendations that they do so. But let us suppose that teachers do act on the recommendations and attempt to alter classroom procedures. There will be a disturbance of the prevailing balance of forces, necessitating a fresh process of conflict resolution and leading eventually to a new balance which can accommodate the new pattern of activity.

If the new balance is a precarious one—with which participants in the classroom lesson are not sufficiently comfortable—the new pattern of activity continues to be a source of insecurity and is likely to be thrown out as soon as an opportunity arises to do so. Once again, however, let us assume that the new balance arrived at is a stable one, with a firm assimilation of the new pattern of activity. Inevitably, there will have been a resolution of conflict between the old routine and the new pattern of activity, with various adjustments and modifications in both, making use of any common ground and toning down the conflicting parts. The recommended pattern of activity has therefore been assimilated in various forms in various classrooms so as to be in most harmony with existing routines. Even where it has not been altered significantly in the process of assimilation, it has at least become a part of a new stable pattern, allied to a new, stable balance of the varied forces at play.

The result of such a development is that the altered procedure will now establish itself steadily as the new routine, serving the same functions as did the old routine and providing little more than the forms of satisfaction that arise from the performance of such routines. This I think is the main reason why in the language teaching profession there has been a succession of new pedagogic approaches and methods on the one hand and, on the other, a succession of disappointments at the implementation of those methods in classrooms and, even more, with the learning outcomes of such implementations as have taken place. While we think that we are providing new teaching procedures capable of yielding better learning outcomes, we are actually providing new classroom routines to replace old routines, the general dynamics of the classroom continuing to be what they are.

When can a new method be more than merely a new routine in the classroom? I said earlier that a method has a conceptual aspect as well as an operational one. The teaching procedures we recommend to teachers constitute the operational aspect and if that is all that teachers take from us and try to implement, the implementation is sure to be a matter of replacing old routines with new. But suppose we put to teachers not just the operational aspect but the conceptual aspect as well—that is to say, our theory of how language learning comes about and how the procedures being recommended are likely to bring it about. We are now asking teachers to take to the classroom not just the teaching activities we recommend but the theory of language learning behind those activities. We want teachers, in other words, to make our theory their own—to be as persuaded by the theory as we are. It is not difficult to see that this is a rather naïve demand to make. It implies that people's concepts and beliefs are as open to a replacement as their behavioural routines. Reference has been made above to the difficulty of altering routines; altering beliefs can only be that much more difficult, unsuccessful, or uncertain in its outcome. If a threat to one's routine is unsettling, a threat to one's belief can only be more unsettling. But perhaps it does not have to be an alteration of beliefs; all that is needed, it may be argued, is that teachers understand the theory involved, not necessarily be persuaded by it. This means, however, that we are asking teachers to operate with a theory that they do not themselves subscribe to. It seems to me a formula for a profound sense of insecurity—to have to carry out, day after day, a set of activities which upset established routines and unsettle the prevailing balance of relationships, and to be trying to justify those activities with a theory which is at variance with one's own belief. It would not be surprising if survival dictated a discarding of the theory and a retention of just the pattern of activity, to be assimilated into existing routines.

The Lesson as an Experience of Growth

For classroom activities to be more than protective routines, it is minimally necessary for teachers to be operating with their own beliefs about the pedagogic value of those activities—with their own notions or theories of how learning comes about and how the teaching that is being done is bringing it about. I do not mean by this that the theories should be original to teachers and different from all others. They may have been received, adopted, or inherited by teachers from various sources, with or without conscious decision, at some time in the past. What I mean is simply that they should be theories to which teachers see the most truth or plausibility and with which teachers are most able to identify, at a given time. These theories will of course vary widely in content between teachers and vary inevitably from the theories being advocated by specialists. Variation (and, indeed, conflict) between theories is, after all, conspicuously prevalent among us as specialists who are admittedly advocating what we see the most truth or plausibility to; so there is no reason to expect any less variation in the theories that different teachers identify with. More importantly, teachers' theories are sure to vary in the degrees of their explicitness and in the level of awareness teachers have of them. In many cases, they may be unarticulated and ill-defined, in the form of intuitions; in other cases, they may be strongly held but unexamined notions, in the form of beliefs or preconceptions; in yet other cases, they may not be easily accessible at all, having been "buried" in the process of classroom routinisation. As a result, the foremost need, if classroom activity is not to be just a performance of routines, is for teachers' own beliefs and intuitions to become more accessible to them and more actively engaged as one of the forces in the dynamics of the classroom.

It is common to think of specialists in language pedagogy as people who are able to develop theories of language learning and teaching, to support those theories with relevant evidence, and to state them explicitly for other people's consideration. In contrast, classroom teachers are thought of as being ill-equipped or at least unengaged in this mode of rational, "scientific" enquiry, though hopefully able to make use of the products of such enquiry. I would like to suggest, however, that there is a more basic level of mental activity which is shared by specialists and teachers (and indeed all human beings). All of us have commonsense views of the world, constituting our minimal response to a human urge to make sense of what we experience and what we do. If one can talk about this commonsense knowledge construction by employing (for want of a more direct means) rational theory construction as a metaphor, one can say that the human psyche includes a large theory-building mechanism, operating subconsciously. It takes in the data of ongoing experience, as well as available/inherited interpretations of such experience, and strives to arrive at what it regards as the most satisfying view through (what may be thought of as) theory construction, theory revision, theory replacement (or data shelving, data doctoring, data dismissal), and so on. None of us has much idea of the "rules" of this activity but that does not justify our ignoring its existence. Indeed, it is possible that some (or much) of the specialist-level, rational theory construction represents an explicit, "rationalised" articulation of this subconscious activity, or at least draws strength from intuitions arising from it.

Teachers have commonsense views of learning and teaching, just as other people do of the activities they are engaged in. The data leading to these views may have arisen from a variety of sources, including teachers' own experience at one time as learners, and existing views of learning and teaching, as noted above. A continuing source of such data is each teacher's ongoing experience in the classroom and, to the extent such experience is being taken in as data by the teacher's subconscious "theory", there may be said to be a further factor at play in the classroom, namely, a form of theorising by the teacher. The process of theorising can be said to be strong when the subconscious theory is active and able to take account of continuing data, and weak (or "frozen" into a prejudice or dogma) when it is not active in that way. It is the strong state of the process that I am calling the engagement of the teacher's theory in the classroom.

When a teacher's own theory is engaged in classroom activity, the teacher has more at stake than an immediate sense of security and the protection of self-image. The theory is something the teacher identifies with and therefore constitutes an intellectual stake in the activity. There is a reason to seek confirmation of the theory from what goes on in the classroom—or to come to terms with any disconfirmation by altering or reinterpreting the theory itself. This makes the teacher's theory a significant factor at play in the classroom—a factor more powerful than the need to conform to a prescribed curriculum or prescribed method because it is a personal, intellectual stake for the teacher, comparable to a sense of security, which is a personal, affective stake. The theory thus acts as an additional, strong influence on the resolution of different conflicts in the classroom and is in turn influenced by the other forces at play and by the confirmation or disconfirmation it receives. There is then an active, ongoing interaction between the theory and its operation in the classroom—between concept and conduct. Teaching becomes something of an intellectual exploration—a process of subjecting one's theory to an operational test, and sustaining or modifying it in the light of outcomes (to employ again the metaphor of scientific enquiry). To experience such a process of exploration is to experience professional growth as a teacher—to learn a little about teaching and learning from every lesson (or every so many lessons) taught in the classroom. The process is also an exciting one, in the same way that specialists find it exciting to explore theories of teaching and learning. For specialists to "give" methods to teachers is for them to pass on a set of outcomes devoid of the excitement of arriving at them. For teachers to engage in theorising is for them to experience the excitement of the process and to be able to continue the exploration as a part of their teaching.

Such an engagement of the teacher's own theory will not eliminate routinisation—indeed, it would be destructive for it to do so, since a certain degree of routinisation is essential to day-to-day teaching, as we have noted—but it can prevent over-routinisation to the point where lessons become merely the performance of routines. It can do so because the intellectual excitement of exploring and developing a theory can act as a rival to a desire for security, and replace it, to various extents, as the dominant factor in resolving conflicts and arriving at a balance of the forces at play. Further, if the teacher engages in classroom activity with a sense of intellectual excitement, there is at least a fair probability that learners will begin to participate in the excitement and to perceive classroom lessons mainly as learning events—as experiences of growth for themselves. My suggestion, therefore, is that for classroom lessons to be more than mere routines, teachers need to be theorists—not in the sense of being able to wield the apparatus of scholarship or the skills of academic argument, but in the sense of operating with an active concept of the cause–effect relationship between teaching and learning, and of developing and modifying that concept in the light of their ongoing experience in the classroom.

This is admittedly an idealistic view of classroom lessons, with limits of various kinds on its realisation. I think, nevertheless, that it is an ideal worth striving for, in order to achieve whatever success is achievable. I think, in particular, that specialist effort in language pedagogy needs to explore possible ways of enabling teachers to operate as theorists, instead of providing them with new methods to be used as new routines. If, as I have tried to show, classroom lessons are highly susceptible to routinisation, it is more worthwhile enabling teachers to counter the forces of routinisation than merely helping them to change from one routine to another. It is of course unclear at this stage what procedures might be useful in enabling teachers to operate as theorists, though it does seem clear that teacher training will need to seek ways of activating teachers' subconscious theories and getting them to interact with available theories. Perhaps there are ways of helping teachers to try to articulate their pedagogic notions and intuitions, such that the process of articulation acts as a form of exploration, and any success in articulation helps to increase confidence as well as ability for further exploration. Perhaps specialists should themselves take teachers' theories seriously and interact with them in the way they interact with each other's theories. I do not think that specialists in language pedagogy have any better source for their theories than their own notions and intuitions, though of course they are more highly skilled in articulating them and supporting them in academically recognised ways. Perhaps it will be a gain for all of us to acknowledge that specialists' theories are on the same footing as teachers' theories, and that both specialists and teachers can benefit through an interaction between their theories. Perhaps teachers will be helped to function as theorists if those who regard themselves as theorists begin to function as teachers.

References

Allwright, D. (1989). *Interaction in the language classroom: Social problems and pedagogic possibilities.* Paper presented at Les Etats Generaux des Langues, Paris, April 1989.

Allwright, R. L. (1984). The importance of interaction in classroom language learning. *Applied Linguistics,* 5(2), 156–71.

Breen, M. P. (1984). Process syllabuses for the language classroom. In C. J. Brumfit (Ed.), *General English syllabus design* (pp. 47–60). Oxford: Pergamon Press.

15

Descriptive and Prescriptive Approaches to the Norms of English in Singapore

The distinction between description and prescription gained prominence in the first half of this century, in the context of the discrepancies that emerged between linguists' statements about the regularities or rules of a language, and corresponding statements in traditional school grammars telling learners what is and is not correct in the language. Some statements in linguists' grammars appeared to be sanctioning some of the things which school grammars regarded as incorrect or improper, and some statements in school grammars in turn appeared to linguists as not reflecting actual, contemporary language use. Linguists accordingly characterised their grammars as descriptive statements of how things are, in contrast to school grammars which were prescriptive statements of how things ought to be.

In the context of language education, the term 'prescriptive' has two possible meanings. One is that language teaching tends to be tradition-bound or authority-dominated, and as a result tries to enforce certain rules of correctness which are outdated, ill-founded or blind to the natural process of language change. This was criticised, rightly, by linguists. But there is another, broader sense in which all language teaching is necessarily, legitimately, prescriptive. Learning a language is being able to use it in the way

---

This essay was first published in 1993. *Source*: Prabhu, N. S. (1993). Descriptive and prescriptive approaches to the norms of English in Singapore. In Anne Pakir (Ed.), *The English language in Singapore: Standards and norms* (pp. 1–5). Singapore: Singapore University Press.

those who know the language do, and the practice of language knowers (including language teachers) is therefore a prescription for learners on what they should and should not do. All pedagogy is in this sense prescriptive, and language pedagogy is perhaps additionally prescriptive in that right and wrong are a matter of language-knowers' practice, rather than of some independent criterion such as logic.

When we talk about norms of English in Singapore or India, where there are large local communities of English-users, "prescriptive" can once again have two different meanings. We can say that people in Singapore or India should be able to use English in the way people in Britain or the United States do, and therefore that the norms of English prevalent in those countries is the proper norm for these people. If we do, we will be regarding English-users in Singapore or India as essentially collections of English-learners, by making a kind of global generalisation of language or language pedagogy. We can, alternatively, regard users of English in Singapore or India as English-using communities (as distinct from collections of individuals), in the same way that the British or Americans constitute such communities. If we do, any enforcement of the norms of English prevalent in Britain or the United States on these communities in Singapore or India will be authoritarian, ill-founded and blind to the natural process of language variation, hence subject to the same kind of criticism that linguists directed against the prescriptivism of school grammars.

There are two concepts about the nature of language that are crucially relevant to this issue. First, language can be thought of as a kind of social or communal organism. Members of a speech community have a language system in their minds which they share with other members. The fact that the system is shared enables it to function as a language, and it also acts as a constraint on individual innovations or transgressions. At the same time, the fact that it is a system in each individual's mind enables it to vary, perhaps very slightly, between one individual and another, and each individual's role as a participant (or constituent, or "stakeholder") in the community gives the individual a right, as it were, to vary from or transgress the shared system, also perhaps very slightly. This makes the shared system largely stable but also open to change over time. It gives each individual both an obligation to conform to the shared system and a stakeholder's right to change it.

Secondly, speech communities can be said to have both centrifugal and centripetal linguistic tendencies. A speech community tends to consist of, or subdivide into, subcommunities expressing group/subgroup identities of various kinds (such as class, status, age or locality) and exhibiting a higher or lower degree of sharing (within and across subcommunities, respectively) of the language system. This tendency leads eventually to the formation of separate speech communities, with distinct shared systems, that is to say, to different "varieties" of a language, or to different languages. But there is also a centripetal tendency working in the opposite direction. Different social values (as distinct from group identities) tend to be attached to the shared (sub)systems of different (sub)communities, some of them being regarded as being more desirable (or of a higher social status) than others. The values themselves may be linguistically irrelevant (having to do, instead, with social, economic or political power, or education and scholarly status) but they do have a linguistic consequence, in that members of the less highly valued shared (sub)systems tend to move towards a sharing of the more highly valued ones, as an expression of their social aspirations. When, as a result, one shared (sub)system receives a higher value than all others in a spread of (sub)systems, that highly-valued (sub)system acts as a norm for all of them, indicating their choice or wish to move towards it and constituting a convergent force.

There is a spread of subsystems of English in Britain and there is also a norm, in the sense just indicated, operating across them. This is true of other places such as the United States as well. When we consider the use of English in Singapore or India, there is clearly a spread of subsystems (whether or not a spread of the same size in terms of population or variation) in these places too. The question of what the norm is or should be for them can be answered in one of two ways. One can say, on the one hand, that the English-using communities in Singapore or India (taking all their internal subsystems together) share a relatively lowly valued subsystem in the global spread of English, and that the norms for them should therefore be the more highly valued ones of Britain or the United States. One can, on the other hand, say that, just as the norm for Britain is the highest-valued subsystem in the spread of subsystems in Britain, and likewise for the United States, the norm for Singapore should be the highest-valued subsystem in the spread of subsystems obtaining in Singapore, and likewise for India.

A choice between these two answers is partly an empirical matter and partly an ideological one. Empirically, one needs to find out what subsystem of English actually constitutes the linguistic aspiration of English-users in Singapore. This is not adequately done through crude methods such as questionnaires or speakers' declarations. More careful and subtle means need to be found to see what subsystem they actually find themselves approximating to (unconsciously more than consciously) in the process of a rise in social status, what speakers they tend to imitate or emulate, what differential perceptions they have of speakers of the different subsystems around them, etc. This is a difficult, descriptive approach to the question of a norm.

Ideologically, there is an important difference between the two answers suggested above. We noted earlier that members of a speech community are not just conformers to the shared system of the community; they are stakeholders, too, in the shared system and have the right or power to change it (however little or infrequently they may use that right or power). This is also true of a spread of subsystems with one of them operating as the norm. Speakers of the different subsystems are not just conformers (or aspirants) to the norm; they are also stakeholders in what comes to be (or continues to be) regarded as the norm, and have the power to change it. Now, if the norm for Singapore is a subsystem in Singapore, speakers of different subsystems in Singapore will indeed have a stake in the choice of that norm, and the power to change it. If, instead, the norm for Singapore is the norm in Britain, it is difficult to see what stake or power any speaker of any Singapore subsystem will have in the matter. All speakers in Singapore will only be (more or less successful) conformers, with no participation in the choice or change of the norm. This would be a very prescriptive approach to the questions of a norm.

Let me, finally, comment on one point which often looms large in such discussions but which seems to me to be largely irrelevant. This has to do with the notion that English in Singapore is a "non-native" language (or variety), in the sense that it arose from an initial set of speakers who learnt it as a "second" language from the native speakers of Britain. It is true that when one is learning a language, one is attempting to develop an individual system which is a replication of the shared system being learnt. It is also true that second-language learners often end up with a system which falls short, in some respects, of the level of replication attained by first-language learners. Suppose, however, that a set of second-language learners, whose replication is less than full, begin to function as a community of speakers of that language. They now have a shared system which they operate as a community and pass on to their successor generations. Their shared system is different from that which they once attempted to replicate but in no linguistically viable sense a deficient or inferior shared system. It is different in exactly the way different shared (sub)systems in Britain are from one another, all functioning as social organisms. To think that its once having been an incomplete replication of some other shared system deprives it perpetually of the full status of a shared system, thus dependent forever on an external norm, is not very different from thinking that a country which was once ruled by a foreign nation remains perpetually less than a nation, less than fully entitled to self-government.

16

English Language as a University Discipline

I would like to explore in this paper the question of what the proper objective might be of a university discipline called English Language. The question I am asking is not "What constitutes the English Language?" much less "What constitutes knowing the English Language?"; nor am I asking why the English language should be taught or learnt. I am asking, rather, what fit there might be between the concept of a university discipline and a subject entitled English Language. What claims can such a subject make to the status of a university discipline?

At one level, this is a question which all university subjects need to ask of themselves, from time to time. A subject is taught much of the time as a body of knowledge, largely as a continuance of past practice. When reviews take place, they usually focus on making changes to the body of knowledge concerned, updating it by adding recent theories, findings or publications, or modernising it by omitting what has become less valid or less relevant as knowledge. These are ways of reconsidering the composition of a subject as a subject. There is a further need, it seems to me, to consider and periodically reconsider the nature of the subject in general as a discipline of the mind. The question then would be: How is the subject, whatever body of knowledge it consists of, envisaged to exercise the learner's mind into a state of intellectual fitness or maturity? The concept behind the term "discipline" is one of mind-training: some faculty of the mind is made stronger, sharper or

---

This paper was presented in 1993 at the Department of English Language and Literature, National University of Singapore.

more refined, more open to controlled application, more capable of gaining an understanding of the world (as distinct from merely engaging in the world's affairs), more sensitive and discriminate in its perceptions and reactions, etc. It is by conceptualising a given subject in these terms that we can define it as a university discipline and state its most general objectives. In the absence of such a conceptualisation (and recurrent reference to it), we would be missing out an important educational criterion in the determination of subject content, and any decisions about changes in the body of knowledge to be dealt with would be based on short-range or ad hoc considerations.

At a second level, the question I am asking has a special relevance and urgency for English language as a subject. Many subjects of study at the university, such as philosophy, mathematics, economics or English Literature, are essentially curricular formulations of specific traditions of such studies in the learned world, a way of fitting into the academic system an existing area of intellectual activity. There are, as a result, certain general objectives and parameters of study, certain expected modes of enquiry as well as necessary constraints, a certain notion of fundamental principles, desirable directions and possible achievements, available or discoverable in the traditions themselves, and usable in defining the subject as an academic discipline. This is not a matter of old as against relatively young subjects of study. Young subjects, such as Linguistics, Electronics, International Law or Artificial Intelligence, can all be seen to represent definable areas of enquiry, with emergent, if not established, principles, parameters and goals. English Language as a university subject is I think different in that it is something of a creation within the academic system, not an acceptance into the system of an ongoing or emergent area of study in the learned world—or at least it is more of the former than of the latter. A space has been created within the university system, with a label to it. The problem is not any dearth of academic content to fill the space with: descriptions of the structure of English, knowledge about the history of English or about the current forms, functions and variations of the language, studies of ideologies embedded in English (such as sexism or imperialism), theories about language acquisition or the human faculty for language, skills of using English appropriately for academic, social or professional purposes, upgradation of the level of accuracy in learners' use of English, and many other things besides, can all fill the available space, with arguable benefits. Indeed, it is the availability (and competing claims) of such widely varied content that points to the problem: it is difficult to see what can hold the different chunks of content together, other than the fact that they can all be linked, in different ways, to the label, English language. It is difficult, that is to say, to ensure any internal coherence to a subject of such composite content, in the absence of an overall concept of what the subject is about and what its central concerns are. To define such central concerns and goals, we need to conceptualise the subject as an academic discipline and identify the aspect of the learner's mind which it can best develop, deepen or strengthen.

One possible central concern for the subject is indicated by the label itself. The English language is a subject of instruction in schools widely in the world, just as mathematics, history etc. are. Mathematics, history etc. are also subjects of study at the university, and generally see themselves as vertical continuations of what is taught and learnt at school. It is also broadly true to say that the basic principles and goals of history as a school subject are the same as those of history as a university subject, ignoring levels of sophistication and depth. Can we not regard English language as a university subject, similarly, as a vertical continuation of the school subject? Whatever is the central concern of the school subject would then be the central concern of the university subject, at an appropriately higher level.

It will be generally agreed that the aim of teaching the English language at school is to enable learners to acquire the language, so as to be able to use it with linguistic accuracy and communicative facility. Learners are led from a state of not knowing the language (or of knowing it only to a limited extent) to a state of knowing it well enough for use in their academic study as well as more widely in society and at work in later life. The aim, that is to say, is to develop proficiency in the language for a variety of uses. The aim is also to ensure full proficiency in these terms by the end of the Secondary school, but one can argue that the process is not really complete by that stage and that there is something left to do at the university. If we take this view, the aim of English language as a university subject is to fill the gaps left in learners' proficiency or to fine-tune or polish up the proficiency acquired at school, in order to complete a job left incomplete in earlier education.

This is no doubt a worthwhile thing to do and, depending on the needs of the situation, can be an urgent or high-priority matter as well. Universities in many parts of the world do in fact recognise a need for such work and have special provision for it in the form of remedial courses, English Language Centres, Proficiency Units, etc. However, the fact that provision for such work tends to be made in some special form—with Centres, Units, etc. offering extra courses to specifically identified students, rather than as a Department offering a regular subject of study—indicates an underlying distinction between instructional provision of that kind and a university discipline. Broadly, the distinction is between repairing, upgrading or face-lifting, on the one hand, and preparing, constructing or developing, on the other. The former is a finishing stage, the latter a building stage. In more substantive terms, although the acquisition of language proficiency is a matter of the mind, it is different in nature from the kinds of mind-training that are indicated by the concept of a university discipline. English language as a university discipline, that is to say, is not a matter of topping up on the teaching of English done at school.

To say this is not to make an evaluative statement about the teaching of English, either at school or at university. Teaching the English language is a very worthwhile educational activity and, in today's world, a matter of meeting one of the fundamental needs of learners at any level. Nor is it a matter of much significance whether an arrangement for teaching the language is called a Department,

Centre, Unit or something else. There is no reason why a University Department should not engage itself in teaching English, German, or any other language. The question I am exploring has to do with a particular concept of what constitutes a university discipline, not with educational respectability, institutional status or hierarchical labels. I am suggesting merely that, given the concept of a discipline I outlined above, topping up on language proficiency does not quite count as a discipline—or, to put it differently, there is a difference in kind between language proficiency seen as a mental ability and the mental abilities relevant to the notion of a discipline.

A common response to the perception I have just stated is to use the subject of English language to provide learners with knowledge about the English language, as distinct from proficiency in it. Knowledge about the internal structure of English (its phonetic, phonological, syntactic, semantic and textual descriptions) as well as knowledge about the varied forms, functions, modes of use, modes of change and social perceptions of the language easily make up a sizeable body of knowledge, comparable to the knowledge content of other university subjects such as economics, psychology or physics. The English language thus becomes a phenomenon to analyse, an object of enquiry, just as other aspects of the world or of human activity are the objects of enquiry in other university subjects. Further, the process of dealing with such a phenomenon—perceiving the nature of the object, understanding and operating the modes of enquiry involved, evaluating the resulting knowledge, attempting to construct such knowledge, resolving conceptual or empirical conflicts, etc.—can be said to constitute a form of intellectual training, or "disciplining", in the same way as in other, knowledge-based subjects. A study of the structure of the English language has a considerable tradition in the learned world, and there is also a tradition of regarding a study of the structure of classical languages—the grammar of Latin or Sanskrit—as a valuable form of mind-training. Analysis and description of the English language may thus appear to be the proper content of a university subject called English language, and it is not surprising that they do in fact fill a large part of the curriculum of such a subject in many universities.

It is, however, not clear if there is an integral link between the title of the subject—English language—and a curriculum of linguistic descriptions and analyses of the language. Analyses and descriptions of different languages, including English, are the recognised domain of a differently titled subject, namely, linguistics; and the body of knowledge about the internal structure or external functions of English, which we referred to above, is in fact the product of pursuits in linguistics. Linguistics is no doubt, concerned not just with the English language but with many other (in principle, all) languages, and English language as a subject can perhaps claim to be different in that it is concerned with only one language—a language, moreover, which is arguably the most widely analysed and described, and therefore pre-eminent in language studies. However, to distinguish in this way between English language and linguistics is in effect to regard English language as a variant of linguistics—or a part, albeit a large part, of it. Either the two are essentially the same, but in a part–whole relationship, or else one is basically derivative of the other, employing a large part of its product. There can, of course, be no serious objection to the use of varied labels to refer to the same subject area—such objections would merely make the matter a quarrel about labels—but it is at least important to recognise that there is in fact only a variation in names—that the differently-titled subjects actually represent the same discipline, and that English language as a subject is in substance that part of linguistics which is concerned with English.

There is, however, more at stake than nomenclature. Linguistics perceives the study of different languages as being contributory to, and supported by, the aim of understanding a more general and abstract object, namely, human language, conceived of as a psychological and/or social entity. There is an important sense in which the analysis and description of any particular language, such as English, derives its relevance and value in relation to the more general pursuit and in necessary interaction with the analyses and descriptions of other languages. There is thus a conceptual integrity between the analyses of particular languages and the aim of understanding human language as a general entity; the description of a particular language can only be ad hoc if it is not constrained by a general theory about language as such, and mutually reinforced with descriptions of other languages. Consequently, the knowledge-claim that one can make from a description of just one language is severely limited. In this sense, English language as a subject, seen as a description of only English, is not just a partial coverage of linguistics but an impoverished version of it as well. A description of English, without reference to a general theory of language, is only a body of facts, which can be seen and stated in any of a number of ways, with no higher-level criteria for preferring one form of statement over another, or for questioning any given statement. The point I am making here is not that English language as a subject cannot select as its content a description of English which can be justified with reference to a general theory of language; it certainly can, and most often claims to. The point is rather that the modes of justification involved will not themselves be available as part of the content. The content of linguistics as a subject includes not just descriptions of different languages but processes of evaluating and validating those descriptions, and it is the latter that gives the subject its claim to being a discipline. The content of English language as a subject will, if we take the view being considered here, consist of a given description of English to be treated as a "received" body of knowledge, open at best to relatively minor questioning and consequently limited in its intellectual demands and its claim to being a discipline.

I have so far discussed two possible views of what English language as a subject might be centrally concerned with—the view that it should aim to top up on learners' English language proficiency and the view that it should provide learners with a description of the English language. A third possible view is that it should be concerned with leading learners towards the uses of English that will be demanded of them after their university education—or perhaps in ongoing or further university education, beyond the narrow, confines of the subject itself. There are particular, institutionally marked modes of English use, constituting specific forms of discourse prevalent in different professions or areas of work, as well as in different university disciplines or areas of research. These are the modes of discourse which university students need to be able to engage in effectively, either for success in university education itself or for success in any of the literate, "learned" professions thereafter. Students, that is to say, need to have a mastery of both academic discourse and professional discourse in English and of different variations of each, to the extent possible, in order to function successfully in the academic or the professional world; and English language as a subject can, from this point of view, best aim to provide them with such mastery. University education is thus perceived as a servicing of learners' later lives and English Language as a subject is perceived as a linguistic servicing both of learners' later lives and of their immediate lives as learners. The servicing consists of enabling learners to perform the relevant forms of discourse, as an essential dimension of success in playing the roles they have to or wish to. Indeed, it can be regarded as a kind of linguistic empowering in anticipation of demand, a way of underwriting success in advance in the activities to be undertaken.

The view of education as a preparation for life seems unexceptionable and curricular orientation to the specific demands expected in later life can be seen as making education so much more purposeful and useful. There is however, another side to curricular orientation to specific needs: it causes a certain narrowness of scope to education and leads towards a focus on performance, at the expense of a general underlying competence. The selection of each specific need for attention entails the non-selection of other specific needs, and the more specific the need-identification is, the larger the proportion of such omissions. The broad division between academic discourse and professional discourse soon turns out to be inadequate when one pursues the goal of specific orientation. There are many forms of academic discourse and many more forms of professional discourse, and each of them can be further subdivided into many at the next degree of specificity. One is forced at some point to stop the pursuit of specificity and look for an underlying generality to different forms of discourse, an underlying discourse ability which can support a variety of discourse forms. There is thus a tension between preparation for specific forms of discourse and the development of an underlying discourse ability, and it is difficult to see what criterion, other than expediency, can determine the balance between the two. Further, preparation for any specific kind of discourse involves a focus on the particular form of that discourse, the more specific the discourse category is, the greater the attention to distinctive features of its form, leading at some point to a large degree of attention to matters of conventional format. In this sense, training in specific forms of discourse is training in the performance of conventional forms and formats of discourse—not a matter of mind-training in any significant sense.

It is also legitimate to ask to what extent the university can be thought of as a place of apprenticeship to the various professions and whether it is in fact the best place to provide such apprenticeship if that is thought to be desirable. If a specific form of discourse is institutional in nature (developed, practised and controlled in its context collectively by the people participating in the profession), does it not follow that the performance of the discourse form concerned is contingent to practising the profession itself and that, for that reason, it is best learnt contingently to learning to participate in the profession? In other words, might it not be that apprenticeship in a profession, including the linguistic apprenticeship of learning to perform the relevant discourse, is best provided by the profession itself? Might it, in fact, be creating a needless difficulty to isolate the linguistic apprenticeship and try to provide it in advance and away from its context? There is also a further point to make: the perception that discourse forms are collectively controlled by participants in particular professions does not imply that individual members of a profession merely comply; they are also part controllers, regulators and agents of change in the discourse forms concerned and their exercise of this regulatory function is a matter of negotiation between the institutional pressures on conformity and their own underlying discourse competence, professional confidence and intellectual strength. It should be the role of a university discipline to develop such an underlying competence, confidence and strength, so that learners can, when they go on to participate in the professions, have greater negotiating power in regulating conventional discourse and be able to act as agents of change instead of having to comply wholly or helplessly. To use the university to provide advance training in the conventional discourse of the professions is therefore not only to provide such training out of context and therefore at greater cost in effort; it is, at the same time, to sacrifice an opportunity to give learners the necessary strength to resist the pressures of conventional discourse and to negotiate the level of their conformity to it.

A fourth possible view of what the subject of English language should be about is that it should be a preparation of specialists for those areas of work where a specially high command of English and/or a special knowledge about English are necessary or desirable. Such areas of work would include the teaching of English or activities which support teaching in the form of teacher-training, textbook writing or syllabus construction, research of various kinds on English, journalism and other mass media, advertising and other promotional work where the appeal may be partly in the way the language is used, and more generally those contexts in which the level of language use is important for success. The perception here is that the role of the subject is to lay the foundation for the practice of certain specific professions, in the way that university programmes in law, engineering, accountancy or medicine do.

I do not wish to deny that certain types of work may make much higher demands on the quality of English use than others, or on an analytic knowledge about English. It seems to me, nevertheless, that linguistic ability is too general and pervasive in nature to be attributed exclusively to particular professions. Professions such as law and engineering have an exclusiveness about them: there are specific bodies of knowledge and skill which act as defining features of those professions, in a way that enables one to say: "All and only lawyers (or all and only engineers, etc.) possess knowledge and skill of this kind". This makes it possible to construct a curriculum of such well-defined knowledge and skill. When we consider the English language, the only profession of which one might be able to make such a statement is the teaching of English, and even that is likely to hold true only of a descriptive knowledge about the English language—grammar, pronunciation, etc. The quality of English use represents a much more general ability, whose importance is not confined to one or a small set of professions. It can be a significant dimension of many or most English-using professions, which indeed is the rationale for seeking to develop a proficiency in the language either at school or at university. It seems to me an act of needless narrowing and exclusion to see the subject of English language as serving a select set of professions.

I have considered four possible perceptions of the rationale of English language as a university subject, and found each of them to be less than satisfying. This is not to say that these different perceptions do not have any educational value. There is a certain promise and plausibility to each of them, and it would clearly be dismissive to rule them out of any conceptualisation of the subject. It is, however, necessary to seek a conceptualisation which is larger in scope than these perceptions and in some way more satisfying. The alternative to doing so would be to pursue disparate objectives at the same time, by putting together a curriculum which is a mix of different things with different kinds of perceived value. There would then be no internal coherence to the curriculum, no conceptual wholeness to it. A pursuit of disparate objectives, with a resultant mix in the curriculum, can in fact be seen often in the English language programmes taught at university; and it is perhaps an inevitable feature, more or less marked, of all curriculum construction, in all subjects. Nevertheless, it is I think important to seek at least a common thread that can hold the different curricular components together and provide a measure of unity to the subject.

I wish to suggest that there is an aspect of language ability which is outside the normal concept of proficiency. Proficiency consists of an ability to *conform* to the norms of language use in society, in terms such as grammatical accuracy, functional appropriacy and discourse forms. What I have in mind is an ability to *negotiate* norms—to decide, from a position of some strength, on the extent to which one wishes to conform to prevalent norms, to harness the resources of language to implementing those decisions with success, and generally to play a part in the emergence or ongoing change of norms, thus influencing what society perceives as norms. Let me call this ability linguistic *confidence*, as distinct from linguistic *competence*. There are of course other forms of confidence which reflect themselves in the language use of individuals in various ways, such as social or intellectual or class confidence in some form, often in disharmony with linguistic competence. What I am referring to as linguistic confidence is distinct from them in that it is firmly based on linguistic competence but goes clearly beyond it.

Linguistic confidence arises, I think, from at least three sources. First, there is a dimension of language use which consists of matching word to thought with a degree of precision higher than is normal in common discourse—a kind of "precision casting" of meaning into the forms of language which distinguishes itself from the "rough casting" that passes muster much of the time. Such precision is not just a matter of greater deliberation or facility in the choice of language forms. It involves a high level of sensitivity to the semantic potential (generally a complex or cluster of possible meanings or suggestions) carried by language forms, on the one hand, and a high level of clarity or conceptual sharpness to the meaning one wishes to express, on the other. Further, the interplay of these two factors is mutually supportive: an awareness of the semantic potential of language forms prompts questions about the precise nature of the meaning one wishes to convey, thus causing a "sharper resolution" of that meaning or perhaps showing it to be quite different from what it appeared to be (hence the notion of using language to explore one's meaning, which is basic to theories of "process writing"); it indicates the aim of mind-training of a certain kind, which is in harmony with the concept of a "discipline".

The two aims may look somewhat idealistic or unrealistic, but it must be remembered that they are being envisaged as *aims*—goals to strive towards, a direction for educational effort and a way of perceiving the value of whatever measure of success is achievable or actually achieved.

The adoption of these aims for English language as a subject does not necessarily call for any major changes in current curricula content: higher-order reading and writing activity, knowledge about the structure and use of English, relationships between discourse and knowledge as well as between discourse and ideology will all be still relevant as content, but there will now be an overall objective which goes beyond each of them and gives a common direction to all of them. There will also be a general criterion by which the different components of the total curriculum can be assessed, renewed or reoriented. The teaching of the different components can, as a result, be perceived and carried out as a shared educational endeavour to achieve a common educational goal.

***GD:** In this article, you have argued that English when taught at the University level should focus on the development of linguistic confidence and focus on empowerment and 'mind-training'.*

NSP: I wasn't very pleased with my argument. I started to define the concept of an acknowledged authority/exemplar/adjudicator on the language but ended up with that of a 'process' writer, that is, one who not only uses the language to articulate thought but uses that process to generate further thought.

17

Communicative Language Teaching: Three Perceptions

The term "communicative language teaching" has come to mean different things to different people, thus making it difficult to identify any single, consistent line of thought or to subject it to a productive professional discussion. It is therefore useful to try to unscramble the bundle of notions involved by isolating particular concepts and arguments. There are at least three distinct arguments involved.

Teaching Language for Communication

It is thought that, when a language is taught as a series of linguistic (structural, lexical) items, each item appears to have been learnt at the time it is taught, but there is not enough cumulative knowledge resulting from the teaching over a stretch of time. Although different parts of the structure of the language have been taught at different times, learners are unable to summon up their knowledge of those different parts at will, in response to the demands of real-life communication. They tend to deliberate too long, recall with overt effort the relevant item of language, string sentences together laboriously or be tongue-tied as a result of frustration. There is, that is to say, not enough spontaneity or automaticity in their language use for successful, natural, communication.

This essay was first published in 1994. *Source*: Prabhu, N. S. (1994). Communicative language teaching: Three perceptions. *Language and Communication Review*, 1, 39–42.

One way of interpreting this phenomenon is to say that the learners possess a good deal of "declarative" knowledge of the language but not enough "procedural" knowledge of it. The knowledge they possess, that is so to say, is not sufficiently amenable to ready, automatic access and use. An older perception is that the language they have learnt has not been sufficiently established as "habit". Although particular parts of the language may well have been practised thoroughly at the time they were taught, thus being established as specific "habits", the sum of those parts is still unable to operate as a general, integrated habit, in the way natural communication demands.

Given that this is the interpretation of pedagogic failure, it is logical to ask what kind of teaching can help to proceduralise learners' declarative knowledge—or promote the general integration and use of the different parts of the language as a habit. A plausible answer is that the usual teaching of a series of items should be followed by a second, equally important phase, namely, pedagogic activity in which learners are called on to activate and employ a variety of those items for the purpose of communication—in exchanging meanings, messages, opinions, wishes, etc. Regular engagement in such activity in the classroom is likely to lead to an increasing automaticity or spontaneity in learners' use of the items of language they have learnt, thus making their language use natural and successful as communication. Such two-phase teaching can be called communicative language teaching in that the separate items of language taught in the first phase are for use in the communicative activities to follow in the second phase, and the teaching operation as a whole is for learners' success in real-life communication in later life. This therefore constitutes one consistent argument about communicative language teaching.

Teaching Language as Communication

A quite different argument starts from the premise that there is a lot more to knowing a language than a mastery of the structure and lexis, and that teaching based on structure and lexis will leave learners ignorant or unskilled in another, major aspect of language use, namely, social appropriacy. Forms of a language have not only an aspect of structural and lexical correctness and of meaning derivable from those sources, but, equally, an aspect of social appropriacy and a different kind of meaning arising from it. The imperative structure, for instance has the grammatical meaning of "command, order, request" etc., all requiring something to be done. But the imperative form "Have another cup of tea" does not state a requirement, but rather makes an offer; "Have a rest" makes a suggestion; "Have a good weekend" expresses a wish; "Have a heart" makes a plea; and "Have it your own way" signals a sense of resignation. In fact, when an actual command, order or request is being made, social appropriacy calls for an avoidance of the imperative form: one does not say "Have this done by tomorrow" but rather "Could you have this done by tomorrow?", "I wonder if you can have this done by tomorrow", "It would be good if you could have this done by tomorrow", etc.—all non-imperative forms. Similarly, the active and passive constructions are equivalent in their grammatical meaning, with only an option of omitting information about the agent in the passive. But they have quite different social meanings in the context of conveying requests to one's superiors and subordinates: one has to say "I request you to do this" to a superior, not "You are requested to do this"! In the creation of discourse, the statements "It is true that the book truly offers valuable information" and "The book truly offers valuable information" are equivalent in grammatical meaning, but they are very different in what may be called rhetorical meaning: the first statement signals that the speaker/writer is only making a concession and will go on to say adverse things about the book; the second statement constitutes an assertion, to be followed by supporting details about the book's value.

If social appropriacy is different from grammatical correctness (and is not derivable from it) and if it is important for learners' success in communication, it is reasonable to think that teaching based on structure and lexis is seriously deficient in meeting learners' communicative needs. Almost thirty years ago, Leonard Newmark produced the imaginary example of a person with a perfect mastery of structure and lexis asking for a match to light his cigarette with "Do you have fire?", "Are you a match's owner?", etc. instead of the socially appropriate "Do you have a light?".

To the extent one is persuaded by this argument, one wishes to see how teaching can be directed to the promotion of social appropriacy in learners' language use. This calls for an identification and categorisation of different kinds of social and rhetorical acts, and a matching of those acts with the forms of language appropriate to them. The social and rhetorical acts are commonly referred to as "functions". Thus, making requests, making offers, expressing a wish, stating a plea, and signalling one's resignation are all different functions, as are conveying requests to superiors as distinct from conveying them to subordinates, and signalling a concession in discourse, as distinct from signalling an assertion. Communicative language teaching then consists of providing learners with classroom practice in using appropriate forms of language to perform the different functions one has identified and included in the teaching syllabus. This line of argument therefore leads to the use of a functional syllabus in language teaching.

Teaching Language through Communication

A third argument begins where the first did, but takes a different direction from it. The problem perceived is, as in the first argument, that learners who are taught a series of structural and lexical items are, at the end, unable to employ the sum of those items at will, automatically or spontaneously in response to the demands of real-life communication. The diagnosis of the problem, however, is not that such item-based teaching is insufficient and in need of supplementation, but that it is fundamentally misguided and in need of replacement. Item-based teaching, it is thought, leads primarily to a form of knowledge that is "explicit" (consciously learnt, stored and recalled), whereas the form of knowledge needed for spontaneous, natural use in communication is "implicit" (subconsciously acquired and automatically activated when needed). Examples of implicit knowledge are readily available in children's developing knowledge of their mother-tongue; and examples of automatic activation can be seen not only in children's use of the mother-tongue they are acquiring but in all adults' normal/natural use of a language (whether it is the mother-tongue or not), since natural use of a language is a phenomenon in which the user's conscious attention is on the meaning, message or content being dealt with while some subconscious part of the mind ensures that the words and sentences are available as needed and are grammatically correct. The knowledge resulting from item-based teaching is different in kind, it is argued, from that developed by children in learning their mother-tongue (or, indeed, by adults learning a language naturally by having to cope in it without being specifically taught), and it is this difference that causes the problem of non-automaticity. It is also argued that normal/natural development of the knowledge of a language is holistic—that is to say, in the form of a whole system of rules, principles and constraints, which undergoes change, revision or elaboration always as a system, not in isolated parts one at a time. If this is so, teaching the structure of a language one part at a time (which is the essence of item-based teaching) goes counter to the natural process of language acquisition and can be a hindrance to it.

Further, the parts that are taught in this way (the items of a structural syllabus) are units which are identified by grammarians in their attempt to describe the language. They may not, in fact, correspond at all to the units of the (as yet unknown) representation of the structure of the language in the minds of normal learners or users of the language. There is, that is to say, no basis for claiming any psychological reality to the units of a structural syllabus.

It is easy to see that this perception of the nature of language acquisition, and of the disadvantages of item-based instruction, points to a form of teaching which is not based on structural and lexical items, nor on functional items (since that is unrelated to the perception), but instead on creating classroom conditions which are as close as possible to natural, untutored language acquisition and maximally conducive to the holistic development of implicit knowledge. A central feature of such classroom conditions is opportunity, encouragement and support for learners to cope in the language being learnt—to make sense of what is heard or read, to construct meaning by making inferences, thinking things out and testing things out through trial-and-error, and to put things across by employing and stretching the linguistic resources available. Such pedagogic activity is necessarily meaning-focused, in contrast to item-based activity which is either structure- (or lexis-) based or function-based and, in both cases, focused on the forms of language more than on meaning or meaning-making. It is hypothesised that while learners are preoccupied with making sense of the forms of language encountered or with giving verbal expression to the meanings made, the linguistic structure of those forms of language is subconsciously perceived, abstracted and internalised as implicit knowledge. This form of teaching can justifiably be called communicative because the exchange of meanings—receiving, re-shaping and transmitting meanings of different kinds—is central to the process of communication, and the condition of a conscious occupation with meaning simultaneously with a subconscious occupation with the forms and rules of the structure of the language is, as we have noted, a central characteristic of normal, real-life communication in a language.

These, then, are three different lines of thought leading to three kinds of teaching, all of them labelled *communicative language teaching* by the supporters of those lines of thought. It will be noticed that not only are the lines of thought distinctly different from one another, and the forms of teaching they lead to also quite different, but the term "communication" itself is used in quite different senses. In teaching language FOR communication, "communication" implies an automaticity to the use of known language forms, or a proceduralisation of existing declarative knowledge; in teaching language AS communication, "communication" is seen as the achievement of social or rhetorical appropriacy to the forms of language used; and in teaching language THROUGH communication, "communication" constitutes a meaning-focused condition of retrieving, constructing and articulating information content.

18

The Mathetic Function of English as a World Language

If one asks why the English language is an important subject of study in Asia today, the answer is likely to be partly in terms of our colonial history, but more importantly in terms of the current and future role of English as a world language. If one then asks what constitutes the role of English as a world language, the answer is likely to refer to international trade and travel, political and economic relations, the flow of technology from more industrialised to less industrialised countries, and the prospect of economic development in the latter. The answer may also, of course, refer to the use of English within particular countries—resulting from the colonial past—as a common or link language, though even this can be said to be largely centred in areas of activity related to economic development. English is, in general, viewed as a vital channel of technical and commercial information, an instrument of economic modernisation (perhaps even of economic survival), of the Third World.

I do not wish to deny that English has this important role in the present-day world, but would like to argue that the language has a more basic role which tends to get obscured by immediate and obvious concerns. What I have in mind is not the use of English for literary creation or artistic expression in the Third World, which is what often receives attention when one moves away from the

---

This essay was first published in 1994. *Source*: Prabhu, N. S. (1994). Mathetic function of English as a world language. *Journal of English and Foreign Languages,* 13 and 14, 53–66.

more utilitarian uses. Creative use is no doubt a significant aspect of the role of English in certain Third World countries, but I take it to be essentially a manifestation of that role, rather than a motive force behind it. What I wish to explore here is the cognitive aspect of language use, rather than the artistic one.

In a discussion of language acquisition by a child, Halliday makes "a fundamental distinction between language as doing and language as learning—the pragmatic and the mathetic function" (Halliday, 1975, p. 3). The pragmatic function is "language as action" while the mathetic function is "language as reflection" (and there is, says Halliday, a third, subsidiary function as well, which is "language as creation, or meaning in the imaginative mode"[p. 87]).

The pragmatic function in language acquisition seems to me to be well-recognised and often exclusively focused on. It is based on the transparent fact that (to quote Halliday again) "the child learns to talk in order to get what he wants, which means getting other people...to give it to him or do it for him". The mathetic function, which receives much less attention, is based on the less transparent fact that "the child learns to talk...to express ideas—ideas about things and their relations" (pp. 106–7). Language in its mathetic function is "the use of the symbolic system not as a means of acting on reality but as a means of learning about reality" (p. 106). It is "language enabling the child to learn about his social and material environment, serving him in the construction of reality—[it] evolves in the context of his thinking about the universe, [as distinct from] the context of his exploiting it" (p. 75). Elsewhere, Halliday observes that "every human language is a potential for meaning in these two ways: it is a resource for doing with; and it is a resource for thinking with" (Halliday, 1985, p. 7).

Halliday, of course, makes this distinction between pragmatic and mathetic (and, as a third term, aesthetic) functions in the context of first language acquisition, and he in fact treats these generalised functions as a transitional phase in the child's development from "proto-language" to adult language. The pragmatic and mathetic functions, that is to say, are seen by Halliday as the child's generalisation of areas of language use, before those functions get codified, in much more abstract and complex forms, as aspects of language structure. I think, however, that the distinction is of great value in discussing areas of language use generally—not only of the first language but of a second language and, in particular, of English as a world language. The prevalent view of the role of English in the Third World tends to focus primarily on the pragmatic function and secondarily on the aesthetic function, thus overlooking the mathetic function. We are very aware of the use of English across the world for information transfer and for what may be called transactional communication; we are much less aware of the role English plays in the sharing and furthering of a certain "construction of reality"—a certain "way of thinking about the universe" (to use Halliday's words).

Unlike the pragmatic function which involves meeting one's material needs, the mathetic function involves meeting a basic need of the mind—the need to make sense of the world one lives in, to develop a conceptual model of causes and consequences, to construct a world-view in which one can locate oneself, or at least to be able to believe that one has done so. It involves the satisfaction of what one commentator on science has called "the rage to know" (Judson, 1985, p. 66) or an intellectual strategy for coping with the unknown, even if this means operating with some form of delusion of knowledge. Some views of the world are clearly more satisfying than others—or more powerful, in that they are able to satisfy a large number of minds, and to replace less satisfying views. Despite the many divisions of mankind into races, continents, nations and cultures, ideas of power tend to reach out to large numbers of minds though the extent and pace of their spread can be hampered or enhanced by other forms of power. Further, ideas of power are not static entities, but change, expand or exhaust themselves in time, as a result of the differential responses they evoke in different minds. They may change gradually over time or violently at certain points of time, setting up what Kuhn (1962) has called new "paradigms" of knowledge, which change not only the content of knowledge but the concept of what constitutes knowledge. The concept of what constitutes knowledge has, as we know, taken different forms in the past—from powerful and widely influential myths and epics, to the great religions and mystic visions, to abstract philosophical and mathematical constructs. Although such concepts originated in particular cultures (and particular minds), their power over other minds enabled them to spread across cultural, geographical and ethnic boundaries, influencing people's views of the universe and providing more satisfying ways of construing reality. It would of course be simplistic to deny that the power of ideas had to contend with more material forms of power, but it seems to me important to recognise that ideas do have power and that power often underlies material power.

To move back from these epistemological matters to more linguistic ones, I think we can distinguish between two kinds of function for a common language which spreads across linguistic groups. A common language may serve a purely or largely pragmatic function meeting the needs of transactional communication, whether in trade or tourism or administration or the transfer of technology. Alternatively, a common language may function as a language of learning, enabling different linguistic groups to share and participate in the same knowledge-paradigm. The notion of a "bazaar language" clearly illustrates the first function, while the role of Latin in medieval Europe illustrates the second. I am not suggesting that a given common language is necessarily confined to one of these two functions; I am only suggesting that the functions themselves are different. More importantly, I am suggesting that English as a world language is not just a transactional medium across large parts of the world but, more significantly the medium of a knowledge-paradigm which has spread across the present-day world. Behind the technology and industrialisation of the West are powerful concepts of the material world providing their knowledge-base. What Newton, Darwin and Einstein developed are views of the universe which have had the power to influence minds in all parts of the world. Nor are such ideas of power confined to the field of science. The concepts of democracy and a democratic organisation of society, the rights of the individual, the possibility of progress and the common good, the value of rational enquiry as well as of criticism, doubt and skepticism are all among the powerful ideas which have, through the English language, exercised a worldwide influence on people's modes of thought. It is this knowledge-paradigm that constitutes much of the academic content of formal education, especially of higher education, in different parts of the world, and it is within this paradigm that the learned professions seek to advance their understanding in different fields. The actual language of formal instruction or professional discussion may not always be English, but it is English which provides the most direct access to relevant sources of knowledge, which makes it a disadvantage in the pursuit of knowledge not to know the language.

We therefore, need to look on the English language not just as a legacy of our colonial past, nor just as a national need for economic survival in the present-day world, but as the medium of a knowledge-paradigm which has reached out to all of us. It is the language in which a powerful construction of reality became available to minds across many boundaries, and was able to influence their perceptions of man and the material world. More significantly, it is the language which offers the possibility of worldwide participation in a shared knowledge-paradigm a language through which a widening circle of thinking minds across the world can function as an intellectual community, sharing, sharpening or changing particular concepts, and together moving the knowledge-paradigm forward. Other languages have played a similar role in the past—among them Latin, Arabic and Pali, each carrying the knowledge-paradigm of its day to sizeable parts of the world and thus bringing into being a learned community which functioned across linguistic and political boundaries. What we have today is not only a different knowledge-paradigm and a different language to carry it; we also have a far wider spread of both the language and the knowledge-paradigm, making it possible to think of a learned community which functions as a world community, employing a world language. It is truly a phenomenon to celebrate: an unprecedented prospect of worldwide intellectual participation and parity.

This is not, however, how the benefits of the spread of English are usually seen. The benefits that get highlighted are those of technology and economic development—the products of the knowledge-paradigm rather than its processes. The current knowledge-paradigm can be said to be different from those of the past in that, to quote Judson again, "the rage to know has been matched by the rage to make" (p. 74). It defines knowledge as that which is empirically knowable; what is not so knowable does not count as knowledge (Goulet, 1981). Knowing a phenomenon is being able to predict, manipulate and exploit it to make it serve our purpose. While this may have shut out other possible forms and concepts of knowledge, it has been able to produce a vastly powerful body of empirical knowledge and a body of technology based directly on it. Indeed it can be said that the power of this knowledge-paradigm derives to a large extent from the technological translatability of the knowledge it generates. However, if the Third World saw in the English language only (or primarily) an opportunity to make use of modern technology, it would be claiming a share of the produce of the knowledge-paradigm, but denying itself a share in the knowledge-generating processes. While the flow of technology from the West can increase the gross national product of the Third World countries and perhaps reduce economic disparities between different parts of the world, it is, at the same time, likely to leave the world divided between, knowledge-generators and knowledge-receivers, the future course of the knowledge-paradigm being shaped in one part of the world while the other part continues to depend on the products arising from that process. A concentration on reducing technological and economic disparity can thus result in a perpetuation of intellectual non-parity.

What I have said about the desirability of Third World participation in the processes of knowledge-development does not imply any assumption that the current knowledge-paradigm is the best, in some absolute sense, or even that it is permanent or long-lasting. What it implies is that it is the paradigm of our time and has deeply influenced not only our lifestyles but our perceptions of ourselves and of the world. We exist within it, simply by living at this time in history. It is a part of our response to "the rage to know"—a part of our mental make-up. The question then is: are we content to let ourselves be influenced by the knowledge-paradigm or do we wish to play a part in its generative processes? We need English in a mathetic function so that it can enable us to play a more equal or integral part in the future development of the knowledge paradigm or the eventual emergence of a new paradigm. Even a radically different future paradigm will have arisen as a response to an exhaustion or atrophy of the current paradigm, and worldwide participation in the current paradigm will also be worldwide participation in that change.

An argument on these lines, which regards English as the medium of a knowledge-paradigm originating in the West, might suggest the possibility of another part of the world returning to an earlier knowledge-paradigm of its own, carried by a more "native" language. I think, however, that this would be a negative approach to take. It would be an attempt to move back in time, instead of moving ahead with it. To the extent the current knowledge-paradigm is already a part of our mental make-up, it would also be an act of rejecting a part of ourselves, instead of building on what we are at this time. More regrettably, I think, it would be a turning away from the prospect we now have of a worldwide knowledge-paradigm, open to participation through a widely spread world language and, given such participation, more and more a possession of intellectuals across the world, rather than of those in one part of it. We should, I think, be looking beyond the notion of native and alien knowledge-paradigms, rather than helping to perpetuate that notion.

Let me now turn to an implication of the view I have outlined to the teaching of English in the Third World. About a hundred years ago, there was a major reorientation of foreign language pedagogy, known as the Reform Movement and led by linguists in Europe such as Vietor, Jespersen and Sweet. It rejected the then prevalent Grammar-Translation Method of language teaching and advocated a Phonetic Method, which gave primacy to spoken language instead of written language. It was an emphatic assertion by linguists that language was speech, and that to give primacy to the written form of a language over its spoken form was to treat that language as a 'dead' language. The Reform Movement was a very influential one, leading among other things to the setting up of the International Phonetic Association (Howatt, 1984, pp. 169–89) and resulting in due course in the emergence of the Oral Method on one side of the Atlantic and the Audio-lingual Method on the other. It started the tradition which has since established a firm precedence to oral skills over written skills in language pedagogy across the world. In more recent years—the Communicative language teaching movement, which challenged the Audio-lingual Method, has nevertheless preserved the assumption that oral skills are primary, and has in fact reinforced that assumption by highlighting interactional activity for transactional purposes. Written language, that is to say, has had a secondary place in language teaching theory for a century now, partly because of the attention given to speech in linguistic analysis and partly because of an increasing emphasis on pragmatic objectives in language instruction. Languages should be taught, it is argued, in order to enable learners to talk to people so as to get what they want or to transact the work they have to in employment.

If, however we want to teach English such that it can serve a mathetic function, in the sense I have suggested, there is reason to give written English a much higher priority than it receives at present. An obvious reason is that written language enables minds to reach out to other minds across distance and time, in a way that spoken language does not. Publications, as we know, play a central role in the operation of a knowledge-paradigm, making it possible for workers in a given field of knowledge to function as a professional community. The more widespread the knowledge-paradigm is, with members of the community being more widely separated, the more crucial the role of written language becomes.

A second reason for the importance of written language has to do with the process of articulating knowledge, as distinct from transmitting it. Unlike informational and transactional content, which is relatively easily coded in language, conceptual content, such as a theoretical argument, demands a high degree of deliberation and precision in its articulation as well as its interpretation. Such deliberation and precision in formulation are characteristic strengths of language in the written mode, rather than in the spoken mode. In general, the spoken mode of language is well-suited to the pragmatic function, as "a resource for doing with", in Halliday's words, while the written mode is well-suited to the mathetic function, as "a resource for thinking with". Indeed, there is a sense in which the process of writing is in fact a process of thinking, with effort at verbal precision helping to sharpen mental perception. This is the essential insight behind what is called the "process" approach to the teaching of writing, which makes assertions such as that writing is a process of discovering meaning (Murray, 1983). It is also, I think, the reason for treating writing as an independent discipline in higher education, quite outside the field of second/foreign language instruction. Teaching people to write, in the sense of enabling them to articulate conceptual content, is an important way of training them to participate in a knowledge-paradigm.

A third argument for giving written English a high priority in teaching is that there appears to be an organic connection between the evolution of the current knowledge-paradigm and the evolution of its chief medium, namely, English in its written mode. Halliday (1985) provides a revealing account of this connection, showing how the forms of conceptualisation involved in scientific thought are related to such structural features of written English as nominality, lexical density and grammatical metaphor.

He concludes: "Thus there are a lot of things that can only be said in nominal construction, especially in registers that have to do with the world of science and technology...that is to say, they can only be said this way in the grammar of modern English (p. 73). Halliday, in fact, goes a step further and makes the large generalisation that "the structure of the modern world and the structure of the language together make the written language what it is" (p. 75). It is therefore not enough to learn English, in some general sense, to be able to participate in the current knowledge-paradigm; it is crucial to learn it in its written mode, in the way it functions as a carrier of the paradigm.

A revision of priorities between spoken and written modes is not the only implication for pedagogy of the view outlined above of English in its mathetic function. I have suggested elsewhere (Prabhu, 1987, pp. 46–51) that communication tasks in the language classroom can be classified into information-gap activities, reasoning-gap activities, and opinion-gap activities, and that reasoning-gap activities have a greater value for language acquisition than the other two types. An appreciation of the mathetic function of English in the world further strengthens the case for a high priority to reasoning-gap activities, since reasoning in English is clearly a good preparation for mathetic uses of the language. There are other pedagogic implications, too, such as that the relatively high degree of deliberation and precision involved in mathetic use engenders a correspondingly high degree of language awareness which can be of value in preventing (or at least reducing) the phenomenon of "fossilisation" in language acquisition, or that a priority to mathetic use makes it more natural (or legitimate) to employ serious, knowledge-based subject-content than the give-and-take which prevails much of the time. But perhaps I have said enough to indicate that an appreciation of the mathetic function of English has consequences for the teaching of English as a second/foreign language.

I have been concerned in this paper with the function of English as a world language, rather than with the status of English as an international language, seen in terms of one or more varieties. I would, however, like to conclude by commenting on the consequence of this view of the function for the current debate on the relative status of native and non-native (or old and new) varieties of English. Briefly, a perception of the centrality of English in its mathetic function does not resolve the issue of varieties, but I think it helps to reduce the proportions of that issue, as well as its significance.

To begin with, variations in the forms of English between different communities occur chiefly in spoken uses of the language, largely in a pragmatic function—or, arising from those spoken uses, in creative uses of the language, in an aesthetic function. Variation can also occur in written uses of English in a pragmatic function (as in office letters and newspapers), but it seems fair to say that it occurs least in written English in a mathetic function (such as professional publications and textbooks). The phenomenon of variation, therefore is far more limited and, in that sense, far less important in the international use of English in a mathetic function. It is also likely that writing—in the sense of articulating conceptual content—is an aspect of language use in which proficiency is acquired mainly through intellectual discipline, and in which, as a result, being a native speaker is a doubtful advantage.

However, it would obviously be a mistake to assume that English in its mathetic function does not operate in speech: the written mode of English, which is what is involved in the mathetic function, is not the same as the written medium, which is a matter of scripting as against pronouncing the language (Halliday, 1985, pp. 42–45). An instance of language use can be in the written mode but in the spoken medium, as in professional debate at a seminar. Mathetic uses of English across the world will therefore involve not just the written medium but the spoken medium as well, and a high priority to the mathetic function (with a correspondingly large reliance on the written medium) can have an effect on the spoken forms of English internationally, perhaps making non-native speakers "sound like a book" or move towards spelling-based pronunciation. There will thus be variations in spoken English, and deviations from native-speaker speech, too large and regular not to raise questions of varietal status, even in the mathetic uses of English as a world language; and varietal status will inevitably bring up notions of superiority and inferiority between native and non-native speech-forms.

It seems to me likely that there is a relationship between the presumption of superiority by native varieties of English and the role of English as the language of the current knowledge-paradigm: it is the fact that the dominant knowledge-paradigm developed and continues to operate largely in native-English speaking parts of the world that supports the notion of native-English superiority over non-native varieties of the language just as it supports other notions of superiority, such as that of ethnicity. To the extent that this is the case, seeking to counter the notion of superiority on linguistic grounds as such would be seeking to remedy a symptom rather than the cause. It is a widening of the knowledge-paradigm, with increasing intellectual participation from different parts of the world, that can lead to a truer sense of parity and, in the process eliminate the symptoms of non-parity. If, on the other hand, the notion of linguistic superiority is in fact unrelated to achievement in the knowledge-paradigm, then it seems to me not very worthwhile trying to counter a notion which involves no more than privilege by the circumstance of birth. A trivial notion is best treated as being trivial, not dignified with the effort of professional argument. Besides, I am unable to see much substance in the measures meant to counter the notion, such as a loud assertion or declaration of linguistic independence or secession—a self-conferment of linguistic status, as unrelated to any substantive achievement as the notion of superiority by birth. I think it is far more worth our while to seek a more equal share in knowledge generation through English than to seek a more equal status for our variety or varieties of English. International English is of greatest value as the language of international collaboration in the mathetic endeavour, and it is by internationalising that endeavour more and more that we can truly internationalise the language.

References

Goulet, Denis. (1981). In defense of cultural rights: Technology tradition and conflicting models of rationality. *Human Rights Quarterly*, 3(4), 1–18.

Halliday, M. A. K. (1975). *Learning how to mean—Explorations in the development of language.* London: Edward Arnold.

Halliday, M. A. K. (1985). *Spoken and written language.* Victoria: Deakin University Press.

Howatt, A. P. R. (1984). *A history of English language teaching.* Oxford: Oxford University Press.

Judson, Horace Freeland. (1985). The rage to know. In Jeanne Fahnestock and Marie Secor (Eds.), *Readings in Argument* (pp. 65–76). New York: Random House.

Kuhn, Thomas S. (1962). *The structure of scientific revolutions.* Chicago: Chicago University Press.

Murray, Donald M. (1983). Writing as process: How writing finds its own meaning." In Timothy R. Donovan and Ben W. McClelland (Eds.), *Eight approaches of teaching composition* (pp. 3–20). Urbana: National Council of Teachers of English.

Prabhu, N. S. (1987). *Second language pedagogy.* Oxford: Oxford University Press.

19

Attempting Educational Change

LECTURE ONE

I consider it an honour to be asked to give this year's H. M. Patel Memorial Lectures at an institution which bears clear witness to the late Shri H. M. Patel's educational vision.

In these two lectures, I hope to place before you an overall view of the effort made to improve the teaching English in India in the past half-century or so, and of what I see as the prospects and problems of a continuance of such effort in the next half-century. The view I present is necessarily personal, informed by my own experience and reflection in the field and constrained by my own preferences and limitations; but I hope it will nevertheless prove to be of use to others in forming their own overall views of this important educational enterprise.

There are, as I see it, two broad dimensions to educational endeavour: (i) an institutional dimension, having to do with schools, education departments, specialist institutions, state policies, etc.; and (ii) an academic or "ideational" dimension, having to do with the development or emergence of ideas, theories or methodologies about what learning is like and what kind of teaching can best bring it about. I will deal with the institutional dimension of English language teaching today and with the ideational dimension in the lecture tomorrow.

The MELT Campaign

Institutional effort in improving English language teaching in India started within a few years of Independence. Around 1950, the

---

These two lectures were delivered as HM Patel Memorial Lectures in 1995 at the HM Patel Institute, Vallabh Vidyanagar, Gujarat.

government of the then Madras Presidency was seeking professional advice from the British Council on effective methods of teaching English, and, in 1952, Dr. Jean Forrester, a British lady working as Principal of a Teachers' College in Madras, produced the first "structural" syllabus, on the lines of the training she herself had received earlier in London. The government quickly conferred official status on this syllabus by publishing it in its Fort St. George Gazette. Implementation of the new syllabus in the state's primary schools, however, took several years' preparation. A massive programme of re-training primary school teachers was launched in 1959, under the name Madras English Language Teaching Campaign—MELT Campaign, for short. It operated at three different levels:

i. a top level Center which acted as administrative headquarters and also as a source of professional expertise, teaching materials, etc.;
ii. four Primary Centres which provided intensive, in-service courses of three weeks' duration; and
iii. over 20 Secondary Centres which provided training courses of about 80 contact hours as a part-time, two-evenings-a-week activity over a period of 5 months.

It was a carefully worked out, tightly structured and highly demanding programme, resulting in the re-training of over thirty thousand primary school teachers of English over about four years (1959–63). Although it had to be stopped prematurely on account of the national emergency arising from the Indo-Chinese border conflict in 1963, it had by then caught the imagination of the other state governments in southern India, and led to the establishment of a Regional Institute of English, sponsored jointly by four southern states, in Bangalore (Smith).

The English Language Teaching Institutes

Meanwhile, the introduction of a new method of teaching English in schools, and provision for the necessary re-training of teachers, were receiving attention in other parts of India, too. The British Council itself established, with financial support from the Nuffield Foundation in Britain, an English Language Teaching Institute in Allahabad in 1957, an institute which was later taken over by the Government of Uttar Pradesh. In 1958, the Government of India established, with financial support from the Ford Foundation and professional help from the British Council, the Central Institute of English in Hyderabad. Over the next five years, the state governments of Bihar, West Bengal, Maharashtra, Punjab, Madhya Pradesh and Rajasthan all established institutes of in-service training in English, in support of a reformed teaching method and with professional assistance from the British Council. There were also three other institutes which came into being in the same time, differing structurally from the others (in not being sponsored by a state government, or not being assisted by the British Council, or not re-training teachers at the school level) but with the same kind of professional content and objective—namely, those in Himachal Pradesh, Kerala and Gujarat, the last of these being the H. M. Patel Institute under whose auspices we have met today. Together, this constituted a large network of specialist institutes devoted to the improvement of English language teaching—larger than any in the rest of the world.

Summer Institutes in English

Quickly following the establishment of the various English Language Teaching Institutes, there was another form of institutional effort at another level: an effort to reform the teaching of English at the tertiary (undergraduate) level and a consequent effort to re-train college-level lecturers in English, not through permanent institutions, but through a series of annual, 6-week Summer Institutes, sponsored by the University Grants Commission and professionally assisted by the British Council and the Central Institute of English and Foreign Languages. This, too, was a large-scale activity, beginning in 1965 and expanding quickly in the next five years, to provide in-service training to over 500 college lecturers each year, over about ten years.

The MELT campaign, the English Language Teaching Institutes and the Summer Institutes in English are three prominent forms in which an institutional effort was made in India to bring about educational change in respect of instruction in English. These were not, however, the only forms of ELT activity. The Government of India Ministry of Education set up two high-level study groups, within five years of each other (in 1964 and 1967) to make recommendations on the measures to be taken to improve the teaching of English, and published for wide use the detailed reports produced by both (Ministry of Education, 1967; 1971). The National Council for Educational Research and Training, concerned with quality improvement in secondary education, paid specific attention to improving instruction in English both through a specialist wing at its headquarters in Delhi and through the teacher-training programmes offered at the different Regional Colleges of Education. The British Council operated more than one scheme of using British Universities to provide the services of British specialists to English Language Teaching Institutes, University English Departments, and some institutions of higher-level science and technology. There were also other initiatives, such as the British Council's initiative in developing and using a 50-hour Bridge Intensive course in English in a large number of undergraduate colleges in Tamil Nadu; the broadcast of radio lessons for teachers or learners of English, prepared by the Regional Institute in Bangalore as well as the Central Institute in Hyderabad; the development of textbook materials at various English Language Teaching Institutes and, in particular, an influential undergraduate course called Language Through Literature at the Central Institute of English; and so on. But perhaps I have given enough examples of the kinds of institutional activity that took place over about thirty years from about 1955. I can now go on to identify some general features of those activities.

General Features of the Institutional Effort

Perhaps the most noticeable feature of the activities we have looked at is that they viewed educational change as a top-down process. The need for a change was perceived, decisions about its form and content were taken, plans of action were made and procedures of implementation were initiated all at the top end of the educational organisation—by government ministries or departments of education, high-powered specialists who advised at that level or leaders who had the institutional status and social trust to plan and initiate such change. The bottom end of the educational organisation represented by teachers and pupils in classrooms, or individual schools as units, had the role of receiving the change when it reached them, complying or coming to terms with it as best they could, and incorporating it in their normal work from then on. Though the educational benefit of the change, in the form of better or faster learning by pupils, was to arise at this bottom end of the organisation, all the enthusiasm for the change, expectation of the benefit, and responsibility and risk in raising the expectation remained very much at the top end. There was, as a result, little enthusiasm, expectation or sense of risk—little feeling of something being at stake or desirable or disappointing or rewarding—marking the actual classroom events from which the benefit of better learning was to arise.

A second feature of these activities is that the top-level initiatives and plans of action were marked by a certain sense of idealism and, indeed a sense of historic mission. India had just emerged as an independent nation, and there were many kinds of nation-building work going on, meant to make the country strong and modern, in contrast to the colonial backwardness of the past. In this general context, it was easy for the English teaching methods of the past to get associated with colonial backwardness, and for the new method being implemented to be seen in the same light as the Five-Year Plans or the Green Revolution. This had the effect of conferring a measure of certainty or truth on the method being implemented; the new method was viewed as the self-evidently right one to follow.

The only risks involved were that the teachers and pupils might not all rise to the occasion or prove worthy of reform.

Accompanying this idealism, and to some extent hiding behind it, was an element of political pragmatism. Independence had brought to the fore the forces of linguistic nationalism, with a demand for the reinstatement, elevation or promotion of Indian languages in various fields, including, in particular, education. The governments of different states had, in response, reduced substantially the classroom time given to English in schools, which now started to teach the language at a later stage or gave fewer hours to it or both. At the same time, the governments were keen to maintain the level of the new generation's knowledge of English—or at least keen to appear to be trying to maintain it—to satisfy certain other demands, including those of learners and parents who associated English with good employment. In this context, the introduction of a new method, which can teach more English in less time, was very attractive, both as an actual educational operation and, apart from that, as a public demonstration of intention. It enabled the governments to resolve, conceal or appear to resolve a basic contradiction in their educational policy. The British Council, too, found it convenient to be involved in a large way in such English language teaching reform. Its original function as an instrument of government propaganda during the war having disappeared at the end of the war, the Council was looking for a more substantial purpose and a more positive identity for itself than those of being a mere peacetime information agency, and helping former British colonies to maintain or improve their knowledge of the English language seemed just the kind of role it was looking for—promoting a British Asset (namely, the language) and through it Britain's long-term international relations and interests, on the one hand, and providing educational aid to less developed countries which had been dependent on Britain in the past, on the other. There was thus a convergence of the quite different political and pragmatic interests of the Indian and British Institutions involved in the ELT reform movement of the 1950s and 1960s.

A further feature of this movement was that the new teaching method being implemented was seen to be an imported one, a form of advanced classroom technology developed in the technologically advanced West, similar to industrial or agricultural technologies which were also being imported at the time. Not only was the new method, that is to say, non-indigenous, but its non-indigenous nature was viewed as part of its strength. It was modern, scientific, effective, etc., carrying the same appeal, glamour or mystique as other Western ideas or techniques in other fields of development and reform.

Overall, the institutional effort in ELT which we have been looking at was a form of educational engineering: large-scale; top-down; ideologically and politically driven; viewed and handled as a form of imported, hence superior technology. The results expected of it were also thought of in terms characteristic of mass-production engineering. There was an expectation of uniform outcomes, with all learners attaining the same pre-specified level of success; there were attempts to achieve a multiplier effect, with each instance of success prompting two or more others; and there was an aim of saturation, with all teachers in all schools being trained in the new method and all following that method in all their teaching thereafter.

The Current Scene

I have so far tried to provide a view of the past in Indian ELT, by outlining the institutional effort that was made over some thirty years following Independence, and identifying some salient characteristics of that effort. Let me now pass on to what has followed this period of institutional effort, that is to say, what the present situation is.

The enthusiasm and optimism that marked the various forms of institutional activity in the past has since given way to a sense of realism, indeed, a sense of disillusionment about past hopes. Two things, I think, became increasingly clear after the institutional effort had advanced to a certain stage. First, the objective of saturation, that is to say, full coverage of all teachers in all schools by the training programme, was clearly unattainable with all the resources likely to be available: saturation simply acted as a receding horizon, calling for a larger and larger effort but not rewarding it by getting any nearer; and secondly, the outcome of the actual effort being made, in terms of learners' attainment in English, turned out to be highly non-uniform, generally below the predicted level and often unconvincing in its quality. It was difficult to persuade oneself that learners on the whole learnt more English under the new dispensation than they did under the old. It was possible for a while to blame the non-attainment in English on the non-attainment of saturation, and the non-achievement of saturation on the non-availability of further resources, etc., but in the end the two realisations together brought about a sense of disillusionment with what was being attempted both pedagogically and institutionally.

The sociopolitical factor that had lent support to the earlier ELT effort, changed in time and pointed to other priorities, both for the state governments in India and for the British Council. Also, the earlier implicit faith in the teaching method imported from the West was shaken by the challenge that arose to the method in the West from more than one newer idea. There has also been a challenge to the process of top-down educational change and to the general idea of educational engineering through institutional effort.

As a result, the current situation in ELT is one of uncertainty, plurality and more than one form of inconsistency. Some of the English Language Teaching Institutes set up in the 1960s have been closed down, though a majority of them continue to function with receding levels of professional energy and morale. The institutional effort they make is on essentially the same lines as in the past but there is no longer an informing vision of educational reconstruction or optimism about achieving saturation resulting in uniformly high learning outcomes. The teaching method introduced in the

1960s continues to be advocated, but not with the same sense of certainty as in the past, and not to the exclusion of other, alternative methods. Teacher re-training courses outside the English Language Teaching Institutes—for tertiary teachers, for instance—continue to take place but not as part of a regular, unified and coordinated programme as with the Summer Institutes in English. There is, on the other hand, much more professional debate, disagreement or controversy than in the past, which can be considered more healthy than unquestioning certainty. There is also a certain intellectual ferment, with various radical ideas such as teacher-autonomy, learner-autonomy, grassroots-level change and classroom-centered action research exerting their influence and stimulating diverse forms of small-scale activity.

A Future Possibility

Let me now, in this last part of the lecture, outline a future possibility for ELT activity in India. In doing so, I make no claim to predicting future events or even making logical projections from the past and present. I am only outlining a possibility and expressing a personal hope—that is to say, stating what I consider to be a desirable development, something worth aspiring for and striving towards.

I referred a moment ago to a state of intellectual ferment and flux at the present time, together with much uncertainty, inconsistency and lack of overall direction. Although this intellectual ferment is, to a large extent, a response to various radical ideas in education, born in the West and imported, like the teaching methods introduced earlier, with some blind respect, there is in its actual operation the possibility of ELT becoming an intellectual activity in the country, in contrast to an institutional activity as in the past. Institutional activity aims at institutional change or reform in the form of replacing one set of procedures and behaviours by another. It necessarily makes demands on the individual concerned to conform and to carry out. Intellectual activity, on the other hand, demands of individuals that they think for themselves, probe, search, question and conceptualise, and follow in their actions and behaviours what appears to be the most promising course, rather than what has been laid down. If this possibility should materialise, we will have thinking teachers rather than trained teachers, teaching as an act of exploration rather than as an act of conformity, and ongoing change in teacher behaviour as an organic development from each teacher's experience of teaching rather than as implementation of a new method.

Institutional effort at educational change is a procedure analogous to that of industrial production: one sets up the institutional machinery, makes the necessary professional inputs (from specialists) and expects the desired products at the end of the process. It treats trained or re-trained teachers as merely desired products—or, perhaps, treats learners' learning as the desired product and trained teachers as a part of the machinery. The one thing it does not do is to treat the teachers themselves as professional inputs—that is to say, as people who have some special knowledge or experience of teaching, learning and the classrooms, who can reflect, judge and make decisions about teaching and whose judgements and decisions have a greater bearing on learners' learning than the judgements and decisions made at the institutional level, away from the daily act of teaching. The institutional machinery cannot treat individual teachers as professionals capable of thought, judgement and decision, simply because it would then be unable to treat them as a part of the machinery. Professionals capable of thought and judgement will make varied decisions between them, as well as different decisions at different times, in a way that cannot be predicted by institutional planning.

It seems to me that we have, in the first major phase of ELT reform in this country, attempted educational change through institutional planning and effort—creating a large institutional machinery for the purpose and planning at the top to bring about the desired educational effects. I would be happy if there was a second phase to come which consisted of educational change at the level of the individual teacher—not planned but spontaneous, not uniform but multifarious, not top-down but bottom-up, not quick and spectacular but slow and continuous. The role of institutions in this phase will not be to plan and cause educational change but to permit and create room for it, to refrain from interfering with it, to observe, tolerate and accommodate it, and to readjust themselves from time to time so as to maximise opportunity for it. The most important agent of educational change is the individual teacher, and the most powerful source of educational change is the individual teacher's mind with its reflections, interpretations of experience, and judgements and decisions made in the daily act of teaching. Any institutional effort at educational change should be supportive of and responsive to change at the teacher's level rather than pre-emptive of it.

LECTURE TWO

An improvement of teaching procedures calls for two things: it calls for teaching conditions favourable to improved teaching; and it calls for teaching procedures which can bring about improved learning. The first is an institutional matter which we looked at yesterday. The second is a pedagogic matter concerned with theories of how learning takes place and what method of teaching can best promote it: it is this aspect that I wish to look at today, with reference to English language teaching in India.

Various methods of language teaching have developed and proved influential in the Western world—in Europe and in the United States—over the past century and a half. The teaching of English in India has been influenced by all or most of these methods, at different times. I will briefly examine these different methods, and also look at two that can be said to have developed within India.

Classical–Scholastic Procedures

Until the early decades of the last century, language education in Europe meant the teaching and learning of the classical languages, Greek and Latin. Only the classical languages, no longer spoken but possessing a body of great, mind-improving texts, were considered worthy of formal instruction and study. The procedures used in teaching the classical languages consisted, broadly, of learners "construing" (or comprehending) a series of important (or "canonical") texts, with the help of teachers' linguistic commentary on them and some understanding of the grammar of the classical language concerned. Learners gave evidence of their successful "construction" of a text by translating it into their own language. Learners' minds were believed to benefit both from the elevated subject-content of the texts being construed and from the "perfect" grammatical structure of the classical languages. For want of an accepted name for these teaching and learning activities, we may refer to them as Classical–Scholastic procedures.

When, following Macaulay's Minute, English came to be taught and learnt formally in the Indian Schools, it was these Classical–Scholastic procedures that were employed—perhaps with justification, since English was as unfamiliar to Indian pupils as Latin was to European pupils and, moreover, Macaulay's main argument for teaching English in India was that English contained a body of knowledge and literature—a body of texts—which will be beneficial to the Indian mind (Viswanathan, 1994). English texts considered to be of great merit were taught in the classroom through a detailed commentary by the teacher, and learners demonstrated their comprehension of those texts by producing paraphrases of them (not translations, perhaps because the British teacher of English could not cope with translations in an Indian language). This soon became the standard procedure for teaching literary texts in English, under the somewhat misleading name "lecture method" (misleading because the activity consists of an explication of the text, rather than a lecture), and led in due course to a cramming by learners of prepared paraphrases/summaries, and the commercial provision of such prepared summaries for learners, in the form of "bazaar" guides. There has, for many years now, been a good deal of criticism and discouragement of this "lecture" method, as we know, but a good deal of the teaching of English at the tertiary level continues to be in that form. Our classrooms are still working with a remnant of the old Classical–Scholastic procedures.

The Grammar-Translation Method

At about the time English was beginning to be taught in India (in the first half of the nineteenth century), languages such as English, French and German (that is to say, modern languages, in contrast to classical languages) were beginning to be taught formally in schools in Europe too. Unlike in India however, there was a movement in Europe against the use of classical–scholastic procedures for teaching these modern languages. It was argued that modern languages, which are living languages, can be taught much more simply and effectively by employing a new method. The new method that was advocated consisted essentially of (i) using ordinary sentences to present the language to the learner, instead of the difficult "canonical" texts; (ii) organising the sentences to be presented to the learner according to their grammatical structure—that is to say, using a form of grammatical grading in the teaching; (iii) presenting only one or two new grammatical points at a time, with brief explanations and examples, and (iv) providing plenty of practice to the learner following the presentation of each grammatical point. The practice was provided in the form of a translation of sets of sentences by the learner—first, from the target language to the mother-tongue, and later from the mother-tongue to the target language (Howatt, 1984, pp. 131–32). This method became quickly popular in the newer secondary schools in Germany, France and Britain, though its popularity also provoked the hostility of the older, more prestigious schools which clung to classical languages to the exclusion of modern languages. Those who criticised the method, many years later, referred to it as the Grammar-Translation Method—a label which was very inappropriate because neither grammar nor translation was an innovation of the method. The innovation actually consisted of sentence-based teaching, in place of text-based teaching; grammatical grading and organisation of material; and an emphasis on practice, at the expense of explanation—all procedures whose value can easily be recognised today.

The Grammar-Translation Method too had an impact on the teaching of English in India, though its influence seems to have been much greater in the preparation of self-teaching materials for adult learners of English, than in face-to-face instruction in schools. Coursebooks in English produced in India for those who wished to take public examinations by private study (for example, Matriculation) continued to employ the Grammar-Translation procedures throughout the first half of the present century.

The Direct Method

In the second half of the last century—in the 1860s and 1870s—there arose, in the United States of America, a procedure of language teaching which did not use any translation—indeed, did not use the learners' mother-tongue in the classroom—and did not use any grammatical explanation, grading or practice either. It relied, instead, entirely on teachers talking to learners in the target language, and making themselves understood as well as they could, with the help of context, gesture, realia, etc. The method, which was developed by two private language schools (one of them the original Berlitz School in Providence, Rhode Island) in the context of teaching English to adult immigrants of other linguistic backgrounds in the U.S. came to be referred to as the Direct Method and exerted an influence on language teaching elsewhere, including English language teaching in India. Textbooks of English in use in Indian schools in the first half of this century often were (or claimed to be) based on the Direct Method meaning thereby chiefly the avoidance of the learners' mother-tongue in the teaching. This principle of avoiding the use of the learners' language in the teaching of English was also emphasised in the training of teachers and continues to receive a good deal of emphasis to this day.

The Structural Approach

At the very end of the last century, there emerged in Europe, an influential school of thought in language teaching known as the Reform Movement. It was influential partly because it based its arguments on the newly prestigious science of phonetics and partly also because it was led by persons of eminence in the scholarly and educational world.

The Reform Movement asserted that all scientific language teaching should give priority to the spoken form of the language, and criticised the then prevalent teaching method in Europe (namely the Grammar-Translation Method) for giving importance only to the written form. It also criticised the constant use of translation, the large amount of attention given to grammar, and the use of uncontextualised sentences instead of continuous texts. It was especially successful in establishing accurate pronunciation as an area of priority in language teaching, and in highlighting the importance of the oral skills of listening and speaking for the learners (Howatt, 1982).

The Reform Movement's insistence on a scientific approach—that is to say, systematicity in terms of the nature of the language being taught—soon led to a search for systematicity in aspects other than pronunciation, in particular, in grammatical structure. People like Harold Palmer gave a great deal of thought to the matter, and came up with the concept of a core grammar of the language, which can be broken up into its parts and listed in a systematic order. Such a list of the core grammatical parts of a language was referred to as a structural syllabus, which, it was argued, could be used to teach that language systematically and efficiently. This concept of a core grammar, divisible into its parts, was further reinforced by developments in American structural linguistics, where syntax was seen as a set of frames for constructing sentences. The use of a structural syllabus in language teaching thus captured the imagination of people in the field, and language teaching which based itself on a structural syllabus came to be referred to as the Structural Approach.

It is the Structural Approach that was introduced in India in the years following Independence, through massive programmes of teacher re-training such as the MELT Campaign, and through the establishment of a network of English Language Teaching Institutes, as noted in the lecture yesterday. Though there may be different opinions about how fully or faithfully the teaching procedures representing the Structural Approach were carried out in the different classrooms, there can be little doubt that the implementation of the Structural Approach has been a large-scale language education programme in India, receiving more governmental, institutional and foreign-aid support than has either been received or is likely to be received by any other programme of English language teaching reform.

Communicative Language Teaching

The most recent movement in language teaching, which arose in Europe about twenty years ago, is what is referred to as Communicative Language Teaching. It argues that teaching based on the Structural Approach develops in learners only a partial ability to use the language—namely, the ability to produce, at best, grammatically accurate language, with some deliberation, but not the ability to produce socially appropriate language with a socially appropriate spontaneity. To develop the ability to be socially appropriate and spontaneous, it is argued, teaching needs to be based on a syllabus of social functions, rather than of grammatical structures, and learners need to rehearse in the classroom those types of social roles which they will later be attempting to perform in real life. There is a shift of emphasis from language learning process to language learning purpose, and it is held that success in language learning is best achieved by directly imitating or play-acting successful language use, rather than by going through a series of intermediate, developmental steps. Communicative language teaching has had a great deal of influence in different parts of the world, especially on private, commercial language schools and on courses in English in technical institutions, though its overall impact on the teaching of English in India has been somewhat limited, probably because English language teaching aimed at adult professionals is not yet a large commercial activity in the country.

The Reading Method

While the different language teaching methods outlined above have all had their origins outside India, though they have often been adapted, modified or further developed in the course of their use in the country, there are two other methods which are worth mentioning and which arose within India. First, an English educationist called Michael West, working in the 1920s in what was then the Bengal Province, developed a method of teaching English based on two important arguments. He argued that, given the high drop-out rate in the Indian Schools and the meagre exposure to spoken English available to pupils, the best use that can be made of the time in the English language classrooms is to develop in learners an ability to read English, without worrying about how far they are able to write and speak the language. West claimed that reading is an ability that can be developed in learners much in advance of the other language skills, that learners can maintain their reading ability in later life more easily than they can maintain the other skills (since exposure to the written word is more easily available than exposure to the spoken word), and that reading in English is also the most useful or valuable skill for learners to possess (since it gives them access to all the information and knowledge of the world available in the language). A second argument was that an ability to read with comprehension depends more crucially on a knowledge of vocabulary than on a grasp of the grammatical structure, and that teaching should therefore be based on a syllabus of common or frequent words, rather than on a structural syllabus (West). The two arguments together led to the formation of the Reading Method, and to the careful construction of a series of coursebooks and supplementary reading books under the title *New Method Readers*.

Task-based Language Teaching

The second teaching method that has been developed in India is what is commonly referred to as task-based language teaching. In the late 1970s a small group of English language specialists and teacher trainers at the Regional Institute of English in Bangalore decided to explore an alternative to the Structural Approach—in particular, the possibility that learners' grasp of the grammatical structure of a language is facilitated best if learners are occupied with exchanging meaning in the language rather than with learning or practising parts of the grammatical structure itself. The group accordingly took up the teaching of a few primary and secondary school classes in Bangalore and Madras and developed, over a period of five years, a procedure of teaching consisting essentially of problem-solving activities in the classroom, with an appropriate degree of cognitive challenge to learners (Prabhu). The arguments and procedures involved in task-based teaching have drawn considerable attention in the language teaching profession, both in India and elsewhere in the world.

Teaching Method as Scientific Theory

I have now mentioned a number of language teaching methods which have been influential at different times in the past and have also had an impact on English language teaching in India. My list is necessarily a selective one: there were other methods or proposals which could have been included in it, and perhaps the distribution of attention to the different methods could also have been different. Further, given this history of a series of teaching methods in the past two centuries or so, it can perhaps be predicted safely that there will continue to arise new teaching methods at various times over the next century as well. At some point, however, one needs to ask what significance there is to these changing teaching methods and how one can evaluate any given teaching method. What, in fact, is the concept of a teaching method, and what is the basis of its appeal for or influence on classroom language teaching?

There are fundamentally two views that can be taken of what a teaching method represents. The first, and most widely held, view is that a teaching method is a form of scientific theory or scientific claim to truth in the matter of how languages are learnt by human beings, what the learning process consists of, and what actions or conditions will help or hinder that process. Whenever a teaching method is advanced or advocated, the arguments put forward involve a particular view of what knowing a language is like, how that knowledge can be developed, etc. The Reform Movement a hundred years ago and the subsequent proposals for the Structural Approach called their views of the nature of language and language learning "scientific", and the notion of scientific truth has been implicit in the claims made and arguments advanced for most new methods when they were developed. Here, each new method seems to say, is a true picture of what language and learning are like—more true than the pictures provided by other, earlier methods and therefore more likely to produce successful learning by learners if adopted.

The concept of truth that is involved here is essentially the same as in the pursuit of science: it is an objective truth, representing the nature of the phenomenon being studied—telling us, that is to say, how things really are in the universe. What we have at any given time may not constitute the complete truth or unmixed truth—we are likely to have only partial truth or an approximation to truth, with further investigation revealing more of the truth in due course. But what we have at any time is more of the truth than what we had before that—that is to say, there is progress in our search for the truth, with each successive statement of the truth being more complete or more accurate or more of an approximation than the last.

There is, however, one problem with this concept of truth in a field like language education. In the field of science, the test of a truth claim is the prediction of phenomena made by the claim, and empirical observation can determine whether or not that prediction has come true. One scientific theory can be said to be more fully true—or closer to the truth—than another if it makes larger predictions that come true. In a field like language education, this should mean that each teaching method predicts greater or faster learning by learners than its predecessor, and that prediction can be verified through empirical observation. In reality, however, it has not been possible to test the predictions made by teaching methods, partly because teaching methods are far less precisely stated than scientific theories, and more importantly because learning, being a mental phenomenon, can neither be observed and quantified empirically, in any precise way, nor attributed to the teaching carried out in accordance with a given method, with any measure of certainty. Human learning, that is to say, is unobservable as it happens, unpredictable from any specific act of teaching, and unrelatable to any specific causes when it happens. It is therefore impossible—or at least has been impossible so far—to select between different teaching methods on the basis of which one of them can be depended on to produce more learning. Although English language teaching in India has employed different teaching methods at different times in the past, and has, at various times, decided to use one method in preference to another, there is in fact no way of saying, or showing, in any objective way, that learners in India have learnt more English or less English as a result of one or another teaching method.

The current state of the language teaching profession is marked by a realisation of this anomaly and a state of uncertainty arising from it. Language teaching specialists today are typically unwilling to uphold any specific teaching method as being superior to all others, in the way advocates of each new method did in the past. Some of them take recourse, instead, in suggesting an eclectic blend of different methods, though they are unable to say what precise blend of what different methods or how the superiority of that particular blend over other possible blends is to be demonstrated or defended. Other specialists point to the possibility that teachers, learners and learning conditions vary from one context to another in many different ways, and that a teaching method needs to be selected with reference to its suitability for each teaching context, rather than on the strength of its greater truth or superiority. But this approach too runs into problems by suggesting that, for any specific teaching context, there is in fact a teaching method which can be predicted to yield better learning outcomes than all others. There are, of course, still other specialists who argue that it will in fact be possible, at some future time, to verify empirically the predictions made by teaching methods, and that our lack of success in doing so in the past is not a sufficient reason for giving up effort in that direction.

There is one consequence of the notion of a teaching method representing a scientific truth that is worth looking at a little further. If a teaching method is based on an approximation to the true nature of language learning, in a scientific sense, its truth is necessarily objective in character, that is to say, independent of the subjective perceptions, or thoughts, or feelings, of those who advocate it, adopt it or operate it. This means that the effectiveness of a teaching method does not depend on the understanding of the teachers who use it in the classrooms, much less on their attitudes towards it. Just as an experiment in the physics or chemistry laboratory yields its results as long as it is carried out in the way specified, regardless of the understanding, attitude or belief of the person who carries it out, so a teaching method should lead to the expected learning outcome, regardless of what the teacher thinks or feels about it. It is this notion that underlies programmes of teacher re-training accompanying the introduction of a new teaching method; the re-training aims to ensure that teachers conform to the teaching procedures required by the new methods. The focus is on what the teacher does, not on what the teacher thinks, feels, understands or believes. But when teachers have to do things in the classroom that bear no relation to their own understanding or belief, they are necessarily acting in the way they are asked to, rather than in the way they would prefer to—that is to say, they are acting mechanically. Teaching as a mechanical activity is therefore a logical consequence of the concept of a teaching method as scientific truth.

Teaching Method as Teacher's Sense of Plausibility

This brings me to the second possible view of what a teaching method represents—a view with which I will conclude this lecture. On this view, a teaching method represents a teacher's subjective understanding of what learning is like and what kind of teaching can best promote it. When a teacher is carrying out teaching which does not correspond to his/her understanding at that time, he/she is not really teaching but engaging in mechanical activity. When, on the other hand, teaching does correspond to the teacher's own understanding, the teacher is making an intellectual investment in the teaching being done, and is likely to derive a measure of satisfaction or dissatisfaction from the activity. Each such instance of satisfaction or dissatisfaction has an influence on the teacher's understanding at that point; it strengthens it, or weakens it, or induces a change in it, or gives it a clearer shape, or plants a question or doubt against it. The teacher's understanding, thus influenced or changed by the last act of teaching, exerts an influence on his/her next act of teaching, which is therefore likely to be different, in however small a measure, from the last; and this new act of teaching is likely, in turn, to influence the teacher's understanding further, in any one of many ways. There is, that is to say, a continuous interaction between the teacher's act of teaching and his/her understanding of the learning process. The best method is that which represents this continuous interaction; it is teaching which is actively supported by the teacher's own perception of the learning process and acts as a source of influence on it. There is no claim to scientific or objective truth; there is only the teacher's subjective perception at a given time, of what learning is probably like and how teaching brings it about—what can perhaps be called the teacher's sense of plausibility about learning. Classroom activity which engages the teacher's sense of plausibility is likely to be productive both of learners' learning and of the teacher's professional growth. That which does not can only be mechanical, no matter what claims of truth are made in support of it.

It seems to me that we have placed too much faith in the past on theories and teaching methods developed by experts and presented with an aura of scientific truth. We have adopted such teaching methods from different parts of the world, hoping, or trusting, that those who developed them had more access to the nature of learning than we can ourselves have. We have not considered the possibility that the people with the most access to the nature of learning may be the teachers themselves. After all, teachers are the ones who are constantly present at the place where learning happens or fails to happen. Whatever learning takes place in the classroom, that is to say, takes place in the presence of the teacher, often as a result of what the teacher does or fails to do, and generally in the course of an interaction between the teacher and the learner. The teacher is therefore more in touch with the learning process in operation than anyone else can be, and more able, therefore to develop a feel for it, over time. Perhaps we should now turn our attention to tapping this rich resource of pedagogic perception or intuition, encouraging teachers to develop their personal theories and teaching methods instead of requiring them to follow what we have decided to adopt. The result will not be a neat uniformity to the teaching procedures followed in different classrooms (since teachers' personal theories will inevitably vary from one to another), but the result can be each classroom acting as a little laboratory for developing teaching methods, and each teacher's mind developing a sense of the nature of the learning process. Perhaps we should try trusting the teacher, for a change.

References

Howatt, A. P. R. (1982). Language teaching must start afresh! *ELT Journal*, 36(4), 263–68.

Howatt, A. P. R. (1984). *A history of English language teaching.* Oxford: Oxford University Press.

Ministry of Education (1967). The study of English in India: Report of the Study Group appointed by the Ministry of Education. Submitted to the Education Commission in 1965, Ministry of Education, Government of India.

Ministry of Education (1971). Report of the Study Group on Teaching English. Ministry of Education and Youth Services, Government of India.

Prabhu, N. S. (1987). *Second language pedagogy*. Oxford: Oxford University Press.

Smith, D. A. (1968). In-service training for teachers of English in developing countries. In G. E. Perren (Ed.), *Teachers of English as a second language* (193–200). Cambridge University Press.

Viswanathan, Gauri. (1993). The beginnings of English literary study in British India. In Janet Maybin (Ed.), *Language and literacy in social practice* (pp. 215–32). Clevedon: Multilingual Matters.

West, Michael. (1926). *Bilingualism (with special reference to Bengal)*. Calcutta: Bureau of Education.

20

Teaching is at Most Hoping for the Best

There is an ambiguity in the way we use the term "teaching". We sometimes talk of teaching as if it meant the causing or bringing about of learning in the learner, so that the performance of teaching necessarily implies the occurrence of learning. Teaching in this sense is the obverse of learning: something can be said to have been taught only if it has been learnt; any failure in learning necessarily indicates a corresponding failure in teaching. The terms "teach" and "learn" thus refer to two sides of the same event, in the way the terms "buy" and "sell" (for instance) do. If something has been sold, it has necessarily been bought, and it is a contradiction to say something like "John sold the house to Peter but Peter didn't buy it". If teaching means the causing of learning, it is similarly contradictory to say that the teacher taught something but the learner did not learn it.

More often, however, we use the term "teaching" to refer to the activities and procedures carried out by the teacher, independently of how successful they are in their aim of bringing about learning. Used in this sense, teaching is a separate event from learning, not another side of the same event. It is entirely sensible to say that the teacher has taught something but the learner has not learnt it, just as it is sensible to say something like "John sent a message to Peter but Peter didn't receive it". Teaching and learning, that

---

This essay was first published in 1999. *Source:* Prabhu, N. S. (1999). Teaching is at most hoping for the best. In Christopher Ward and Willy Renandya (Eds.), *Language teaching: New insights for the language teacher.* Anthology Series 40 (pp. 48–57). Singapore: Singapore University Press.

is to say, are not the obverse of each other; they are like sending and receiving, rather than like selling and buying.

Which of the two senses of "teaching" is preferable or desirable in the discussion of language pedagogy? It is tempting to say that "teaching" should mean the causation of learning because the causation of learning is, after all, the only real purpose of all teaching. It seems clear that teaching which is divorced from learning is of little educational value, being at best a form of routine or ritual, and it therefore seems necessary to resist any discussion of teaching as a separate event from learning. Indeed this line of thought often leads to (or gets reinforced by) an idealistic stance, from which it becomes unenlightened to talk of teaching as distinct from learning.

But in reality we do talk of teaching most of the time as an activity distinct from learning. We discuss teaching objectives, teaching content, teaching materials, teaching procedures, etc., which are all matters different from the occurrence of learning, though meant to be conducive to it. We do of course discuss learners' needs, learners' background, learners' role in classroom activities, etc., but these too are matters of teaching, rather than of learning, since they are all inputs to decisions about what should be done in a given classroom, how, when, etc., that is to say, decisions to be made in teaching.

The point I am making is not that we always discuss teaching and seldom learning, or even that we discuss teaching more often than learning. We do discuss various concepts and theories of what the process of learning might be like—concepts such as memorisation and retrieval, habit formation, intake and internal representation, sequence of acquisition, etc. But we regard this as a discussion of learning, as distinct from that of teaching. Even when we consider what forms of teaching might be supportive of a certain process of learning, we see ourselves as interrelating two distinct matters, namely, the activity of teaching and the phenomenon of learning. Teaching is thus seen to be a separate matter from learning, not just the other side of it. Teaching is what the teacher does; learning is what happens to the learner.

The question I want to ask here is: why is this so? Why do we treat, or need to treat, teaching and learning as separate, though related, events, like sending something and receiving it, rather than as two sides of a single event, like selling something and buying it? Why do we not (or can we not) treat teaching as strictly the causation of learning, so that there is only one event involved, seen as teaching from one point of view and as learning from another? I want to discuss three possible answers to this question.

The first and most obvious answer is that we are unable to consider learning to the same extent as teaching. There is a large disparity in our knowledge of the two. As Brumfit pointed out forcefully some fifteen years ago (1984, p. 59), teaching is an intentional activity which can be planned, carried out with deliberate effort, controlled or regulated, and observed as it happens. One can decide to do it or not to do it, to do it one way or in another, to speed it up or slow it down, to stop or continue it, etc., and what is done can be observed, recorded, reviewed or studied. In contrast, learning can happen with or without the learner's intention, or even willingness, and cannot be started or stopped, speeded up or slowed down, either by the teacher or by the learner. It is something that cannot be planned, deliberately put into operation, controlled, observed or recorded. Learning, that is to say, is unpredictable and intangible, unlike teaching which is much more tangible and fully predictable. This means that we cannot talk about learning with anything like the certainty and specificity available for our discussion of teaching; and, further, we cannot claim, or assume, that what we know and say about teaching is relevant, to any extent, to learning. We cannot, that is to say, treat learning as the obverse of teaching because we have too little knowledge or control of learning, and also because our differential knowledge of teaching and learning is indicative of a major difference between the nature of teaching and that of learning, quite unlike the case with two sides of a coin.

A second possible answer to the question of why teaching and learning cannot be treated as the obverse of each other is that there is a large mismatch between the workings and outcomes of the two. Not only does teaching not always result in the relevant learning but also the learning that does result is often unrelated to what the teaching has aimed at. Allwright (1984) highlighted this fact, several years ago, when he asked, "Why don't learners learn what teachers teach?" He was concerned not with the problem of learners' failure to learn but rather with the puzzling fact that what learners do learn is frequently quite different from what teachers try to teach. As an explanation of this puzzle, Allwright suggests that learners have their own intentions, preoccupations and priorities in the classroom, which are not based on the teacher's intentions, aims and expectations. Learners, that is to say, have their agendas for learning, based on what they consider important, what they find interesting, what they experience as a problem or hurdle on the way, etc., as well as on what they see of fellow-learners' agendas, efforts, successes and failures. Seen in this light, what happens in the classroom is that teachers pursue their teaching agendas while learners pursue their (varied, individual) learning agendas, and the different agendas work at cross purposes much of the time. Far from being two related events, teaching and learning appear as independent, unrelated events, often in conflict with each other. Learners' agendas are no doubt less explicit, less stable and less perceptible than teachers' agendas but one can see enough evidence of their existence, says Allwright, if one sheds a preoccupation with the teaching agenda.

Perhaps we should pause here to ask what "learning" means in this discussion. The term "learning" can refer to two distinct things: one, the thing that happens in the learner's mind when something gets newly internalised, assimilated or organised; and two, the thing that a learner does with the aim of internalising something new. The former is a piece of development; the latter a piece of action. When Brumfit says that learning, unlike teaching, is imperceptible, unpredictable and unavailable for advance planning, he is thinking of learning as a mental event, a form of internal development. When, on the other hand, Allwright talks about learners' agendas, perceptions and efforts to learn, he is thinking of learning as physical or verbal procedure, a form of activity.

"Learning" in this sense of physical activity is quite close to the sense of teaching: learners doing such work as asking questions, referring to books, participating in group work or conferring with one another about what should be done, would all be learning, that is, effort by learners to learn, for Allwright. It can equally well be called self-teaching, that is, effort by learners to teach themselves. Allwright's argument would then be that teachers' agendas for teaching differ from learners' self-teaching agendas, and that "learning" (in the sense of a mental event) is relatable to learners' self-teaching rather than to teachers' teaching.

Let me now go on to a third possible reason why learning cannot be the obverse of teaching. This takes its cue from Brumfit's point about learning being internal to the learner's mind, and considers the possible nature of that mental phenomenon. Learning, as we have noted, can happen with or without a teacher's teaching. It can also happen with or without the learner's intention or conscious effort, or even willingness. Neither the teacher nor the learner can tell whether it will happen or not, or even know whether it is happening or not at a given point of time. It is something that happens, not something that is done. We can only recognise it after it has happened, from the resultant ability or behaviour of the learner, and, based on our experience of recognising similar happenings in different learners, we can sometimes say what sort of learning is likely to happen if and when it happens. What makes it happen is completely internal to the learner's mind, therefore completely inaccessible to us. Further, it may be the case that nothing is certain to make it happen even within the learner's mind; the happening (which we can conceive of variously as a connection being made, a pattern being formed, a reorganisation taking place, etc.) may be a matter of probability or chance. Learning, that is to say, is essentially an accident. It is an accident as far as our knowledge as teachers or self-teachers goes; it may also be an accident more inherently—a truly chance phenomenon in the mind, subject at most to a degree of probability. Seen this way, learning is similar to a thought, idea or image arising in our minds. We cannot make an idea arise, or tell when or whether it will arise; we can only recognise it after it arises. The arising of an idea is an accident, as far as we can tell and perhaps also by the very nature of that phenomenon. I am suggesting that learning as a mental event is similar to the occurrence of ideas, images and thoughts—beyond our conscious control and probably a matter of chance by its very nature.

Learning is also an individual phenomenon, varying from one learner to another in terms of the time at which it happens, the pace at which it progresses and the stage which it reaches either over a given period or ultimately. This is in a sense obvious, in that we know from experience that no instance of teaching leads to the same learning, or non-learning, in all the learners. Learning happens in some learners at some points of time, and does not in others. It happens more often in one learner and less in another, or more often over one stretch of time than over another. No group of learners ends up with the same amount of learning, even though the teaching has been the same. It is common to attribute this variation to such things as the learners' varied backgrounds, varied levels of motivation, varied learning styles, etc., but the point we have just made about the accidental nature of learning provides a different—I think more natural—explanation of it. If learning is inherently a chance phenomenon in the mind, it follows that its occurrence will vary from one mind to another, from one time to another, etc., in a way that is unpredictable and unexplainable in terms of other factors. Differential learning need not be the result of differences between individuals; it can simply be due to the fact that there can be no consistency where accident and chance are involved.

Learning is not just an individual event; it is a personal—in some sense "private"—event. I have already likened the occurrence of learning to the occurrence of an idea in the mind. When one is looking for an idea, one is in a state of uncertainty about whether or not the search will be successful; the more intently one is looking the more acute is the uncertainty, amounting to a state of vulnerability. Something like this is true of the occurrence of learning: there is always an accompanying uncertainty or sense of risk, especially when there is an effort being made to learn, and a corresponding expectation or hope that learning will occur. Also, when a piece of learning or an idea does arise—or, rather, when there is a recognition of its having occurred—there is a moment of intense intellectual pleasure or satisfaction, which is entirely personal and private in that it is independent of any recognition or reward from outside. It is facts such as these—that there is a state of insecurity and vulnerability when a piece of learning is being looked for or hoped for, and there is a feeling of intellectual fulfillment when a piece of learning is seen to have occurred—that make us regard learning as a personal and private event. Neither the sense of vulnerability nor the feeling of fulfillment is open to a sharing with others; indeed, they are states of mind which react negatively to intrusion from others, thus making the occurrence of learning less likely to occur.

Learning, then, is accidental, individual and private—the opposite of teaching which is deliberate, public and most often directed to groups. Not only are teaching and learning separate, but they have characteristics which firmly rule out their being two sides of the same event.

And yet, learning does occur when teaching is done, or occurs much more than if no teaching is done. No one would doubt that, other things being roughly equal, a group of learners who are taught a language will learn some of that language while another group which receives no teaching will learn none. The conclusion to be drawn from our discussion of the difference between teaching and learning is not that teaching does not help learning. The conclusion is only that specific pieces of teaching cannot be expected to bring about corresponding pieces of learning, and that teaching in general can only help to promote learning overall—perhaps by creating some conditions which increase the probability of the occurrence of learning.

This has implications for the way we discuss teaching and the direction of our effort to develop better teaching. It is in general futile to try to match teaching to learning more and more precisely, or to prefer one form of teaching over another on the grounds that it provides a more direct (or more perceptible) route to learning. Teaching can only help learning indirectly and as a general, overall support. We need to accept that we can have no direct access to or influence on learning whatever form of teaching we may do, and then ask if there are certain things which are nevertheless more of a support to learning than others and, equally, if there are things which are likely to be unhelpful. I will draw attention to one or two such things in the rest of this paper.

Let us consider syllabuses. A language teaching syllabus is thought to be a specification of what is to be taught and learnt, that is to say, what learning is to be caused by the teaching. It is not a specification of what the teacher is to do, indicating the teaching activities or procedures to be employed; it is a statement of what the learner is to learn, that is to say, what is to happen to the learner. What the teacher is to do is thought to be a matter of methodology, quite distinct from a syllabus. A syllabus, it is argued, has to indicate what the learning outcome or "content" is to be, both overall and in relation to each part or unit of teaching. But such a "content syllabus" (as it is often called) assumes implicitly that learning outcomes can be specified in advance of teaching, and that specific pieces of learning can be brought about by specific units of teaching. This assumption is so prevalent and so firmly set in the profession that any proposal for a procedural syllabus, specifying teaching activities instead of learning outcomes, is resisted or rejected, sometimes painstakingly (for example Widdowson, 1990, pp. 144–150). A procedural syllabus is, however, much more in line with the observations we have made about the nature of learning and the possible relationship between learning and teaching. A content syllabus is at best a form of pedagogic delusion.

There is also a form of pedagogic idealism which claims to increase the efficiency and accountability of teaching by targeting it more and more precisely, and minutely, to expected learning. It advocates specific objectives for all teaching—the more specific, and clearly specified, the better. Each little piece of teaching should be carried out with a corresponding piece of learning clearly in mind, and evidence on the achievement of the piece of learning is to be sought as soon after the teaching as possible. This can be an effective way of promoting the teaching enterprise either in the eyes of the public or with people like sponsors and clients, but it is so unrealistic that the only way of sustaining it is by reducing learning to some form of intentional activity (for example, memorisation or recall of facts or statements; repetition of a rehearsed piece of behaviour) or by telling the learners themselves what they are going to learn, what they are learning or what they have just learnt, at every stage—that is to say, by making the learners partners in the pedagogic delusion.

One effect of a preoccupation with expected learning outcomes is that it prevents one from recognising unexpected outcomes when they occur. I have argued that teaching is in no position to predict specific learning, but that does not mean that learning does not occur, unpredictably, when teaching is done. A great deal of learning does in fact happen in this way—so much so that I think the bulk of what gets learnt, and perhaps the most important elements of it, constitute such incidental, untargeted learning, triggered by the general condition of teaching rather than aimed at specifically by it. As Newmark (1966) put it some thirty years ago, "if each phonological and syntactic rule, each complex of lexical features, each semantic value and stylistic nuance had to be acquired one at a time ... the child learner would be old before he could say a single appropriate thing, and the adult learner would be dead". Learning is so normal and natural to human beings (in particular, language learning) that it happens all the time. If it cannot be directly caused, it cannot be stopped either. We tend not to see it as teachers only because we tend to be over-focused on the pieces of learning we aim to bring about. If we reduced the focus on such expected learning, we will perhaps begin to see more of the unexpected, incidental learning that occurs.

Not only does teaching help to bring about learning, in some general and indirect way, but it is also very likely that one form of teaching helps more than another. We are familiar with the sad story of method-comparison research in the past, which based itself on what learning was specifically aimed at by each form of teaching. It was assumed, in fact, that the more specifically teaching was related to learning, the more dependable or revealing the comparison would be. But there is a different way of approaching the matter. If learning is normal and natural, given some general condition, one can ask what the norms of the phenomenon are. How much learning can be expected, for example, from certain (sizeable) quantities of exposure to, or contact with, the language? A careful pursuit of this question can hopefully lead to a broad specification of the level of learning (more likely, levels over a certain range) that can be regarded as the norm—in a way comparable to the norms of IQ in relation to a young person's age. The availability of such norms would make it possible to judge particular forms of teaching over fairly large stretches of time. It would also, from another point of view, stop us from setting educational goals too ambitiously. There is at present no usable basis for indicating possible attainment levels for language teaching programmes: attainment levels are set wishfully, rather than knowledgeably, sometimes to please the powers-that-be or under pressure from them. Such unrealistic targets can have the same kind of effect as over-specific objectives, namely, a substitution of the appearance of learning for actual learning.

Developmental norms for language learning can help us make what may be called macro-judgements about forms of teaching. But the daily act of teaching calls for a variety of micro-judgements about one or another aspect of the ongoing teaching activity. These judgements cannot be based on whether or not particular teaching activities result in particular learning outcomes, as teaching cannot be related to learning in that way. The micro-judgements need to be guided, instead, by what may be called the teacher's cumulative experience and, arising from it, an evolving feel for the occurrence of learning. Perhaps when teaching is free of the blinkering effects of a content syllabus and the negative effects of over-specific objectives, teachers in the classroom will be able to recognise, in an intuitive way, more and more of the learning that takes place in learners as a general effect of the teaching being done. Perhaps, too, these small-scale intuitive judgements at the classroom level and the larger-scale judgements to be made in relation to developmental norms will together (and in interaction with each other) give us the best basis we can have for preferring one form of teaching to another.

Let me conclude with a brief, point-form summary of my argument:

1. Teaching and learning cannot be related to each other directly or specifically, as they are very different kinds of event.
2. But teaching does help to bring about learning in a general way, and it is likely that one form of teaching does this more than another.
3. We therefore need to explore ways of organising teaching without making assumptions of a specific relationship between teaching and learning, and also ways of making judgements about different forms of teaching.
4. Such exploration leads us to propose that teaching needs to use a procedural rather than a content syllabus, and needs to avoid specific objectives. It also needs to have some developmental norms to relate itself to, and a larger scope for the teacher to exercise intuitive judgements.

Proposals such as these do not aim to make learning more directly relatable to teaching; they try, instead, to be consistent with the fact that the two are not directly relatable. Given the wide difference between the nature of teaching and that of learning, teaching will always be a matter of hoping for learning to occur, rather than of making it occur.

References

Allwright, R. L. (1984). Why don't learners learn what teachers teach? In D. M. Singleton and D. G. Little (Eds.), *Language learning in formal and informal contexts* (pp. 3–18). Dublin: Irish Association for Applied Linguistics.

Brumfit, C. J. (1984). *Communicative methodology in language teaching.* Cambridge: Cambridge University Press.

Newmark, Leonard. (1979). How not to interfere with language learning. In C. J. Brumfit and K. Johnson (Eds.), *The communicative approach to language teaching* (pp. 160–66). Oxford: Oxford University Press.

Widdowson, H. G. (1990). *Aspects of language teaching.* Oxford: Oxford University Press.

21

Should Materials be Prescribed?

Projects of English Language Teaching reform often concentrate their energies on the design, construction and classroom implementation of a new set of teaching materials. There are several good reasons for this practice. Since teaching, for most teachers, is a matter of taking learners through the materials prescribed, the prescription of a new (and different) set of materials is most likely to make teachers change their teaching procedures as demanded by the new materials. New materials can thus act as a powerful instrument of change in classroom teaching. Materials are also a good, concrete way of capturing, representing or demonstrating the nature and content of the reform being attempted, much preferable to more general or abstract statements which do not translate directly into classroom action. Besides, the construction of a new set of materials is a conveniently project-like activity: it enables a relatively small group of people to play a leadership role, to receive specific training as necessary, to interact, collaborate and divide the labour involved among themselves, and to take the work through a series of planned stages over a period of time. The outcome of this work then becomes available for use in a large number of classrooms, to the benefit (it is thought) of a vast number of learners.

Traditionally, prescribed materials, or textbooks, have been playing a pervasive role in the teaching of English: they are taken to represent the specification of curricula or syllabi, to indicate

---

This essay was first published in 2000. *Source:* Prabhu, N. S. (2000). Should materials be prescribed? In Rama Mathew, R Lalitha Eapen, Jacob Tharu (Eds.), *The Language Curriculum: Dynamics of Change. Volume 1: The Outsider Perspective* (pp. 22–27). Hyderabad: Orient Longman.

what teachers are to do in their classrooms, and to embody what learners are to master for passing their examinations. When new projects which aim to change curricula, classroom procedures and examinations also give a central role to teaching materials, albeit for different reasons, the traditional importance of prescribed materials receives considerable reinforcement.

I believe that this is a situation that can shut our eye to the possible disadvantages of prescribing materials, whether traditional or reformist. I will therefore try to bring together in what follows different arguments, as I see them, against prescribed materials. I take the term "prescribed" to mean either that the materials are directly linked to examinations (constituting their "content"), or that a large number of schools and classrooms are to use the same set of materials (or, as often is the case, both).

De-linking Textbooks and Examinations

The first argument has to do with the first sense of the term "prescribed" and it is quite straightforward. When exams demand a knowledge of the specific content of textbooks, whether it be the topic content of the reading materials provided or the language content of particular exercises/explanations of structural/lexical items, they often lead to learners attempting to memorise the specific content concerned, instead of using that content to improve their general ability to handle other such content. Thus, when examinations call for essays on the topic content of textbooks, students tend to obtain prepared essays of that kind and rote-learn them for reproduction at the examination. When exams call for some of the grammar rules, word meanings, error corrections, etc. that are included in the textbooks, students tend to commit to memory as many of the rules, word meanings, etc. as possible, for a similar reproduction. Where such practice is widespread and long-lasting, as it has been in India, an entire market develops for providing students with prepared essays, lists of language items, etc. all based on the prescribed textbooks.

Once this happens, textbooks lose their crucial function of helping to develop in learners a general language ability with which they can handle a wider range of topic content or language items than has been dealt with in the textbooks; and exams lose their crucial function of assessing the extent to which particular learners have developed such a general ability. Worse, both textbooks and exams are able to maintain a pretense of fulfilling those crucial functions while actually subverting them by encouraging a reliance on memory and reproduction.

In this situation, it is necessary to break the direct link between textbooks and exams, by basing the latter on reading materials and/or language exercises that are "unseen", that is to say, not in the textbooks, though of the same kind as those in the textbooks. This renders memorisation a useless procedure, and is likely to restore to textbooks and examinations their central roles of developing and accessing such general language abilities as reading with understanding, writing with a sense of purpose and precision, or manipulating words and sentences with a feel for linguistic accuracy.

When teaching materials are thus de-linked from exams, they cease to be "prescribed" in the sense of constituting the content of exams. Their role now is to help students develop the kinds of general ability that are demanded by exams. Further, since different sets of materials may provide alternative means of developing the same general abilities, and besides, one set of materials may be better suited than another to a particular set of students (for any of a variety of reasons), it becomes possible/desirable for different classrooms to be using different sets of materials, and the materials, as a result, become no longer "prescribed" in the second sense of the term. On this argument, then, teaching materials should not be prescribed because, if they are, students will tend to memorise content instead of building up general abilities, and examinations tend to lose their validity as assessments of general abilities.

Distance between Teaching Input and Learner's Investment

Let me now go on to a second argument against prescribing materials. The widely held view that it is good for a large number of classrooms to be using the same set of materials is based on a certain concept of quality in materials and the belief that, all other things apart, learning is bound to benefit from materials of good quality. Quality in materials is thought of in terms of how well-refined they are as inputs to the learner: how carefully (systematically, knowledgeably, comprehensively, etc.) the pieces of language to be presented to the learner are selected, how thoughtfully (ingeniously, consistently, inter-connectedly etc.) the activities to be undertaken by the learner are designed and specified, and how helpfully (usably, gradedly, cyclically, etc.) the different inputs and activities are sequenced. Such input-refinement requires a level of specialised knowledge—of the language, of learning processes, of the learner, of the teaching conditions, of past instructional successes/failures, and so on—and the practice of prescribing materials makes it possible for a large number of classrooms to benefit from the work of a small number of specialists. By the same token, it becomes necessary to ensure that the large number of teachers teaching in those classrooms are sufficiently trained to use the materials in the way intended, without tampering with them and thereby causing a loss of their quality.

There is, however, another concept of quality in materials, which does not depend so much on specialised knowledge and does not assume that learning improves with a refinement of inputs. Learning can be seen not as a process of the learner receiving and assimilating inputs, but rather of the learner "investing" (deploying, exploiting, bringing to bear) his/her existing knowledge and ability in an effort to deal with the input. When the knowledge/ability needed to deal with the input is a little beyond what the learner is able to invest, there is what may be called an interaction between the input and the interaction—an effort by the learner to connect the two, by stretching his/her current knowledge/ability to the level called for by the input. This interaction can happen only when the distance between the input and the investment is an appropriate, "bridgeable" one—neither too large (thus making it impossible for the learner to connect the two, whatever effort he/she makes) nor too small (thus requiring little or no effort, that is to say, no stretching of existing knowledge/ability). Learning takes place only when investment and input are in appropriate proximity—within what Vygotsky (1978, p. 86) called "the zone of proximal development". There can be little learning when the input is either too far from the learner's current resources or not far enough from them, no matter how highly refined (well-selected, well-designed, well-sequenced) the input may be by itself.

Given this view, it is not enough to refine inputs on the strength of a specialised knowledge of the language, learning processes, the learner and the teaching conditions; what is crucially needed is a judgement about what the learners' current state is and what input they are likely to find difficult but manageable with an effort. Now this is a judgement that is much better exercised by each classroom teacher in the course of his/her teaching, than by a small group of specialists in advance of the teaching, for at least three reasons. First, learners are varied in their knowledge/ability, at any given time, in any teaching situation—just as all human beings are, in any field of activity. They are varied within any given classroom and are likely to be more varied between classrooms, between schools, between different places, etc. Any team of specialists constructing materials for use in a large number of classrooms will have to be guided by some perception of the "average" learner's knowledge/ability—an average which, by its very nature, will not represent any individual and will differ more from individuals as it ranges over larger populations. In contrast to this, particular classroom teachers need to make judgements only about the particular groups of students they teach, with much smaller variation within each group, and can therefore work with a more matching average in mind. Further, classroom teachers can modify their judgements, as frequently as necessary, in the light of the actual evidence they get of learners' ability to cope, whereas specialist writers of materials can only make the judgement once, based on all the evidence or information available at that time. Though specialists may well be better at making judgements, drawing on their specialised knowledge, classroom teachers have less difficult judgements to make, in that the judgements are about much smaller groups of learners, and, in addition, they have opportunities to adjust and improve their judgements repeatedly through a process of trial and error. Inputs to learners are more likely to achieve the desired proximity to learners' states from classroom teachers' judgements than from specialists' judgements.

Secondly, learners' states are not static; they change with every successful piece of learning. An input which achieves appropriate proximity to a learner's state at a certain time has the effect of bringing about a certain amount of learning at that time. As a result of this, the learner's state changes and now requires input at a slightly different level to bring about the next piece of learning. At the same time, it is impossible to predict with any certainty at any time what input will in fact achieve appropriate proximity to a learner's state and promote the relevant learning. However well-judged the inputs are, predictions of successful learning are at best probabilistic. Learning can at best be observed (or sensed) when it happens; it cannot be presumed to happen in response to some piece of teaching. This means that learners' states need to be reassessed continually in the course of the teaching, not only because the teacher's earlier assessment may have been wrong, but, equally, because that earlier assessment may have been right and the learners' state may as a result have changed. Reassessment for this latter reason, too, is better made by classroom teachers as part of their teaching than by a team of specialists in advance of the teaching. A team of specialists can at best incorporate one or more forms of grading in the materials, thus providing for successive learner states resulting from earlier learning, but this necessarily involves a presumption of specific pieces of learning from specific pieces of teaching, repeatedly over the stretch of time that the materials are meant to provide for.

Thirdly, making pedagogic judgements—judgements about learners' current state, about what input might constitute an appropriate challenge in that state and about whether some piece of learning has or has not taken place after the teaching done—is (or ought to be) the central part of practising the profession of teaching (since it is central to the promotion of learning), and the development of an ability to make such judgements is what constitutes the teacher's professional growth. An ability to make such judgements can develop only in the process of an actual effort to make them, to revise them in the light of their results, and to make them again with the advantage of the earlier experience. Now the prescription of a set of materials prepared by specialists is really an attempt to preclude or at least to reduce the need for teachers' judgements about learners' state, etc., on the grounds that many, most or all teachers are less than good (or less good than specialists) in their ability to make such judgements. But teachers' ability to make such judgements can, as just noted, develop and become more adequate only to the extent that their classroom teaching calls for the exercise of that ability repeatedly. Indeed, the lower the current level of the ability, the greater the need for teachers to be making the judgements. From this point of view, the prescription of materials is a very short-sighted response to teachers' low professional competence; far from helping to improve that low competence, it can be said to ensure that the competence continues to be low.

The three reasons outlined above do not necessarily lead to a denial of any role for specialist-level preparation of materials for use on a wide scale. They do, however, demand a role for teacher judgements and decisions in what specific pieces of material (that is to say, input) are used in different classrooms at different points of time. This means that specialist-level materials should attempt not to pre-empt teacher-level judgements and decisions by laying down a uniform set of specific inputs but, on the contrary, to permit, provide for or require judgements and decisions as part of the daily teaching done by teachers. We can perhaps make a distinction here between "course" materials, which consist of a specification of all and only the inputs to be made to learners in all classrooms, and "source" materials, which deliberately demand further work (in the form of choices, changes, adjustments and specific shapings) before they are used in any classroom. Source materials can be regarded as a kind of half-way house between teacher-made materials (which leave to classroom teachers all the decisions and judgements but which also require of them a great deal of time-consuming work as well as some specialist level knowledge) and "teacher-proof" materials (which leave little or no room for teachers' decisions and judgements, trying instead to prevent them) (Allwright, 1981). If we take seriously the points made above about learning resulting from an optimal distance between teaching inputs and learner states, and about learner states being necessarily varied and unpredictably changeable, it is source materials that specialists should design and produce, not course materials. There needs to be a good deal of exploration and experimentation about possible or desirable forms of such materials but, very broadly, they can either be "semi-materials", being less than fully prepared/specified for classroom use, to different extents, or "meta-materials", being essentially guidelines or frames for the preparation of materials, in different forms (or, of course, some combination of the two). Whatever form they take, they will not represent a set of inputs to be made uniformly to a large number of learners; they will, instead, ensure that different (groups of) learners receive different inputs as decided by their teachers. In this sense, source materials cannot act as prescribed materials; at most, they can be a prescribed (that is to say, uniform) source of the different materials to be used in different classrooms.

Teaching and the Teacher's Sense of Plausibility

We can now go on to the third argument against materials being prescribed. This has to do with the nature of the theory that guides or influences one's decisions and actions in language pedagogy—

broadly, the theory (or conceptualisation) of how language learning takes place and how that learning is caused, furthered or hindered by one or another form of teaching. It is generally thought that such theory is, or ought to be, scientific in nature, that is to say, justified or supported by objective observation or evidence, through explicit/agreed forms of reasoning. The theory, that is to say, is thought to be a form of objective knowledge resulting from agreed forms of research—knowledge that is explicitly stated, empirically supported, rationally justified, publicly debated (among researchers), etc. and is therefore valid or true independently of the persons proposing, espousing or applying it. A theory about language learning and teaching that can claim to be true or valid in this sense can, it is thought, best be the basis of what very many teachers do in very many classrooms and therefore the basis of materials meant for widespread classroom use.

It is, however, possible to think of a different kind of theory that can and often does operate in language teaching. This is a personal sense or feel in a teacher for the occurrence of learning and for links between the teaching being done and the learning being promoted (or not being promoted) by it, in the classroom. The classroom teacher is someone who is constantly in touch with the actual phenomenon of learning, through his/her physical presence at the site of the phenomenon (taking place in different learners at different times, in several learners at one time, in a few learners at another time, etc.), through his/her being involved in the different classroom activities which trigger (or fail to trigger) the phenomenon, and through his/her having a direct interest in detecting, assessing and increasing the phenomenon. As in many other professions, a form of practitioner's intuition develops, over time, about the phenomenon one is dealing with, quite distinctly from the body of professional knowledge one may have acquired in order to practice the profession. Such intuition can be regarded as a personal understanding of the phenomenon, an inexplicit theory or unarticulated knowledge. It is also knowledge that is continuously in the making, as it were, since it not only influences what one does (and how one sees it) in any given act of teaching but is itself influenced by what goes on (and how one sees it) in that act, thus perhaps changing a little in the process. Compared to theory as scientific knowledge, which is explicit, objective and sufficiently stable to be publicly debated or disseminated, this intuition of the teacher is undefined, subjective and changeable all the time. It may be best to refer to it not as theory or knowledge but as a sense of plausibility, an individual's perception that is persuasive (at a given time) to the individual concerned.

Any materials prepared by specialists are necessarily based on (or guided or influenced by) some theory of learning and teaching, and a prescription of those materials for many teachers' use must imply that all of those teachers are to act in their classrooms on the basis of that theory. But the theory (however good or sound it may be in its own, scientific terms) is unlikely to be in harmony with different teachers' differing senses of plausibility, except at most by rare coincidence in a few cases. There will thus be a mismatch, in most if not all cases, between the classroom teacher's individual sense of plausibility and the theory that the prescribed materials incorporate. In order to use the prescribed materials as intended, individual teachers have to suppress or suspend their own feel for the nature of learning (or fail to develop it in the first place). Seen in this light, the prescription of materials involves a heavy reliance on knowledge as scientific theory, to the point of denying or dismissing the value of the individual teacher's sense of plausibility and of trusting the physical activity in the classroom envisaged by the prescribed materials to bring about the expected learning. If, instead, we give value to each teacher's individual sense of plausibility, recognising its validity for that teacher's act of teaching, any classroom activity that is carried out merely because it is demanded by some prescribed materials, that is to say, in dissociation of the teacher's own perception, is mechanical in nature—merely a prescribed routine. There is thus a stark choice to be made between teaching as a mechanical activity and teaching as an activity meaningful to the teacher concerned (that is to say, in consonance with his/her sense of plausibility), and the prescription of materials can only promote the former. If the latter is to be promoted, each teacher needs to be free (indeed, called upon, obliged) to tap his/her personal sense of plausibility in making at least some of the decisions and judgements involved in the act of teaching, including judgements in the choice, form and level of the materials employed.

This does not imply any claim that all or most teachers possess a sufficiently developed personal pedagogic perception to draw on in their choices, decisions and judgements in the classroom. The claim, rather, is that teaching in the classroom derives its value from the fact, and extent, of the teacher's own professional involvement in it (in the form of an exercise of judgement based on a personal sense of plausibility) and that the teacher's ability to carry out such teaching can grow and strengthen itself only if there is repeated opportunity (or need) for the exercise of judgement in the classroom. The development of a teacher's sense of plausibility, and his/her ability to engage it in the act of teaching, can be helped if the teacher is allowed (or called on) to make the various judgements involved in the preparation (or completion or adaptation) of the materials to be used in the classroom (thus evolving, over time, a personal set of materials which are in harmony with his/her personal sense of plausibility and which will grow or change as the sense of plausibility does); it is ignored, suppressed or hindered if a set of fully-prepared materials is prescribed for all teachers' use.

Let me now conclude by referring briefly to the three arguments put forth against the prescription of materials. Prescribed materials often have a direct link with examinations, which tend to encourage memorisation by learners rather than the development of a general ability in them, thus undermining the value of both the materials and the examinations. Prescribed materials also represent judgements, made in advance of the teaching, about what the learners' levels are at different stages of the teaching—judgements which are much better made by individual teachers in the course of their teaching and in relation to the particular classes they teach.

Finally, the prescription of materials necessarily leads to mechanical teaching by teachers and comes in the way of a development in each teacher of a personal sense of plausibility about the phenomenon of learning and its relation to teaching.

References

Allwright, R. L. (1981). What do we want teaching materials for? *ELT Journal*, 36(1), 5–18.

Vygotsky, L. S. (1978). *Mind in society: The development of higher psychological processes.* Cambridge: Harvard University Press.

22

Ideation and Ideology

In this paper, I make a distinction between two forms of intellectual activity and argue that it is important for us in the field of language pedagogy to bear that distinction in mind so that each form of activity can be pursued with greater clarity and integrity. I call the two forms of thought ideation and ideology.

I emphasise their distinctness from each other because there seems to me to be a steady blurring of the difference in much academic discussion at this time. By ideation, I mean the process of developing ideas or concepts with which we can gain an understanding of the nature of the world we live in. Ideation is knowledge-construction. We try to understand some observable entity or phenomenon by forming a conceptual model of it, that is to say, by conceiving of possible properties, processes and mechanisms which can account for what is observed. The basic motive for such model-making is a fundamental need of the human mind—the need to make sense of the world one is living in, to have an understanding (or at any rate to be able to feel that one has an understanding) of the many puzzling entities and events one sees or experiences around one.

The human being, it appears, needs to have an idea of what the world is like and how he or she relates to it. One writer (Judson, 1985) has referred to this as "the rage to know"—an instinctive, insistent demand of the human mind which has been at work throughout human history. Perhaps it is an inner urge to puzzle

---

This essay was first published in 2002. *Source*: Prabhu, N. S. (2002). Ideation and ideology. In S. C. Chaudhury (Ed.), *Teaching English in non-native contexts: Essays presented to V. Saraswathi* (pp. 12–22). Chennai: Prof. V. Saraswathi Felicitation Committee.

things out and solve problems; or perhaps it is a response to the threatening nature of what one does not understand, a deep-seated fear of the unknown.

The conceptual model that is created and found to be satisfying—that is to say, able to account for the relevant phenomena in a way persuasive to many people—is what we call knowledge. Knowing something is having a satisfying concept of the way it is made, the way it works, etc. Ideation is thus a matter of developing conceptual models and testing their power to satisfy.

Knowledge, seen in this way, is not the same as truth, if truth is thought to be some absolute or ultimate reality. Knowledge is changeable, and is in fact, in the process of change all or much of the time.

A conceptualisation that is found to be satisfying today may no longer be satisfying tomorrow, either because there is more to account for than can be done by it, or because there is some other conceptualisation which provides a better account. Further, not only does knowledge change, but our notion of what constitutes knowledge, and when knowledge does or does not account for phenomena, also changes over time.

We have had conceptualisations of supernatural beings, forces, injunctions, etc., to which natural phenomena can be attributed. We have also had conceptualisations of certain sources from which knowledge ensues, the conceived superiority of the source ensuring the authenticity of the knowledge involved. Today we have conceptualisations of natural forces, logical relations, the laws of nature, etc. which account for phenomena as their rational consequences. It is entirely possible that there will be other, quite different conceptualisations in the future, which will be regarded as knowledge.

In speaking of ideation, therefore, we are speaking not of a particular form of knowledge but of the more general processes, which lead to knowledge in different forms at different times. What distinguishes ideation is that it is a search for knowledge—an effort to gain understanding in response to an inner need of the mind.

In contrast, ideology is a matter of pursuing certain ideals or, more precisely, attempting to bring about a better state of affairs in the world. It is based on notions of what is right, just or desirable in human society, and it is driven by a wish to change the existing state of affairs to something better. It is activity devoted to a cause, supported by a sense of conviction or faith in that cause. Perhaps, this too can be regarded as a fundamental human urge—to conceive of an alternative to what exists, and to strive to make that alternative a reality.

While ideation is concerned with understanding the world, ideology is concerned with changing it for the better. If ideation is driven by a rage to know, ideology is driven by a rage to reform or improve. As with ideation, ideology too can take different forms and change from time to time. There have been ideologies of achieving order and stability in human society by defining or imposing a hierarchy among people. There have also been ideologies of organising human societies in accordance with what is believed to be divine will or intention.

Today, we have the ideologies of equality between human beings, universal human rights, protection of the environment, etc. There will no doubt be other ideologies in times to come. It is interesting to recall that, in his study of a child's acquisition of language, Halliday (1975) identified a very early stage when the child had not acquired any language in the ordinary sense of the term but was nevertheless using sound as a vehicle of meaning, in what Halliday terms a "protolanguage". At this stage of development, Halliday could see two distinct functions or purposes to the child's use of sound as symbol. One is what Halliday calls the "mathetic" function, that is, learning, thinking and making sense about the world; and the other is what he calls the "pragmatic" function, that is, doing things that one wants to do, getting things that one wants to have, or making others do things for one. The mathetic function is "language as reflection", as Halliday puts it, while the pragmatic function is "language as action". The protolanguage is used by the child either as "a means of learning about reality" or as "a means of acting on reality" (p. 7). Halliday elsewhere makes the generalisation that "every human language is a potential for meaning in these two ways—it is a resource for doing with; and it is a resource for thinking with" (1985, p. 7). What Halliday calls the mathetic function in a child's protolanguage is very close to what we are calling ideation—in fact, Halliday's model of grammar for normal, adult language has a related macro-function which is named the "ideational" function. What we are calling ideology is a part of the child's pragmatic function, or rather an offshoot of it.

Ideology arises when the child moves on from wanting things for itself and wanting others to do things for it to the stage of wanting the world to be in a certain state and wanting to do things to bring about that state. Halliday's analysis thus indicates that ideation and ideology are basically different functions and that the differentiation starts very early in human linguistic development.

How does the distinction between ideation and ideology look from the point of view of what is referred to as formal linguistics as against Halliday's functional linguistics? The distinction is relatable here to linguistic competence as a mental phenomenon and language as a social phenomenon. It is thought that human beings are endowed with a specific capacity for language, that is to say, a specific set of expectations, options, constraints, etc., on the strength of which each child is able to construct in its own mind the complex grammar of the language it is exposed to. Grammar is a system of rules or relations that operates in each individual's mind and enables that individual to use the language grammatically and tell grammatical from ungrammatical sentences.

Language seen as grammar (that is, grammatical competence) is therefore an individual possession. But the individual is not self-contained in developing grammatical competence. The innate capacity for language needs to be activated and provided with language data for grammatical competence to emerge. That is to say, the individual needs to engage in interaction—try to understand others, try to put things across to others, and try to work out what the world is about—so as to acquire the language of the community around. There is thus a necessary social side to the development of grammatical competence, even though grammatical competence is an individual rather than a social possession.

There is of course more to language than grammatical competence. There are conventions of appropriacy in the choice and use of language forms, conventions which are developed and shared by the language community and are therefore a social possession. There are also traces and impressions of social and political events, arrangements, attitudes, beliefs, etc., carried by language forms, constituting something like a cumulative history of the speech community.

Language is a carrier of evidence about the community's sociopolitical past, and acts as a vehicle of expression for the sociopolitical forces currently at work. It maintains a record of the thoughts and deeds of its speakers. One dimension of language, therefore, is that it is a formal grammatical system in the minds of individual speakers. Another dimension is that it is a carrier of evidence about the sociopolitical workings of the community in which it is spoken. The first is relatable to ideation; the second to ideology. Formal grammar reveals language as a complex means of representing the numerous entities of the world and the varied relations between them. This is essentially a representation of the world as objective, impersonal phenomena; and it is close to the way we try to conceptualise phenomena in the world in an effort to understand them—by identifying or visualising entities, processes and relations in an objective, impersonal way.

Language as an indicator of sociopolitical workings, on the other hand, reveals the many subjective beliefs, attitudes, biases and discriminations that have prevailed in the community and continue to be at play. Language is witness to the different forms of dominance and suppression that the community has experienced; and language has itself been an instrument of some forms of domination and suppression (as when one language or accent is projected as being superior to another). This is a clear stimulus to ideology, evoking a sense of outrage at social injustice, and a strong desire to help make human communities more just and equal.

Although the outrage is at the injustices, rather than at their reflection in language, language too is perceived to play a role in the matter by transmitting, in more or less covert ways, the beliefs and biases that lie behind the injustices to successive generations of speakers and thus helping to perpetuate them. Ideology seeks to make these covert workings overt, so that the injustices can be seen for what they are and fought against more widely. The dominance and suppression in society arise from an unequal distribution of sociopolitical power, and ideology's aim is to increase the power of the less powerful so as to make the distribution more equal.

Power is thus a central concern in ideology. But there is more than one kind of power and power of a different kind is of relevance to ideation. As we have noted, ideation is concerned with ideas of what the world is like, and a variety of ideas arise, or are developed, as competing accounts of the same phenomenon. Some ideas, however, turn out to be more powerful than others—more persuasive, either intuitively or rationally, better supported by observation or experience, more successful in experimental testing or more consistent with other ideas about other phenomena.

Ideas, that is to say, have power, and some ideas have more power than others. The knowledge we possess of the world at any given time can be said to consist of the most successful (or most powerful) ideas available at that time. But this power of ideas is very different from the sociopolitical power of people in a society. The latter is ultimately physical or material power, which works on the strength of fear, unlike the power of ideas which works on the strength of intellectual appeal and response. Both kinds of power have operated widely in the world. The ideas of the European classical world, ancient India's Buddhist philosophy, Arabic art and learning, and the inventions of ancient China have all travelled across large parts of the world influencing people's minds and replacing earlier understandings of the world with new ones; and the more recent knowledge from science and philosophy in Europe and the United States has been so successful that it constitutes the curriculum of formal education today in all parts of the world.

The other kind of power too has stalked the world in the form of military conquest, colonisation, and dictatorial rule, discrimination based on rigid hierarchies, etc., as we all know. We are indeed so conscious of the prevalence of this material power that we do not always remember the power of ideas, thoughts or theories that operates in the field of ideation. Notice, incidentally, that the two kinds of power are of relevance within ideology itself. Ideology deals with sociopolitical power, in that it desires to reveal and reverse the unjust effects of an unequal distribution of such power. But ideology also aims to make other people see those effects as being unjust and to share with them the desire to reveal and reverse them.

Ideology, that is to say, is a particular perception of the working of society and a particular line of thought about what needs to be done. This perception and line of thought have their persuasive power which is what draws other people to it. The power involved here is the ability to appeal to other minds and evoke a response in them, as with the power of ideas and unlike sociopolitical power. Further, there can clearly be ideologies of different kinds, all similarly seeking to influence people's minds. The fact that one particular ideology—that based on a perception of unequal power and a desire to redress it—is more widely shared and more successful than many others is evidence that it has more persuasive power than the others. Ideologies, too, are unequal in the power they possess.

The distinction between the power of ideas and sociopolitical power is important because a non-recognition of it can lead to some strange claims and conclusions. It is sometimes claimed, for instance, that all knowledge is interested, meaning that the power behind successful ideas and theories is the same as sociopolitical power, wielded by those who produce or promote such ideas and theories. Now, it is true that human beings are power-seeking creatures, and those who are involved in the ideational endeavour are as human as anybody else. It should be no surprise, therefore, if those who produce ideas and theories have their power-seeking or self-seeking side, and if some of them have used the success of their ideas to gain sociopolitical status or power.

It is also normal for those ideas that are specially successful to earn professional or public respect for their progenitors, and quite often fame and status with it. But none of this is evidence that the success of ideas in the field of knowledge is in general due to the workings of sociopolitical power, or that there is no power to ideas other than the sociopolitical power of those who produce them. If we find that a single individual has produced an idea of power and also wielded sociopolitical power, it does not follow that there is only a single form of power. Nor does it follow from the fact that successful ideas can lead to sociopolitical power that sociopolitical power is what leads to successful ideas.

The two kinds of power are very different, even though they may coexist, coincide or be related in some ways. Notice, again, that this argument is as relevant to ideology as it is to ideation. If there is only one kind of power and the success of ideas is due to sociopolitical power, then the success of ideologies too has to be a matter of the sociopolitical power of their supporters. This reduces ideology to just another form of dominance and suppression in society or, worse, just another instrument of the powerful against the powerless.

Another strange effect of a non-recognition of the power of ideas is that all ideas then become equally good or bad, equally strong or weak, with no inherent reason for any idea to be more successful than another. This may have a certain appeal to an egalitarian ideology in that it depicts an egalitarian world of ideas and, more importantly, enables one to point out possible alternatives to all successful ideas and to claim that the success of certain ideas in the past was in fact an unjust suppression of the others. But such arguments involve a gross misunderstanding of the nature of the ideational endeavour, that is, the nature of knowledge-seeking.

True, there can be no claim of absolute truth or ultimate rightness to any idea, and no such claim is made by anyone in the field of ideation. But this cannot mean that all ideas have an equal claim to truth or rightness; if it did, there would be no knowledge resulting from ideational effort and, indeed, no serious knowledge-seeking. Knowledge, as we remarked earlier, consists of the most successful (or most persuasive or most powerful) ideas and theories about the nature of things available at any given time, and the success of some ideas over others is crucial for such a body of ideas or theories to emerge or exist.

An idea or theory can be said to be true or correct not in relation to any absolute or ultimate form of truth or correctness, but only in relation to some other idea or theory which is seen or shown to be less true or correct. The selection of one idea over another, and the development of criteria for doing this—that is to say, the testing of a given theory through various efforts to falsify it—is the essence of knowledge-seeking or ideation. A situation where neither of two competing ideas can be preferred over the other is an instance of failure in knowledge-seeking, however much it may look like a piece of desirable equality. It is of course true that the selection of one idea over another that I am talking about, and the criteria relevant to doing so, are all subject to some particular notion of what constitutes knowledge and how it is to be pursued.

There has been more than one notion of what constitutes knowledge in the past, as I pointed out earlier; and there will no doubt be new notions in the future. To cite a contemporary instance of this, the notion that has prevailed for some time now of knowledge as a body of general principles, high-level abstractions, explicit and objective theories, etc., has recently been challenged, as we know, by a notion of knowledge as a set of personal understandings, subjective perceptions in specific situations, experiences rather than abstractions, and so on.

There is a form of truth to the personal and the particular, according to this new notion, which is lost in the process of generalisation and abstraction. There is a good deal of intuitive appeal to this notion, and it may become the prevalent form of knowledge some day, replacing the one based on generalisation. But, if it does, it will still be an ideational construct—a way of making sense of the world around us, with its own criteria for deciding what is and is not a piece of personal and particular truth, what claims to such truth are to be preferred to what others, on what basis, etc. The fact that forms of knowledge can vary and change is not an argument against knowledge-seeking as such or against the need for resilient procedures and constraints in that pursuit.

Whatever may be the prevalent form of knowledge, it will still be an ideational activity, with some claims to knowledge proving to be more successful than others, rather than an ideological one, which treats all claims as being equal. Yet another effect of not recognising the power of ideas is to treat ideation as merely an instrument of ideology. I am not referring here to an application of ideation in ideology, that is to say, the use of available knowledge (ideas, theories) as a source of support in demonstrating the prevalence of inequality or arguing the case for equality. This would simply be a kind of applied ideation, similar to applied science, mathematics or linguistics. The knowledge that is applied (or drawn on) in such cases is justifiable in ideational terms, not in terms of what purpose or cause it is made to serve. I am referring, rather, to an effort to create or construct a theory suited to an ideological pursuit, as a kind of resident and purpose-made body of knowledge.

What is being projected as critical linguistics and critical discourse analysis seems to me to consist wholly or partly of such purpose-oriented theorising and, not surprisingly, its outcome so far does not stand up to scrutiny as theory in ideational terms, as Widdowson (1998) has recently shown.

Theory that is put together for an ideological purpose cannot be a claim to knowledge in ideational terms; it can only be an instrument or appendage of the ideology it is meant to serve, a form of knowledge guaranteed to be tendentious.

Let me conclude this discussion by giving two examples of how the distinction between ideation and ideology is relevant to language teaching. Ideation in language teaching is a conceptualisation of what it is to be competent in a language, how that competence develops and what form of teaching might help or hinder the development. It is an understanding of the phenomenon of language learning and the relationship between learning and teaching. The phenomenon of language learning has been conceptualised in different ways—as a process of bearing in mind and deliberately applying the rules of grammar, as memorisation and recall of actual expressions in the language, as habit-formation, skill-development, rehearsing of target behaviour, etc.

One current conceptualisation is that an abstract grammatical system takes shape in the learner's mind when the learner is preoccupied with understanding and saying things in the language, the more intensely the learner is so preoccupied the better the system-formation. This indicates that language teaching should identify those subjects or topics that are likely to engage learners' minds and organise classroom activities focused on them. It is very likely that ideological issues concerning sociopolitical discrimination, dominance and suppression are a rich source of such activities and therefore useful in teaching. But this is still an ideational approach to language pedagogy.

As against this, there is an ideological approach to the enterprise, or rather two ideological approaches. One is that the concern in language pedagogy should not be confined to developing a grammatical system in the learners' minds but should extend to making learners aware of the traces of sociopolitical beliefs and attitudes carried by language forms, as a safeguard against an unwitting conditioning of learners to those beliefs and attitudes. This is an approach that seeks to add an ideological dimension to the ideational enterprise, sharing out the pedagogic space between the two. The other ideological approach is to use the fact that language carries indications of sociopolitical attitudes to develop in learners a perception of the injustices resulting from unequal sociopolitical power and to generate in them a desire to counter those injustices. This approach replaces the ideational enterprise with an ideological one, making a radical change in the objective of language pedagogy.

All three approaches deal with ideological matters, but there are crucial differences between them. The ideational approach restricts language pedagogy to the development of an internal grammatical system, while the former of the two ideological approaches seeks to divide pedagogic attention between system development and social awareness. The latter ideological approach can be said to hijack language pedagogy to serve the cause of social justice.

The second example has to do with the role of the classroom teacher in language pedagogy. There is a current view that the classroom teacher should not be seen as merely an implementer of pedagogic decisions made at higher levels of the educational hierarchy or as a mere consumer of pedagogic knowledge or theory arrived at by specialists. Teachers have their own form of pedagogic knowledge, arising from a continual involvement in classroom events and recurrent contact with the phenomenon of learning. It is likely that teaching will be more productive if teachers are able to develop and draw on their own knowledge and make it the basis of their classroom decisions. This is an essentially ideational view, which conceptualises a form of knowledge possessed by and available to classroom teachers and a causal relationship between an engagement of that knowledge and the occurrence of learning.

There is also an ideological view, which sees teachers as being relatively powerless in the educational hierarchy, and seeks to redress this imbalance of power by moving decision-making down the hierarchy. Both views favour more decision-making by teachers, but, once again, there is a crucial difference. In the ideational view, it is a form of knowledge possessed by teachers that justifies teachers' decision-making. In the ideological view, it is the low position of the teacher in the educational hierarchy that justifies it. The ideational view would need to be modified if the engagement of teachers' knowledge did not in fact prove to be more productive of learning. The ideological view would presumably be modified if teachers became more powerful than people at some other level of the hierarchy.

I can perhaps conclude by trying to summarise my view of ideation and ideology. I see ideation as the formation of ideas or theories about the nature of various phenomena, and I see it as a response to a fundamental human need to understand the world. I see ideology as the pursuit of an ideal state of affairs in the world, such as equality between people, and I see it as an understandable response to the existence of injustice in society. I see no necessary conflict between the two. I think it is natural for different people to wish to engage themselves in one or another, or in both, as Noam Chomsky does.

I do, however, have difficulty with one or two of the arguments advanced in support of ideology. One is the argument that there is no ideation distinct from ideology, and that the formation of ideas and theories about the nature of things is all part of a power-seeking enterprise. In response to this argument, I have tried to distinguish between two kinds of power—the power of ideas and sociopolitical power—and to show how a non-recognition of the difference between the two leads to a number of misconceptions. The other objectionable argument from ideology is that no one can be disinterested in the ideological pursuit—that those who are not in the movement are necessarily against it, since not trying to change things is in fact allowing things to go on as they are and thus supporting the existing state of affairs. I have not tried to discuss this argument because it does not seem to me to be open to discussion. It is a form of argument that can be advanced in favour of any cause or ideology (including one that is diametrically the opposite of egalitarianism), if its advocates are fervent enough in their faith to be intolerant of dissent and even dissociation. I am disturbed by the touch of fanaticism signalled by such an argument.

References

Halliday, M. A. K. (1975). *Learning how to mean: Explorations in the development of language*. London: Edward Arnold.

Halliday, M. A. K. (1985). *Spoken and written language.* Victoria: Deakin University Press.

Judson, Horace Freeland. (1985). The rage to know. In Jeanne Fahnestock and Marie Secor (Eds.), *Readings in Argument* (pp. 65–76). New York: Random House.

Widdowson, H. G. (1998). The theory and practice of critical discourse analysis. *Applied Linguistics,* 19(1), 136–51.

23

The Appropriation of ELT

I use the term ELT to refer to the teaching of the English language to those who need to be taught that language, that is to say, those who have not learnt it as their mother tongue. The term thus covers areas and activities variously referred to as ESL, EFL, ESP, ESOL, TESL and (at least a large component of) applied linguistics. I also use the term to refer to different levels of the pedagogic enterprise—from classroom activity to the construction of materials, the designing of courses, the training of teachers and the development of different teaching methods, ideas and theories. ELT is all that is involved in providing English language instruction.

What is the intellectual content of this enterprise? It arises from the fact that when a language is taught—or needs to be taught—it does not get learnt as well as when it does not need to be taught; that is to say, a second or subsequent language is not learnt with the same success as the first language. Success in learning the first language is universally, almost exceptionally, certain and remarkably uniform. No normal child fails and, barring perhaps some subtle differences between individuals, all children in a speech community internalise the same system to the same extent. In contrast to this, success in a second language is both uncertain and rarely uniform. Some children learn more or better than others within every school and every classroom, or from within the same family, and only a small number of them end up with levels of success comparable to that in the first language. Understanding why this is so is a large

This essay was first published in 2003. *Source*: Prabhu, N. S. (2003). The appropriation of ELT. *Readings: A Biannual Journal of English Studies*, 1(2), 1–10.

intellectual challenge. Why is it that the same language gets learnt so uniformly and completely when it is the first language, and so variably and incompletely when it is a subsequent language? Why do the same set of children learn the first language perfectly and a second language imperfectly?

An important step in understanding something is to conceptualise or re-conceptualise it so as to achieve a sharper focus on what is to be understood. I have already made use of the concept that learning a language is internalising a system. The learner encounters a language which is essentially an abstract and complex system of rules, principles, constraints, etc., and the learning task is to reconstruct or replicate that system in one's mind. A full replication results in complete success in learning the language, while partial replications to various extents represent a lack of success in different degrees.

It is of course possible to conceptualise the learning of a language in quite different ways—as a process of forming behavioural habits or acquiring cognitive skills, as a matter of imbibing descriptive knowledge and using it repeatedly to guide behaviour, as a linear process of understanding and practising one small part of the language at a time or one specific use of it at a time, as a matter of developing the system in the mind in the course of successive efforts to understand and say things in the language or of simply receiving and retaining large samples of the language by putting oneself in a specially receptive psychological state, and so on. Each such conceptualisation is a response to the intellectual challenge in second language instruction—a search for knowledge that can account for the phenomenon of partial and varied success in learning a second language and can hopefully also help to increase the level and consistency of the success. Partial success is seen to be indicated, understandably enough by learners' errors, that is to say, differences between the learners' language and the language of the relevant speech community, indicating that the system of the community's language has not (yet) been fully replicated. Learners' errors are in this sense central to the knowledge being sought and, not surprisingly, there have been different conceptualisations of what these errors represent—for example, interference of the mother tongue, lapses or gaps in the course of learning, evidence of a tentative or transitional system developed by the learner as an approximation to the system being aimed at.

There are of course other aspects of language learning that have been conceptualised in different ways, such as the role of the learner's mother tongue in the learning of a second language, the role of memory or memorisation, the relationship between a descriptive or explicit knowledge and an operational or implicit knowledge of the system being aimed at, the relationship between the system of the language itself and what may be called the system of its use in society, the relationship between passive or receptive use of the language and its active or productive use. The formation of such varied concepts and their engagement in interaction with one another, as well as attempts to judge the plausibility, validity or usability of particular concepts with known or new evidence from language learners or with planned pedagogic action with sets of learners are all integral to what I have called the ELT enterprise.

Notice, however, that what I have outlined has to do with the learning of a second language—any language as a second language—rather than specifically with the learning of English. As I see it, the importance of English to the ELT enterprise lies largely in two facts. First, the international spread of English in the past century and the demand for teaching and learning the language have created the context and provided support for the search for knowledge involved in second language instruction and, secondly, this search for knowledge has, as a result, largely used English, rather than another language, as its "data" or source of relevant facts and evidence, producing in the process very detailed studies of the system of English, a large record of learners' errors, failures and successes, many reports and accounts of planned pedagogic action, etc., not to mention opportunities for intellectual interaction between different concepts and different scholars in the field. As far as the intellectual challenge and the nature of the knowledge sought are concerned, this data could have come equally well from any other language or, perhaps more usefully, several different languages all together. Any special significance of English in ELT is social, economic or political, neither linguistic nor pedagogic.

But the fact that English is being used as the source of data as well as a source of support creates its own problems or aggravates problems that would otherwise be less serious. I want to draw attention to three such problems and to show how they intervene to the point of undermining or appropriating the ELT enterprise as I have described it.

Recall, first, that the learners can be visualised as replicating in their minds the system of the language they are learning. More precisely, they replicate the system of the particular dialect or variety of a language which they receive exposure to, whether they are learning it as a second language or as the mother tongue. What they are exposed to may or may not happen to be the dialect or variety regarded on social grounds as the standard or desirable one, and whether it is or not is of little significance to the process of language learning (or to the intellectual effort of understanding it). When learners are exposed to a non-standard variety and succeed in replicating its system, they cannot then be held to have failed to replicate the system of the standard variety. Errors are of significance only in relation to the target being aimed at. To confuse the two is to obscure or lose sight of the essential search for knowledge involved in second language instruction.

The learning of non-standard and standard varieties may, however, have some value for the search for knowledge we are concerned with. When learners have learnt a non-standard variety and then try to learn the standard one, how similar is the situation to the learning of a second language, in terms of the level and uniformity of success? Is learning a second variety the same in character as learning a second language, though different in size? If so, can a study of the former reveal things which are of value in the study of the latter? There is at least a case for asking these questions and probing these matters as a part of our understanding of second language learning. But these are not the matters that receive attention in relating varietal differences to the learning of a second language. What receives attention, instead, is the social need to learn the standard variety and learners' failure to do so. In the process, errors in learning one variety of the language can be wrongly seen as errors in the use of another variety, and success in learning one variety can still be labeled failure in learning another. This obscures the actual phenomenon of second language learning and undermines any effort to understand it.

Such intervention of the social dimension of language in the cognitive dimension of its acquisition can be a problem in understanding the learning of any language as a second language, since dialectical variation is a general characteristic of languages. The problem is, however, magnified greatly by the fact that in ELT the language in question is English, with its global spread, global demand and global pedagogic industry. There are much higher stakes to the assertion of a socially superior standard variety and a correspondingly stronger intervention in the pedagogic activity. Also, there is much larger variation to the language itself, extending to varieties used by communities as a second language, in different parts of the world. Assertions of the superiority of a standard variety in this context acquire overtones which go beyond social preference to cultural, economic or ethnic superiority. As a consequence, differences between a second language variety and the mother tongue variety regarded as the standard come to be seen as merely a bunch of errors, and entire communities using a second language variety come to be regarded, more or less, as permanently unsuccessful learners. This game of superiority completely distorts and vitiates the intellectual endeavour of understanding second language learning. If English learners' success in Hyderabad, Singapore or Bangkok is studied in relation to the varieties of English they are exposed to in Hyderabad, Singapore or Bangkok, something of value as knowledge can probably be gained. If their success is assessed, instead, in relation to the variety of English used (by some classes of people) in London, Boston or Toronto, nothing at all of any value can be hoped for. ELT then becomes a worldwide enterprise of one-up-manship guaranteeing perpetual non-success of all second language learners and users.

The second problem I want to discuss is, ironically, meant to be a counter to the first. The attitude that second language varieties (or New Varieties) of English are somehow less legitimate than mother tongue varieties or that communities which use English in addition to their mother tongues are, for that reason, deficient in their use of English is strongly challenged and the status of second language varieties is cogently argued to be equal to that of any language variety. The emergence of second language varieties in our time on a scale unprecedented in history, and a consequent multi-polarity in standards, uses, reference-points, etc., are forcefully shown to call for a major change in the older notions of language variation, multilingualism and the basis of standards.

This can be seen as a very positive development not just in terms of combating unwarranted notions of superiority but as an opening up of new opportunities for understanding both language standardisation and second language learning. What, for instance, marks the emergence of a speech community in a second language, as distinct from merely a set of persons who have learnt and use the second language? How does the fact that success in learning a second language is typically non-uniform and frequently incomplete relate to the continued maintenance of a second language in a speech community in which language use is typically homogenous and participants' competence is, by definition, uniform? Equally what are the dynamics of variation and standardisation within a second language variety and, in particular, what leads to the perception and recognition of an endocentric standard? An understanding of standardisation in a second language variety is both valuable and crucial—valuable because it can be studied as an emergent, inchoative state and may well provide knowledge that is unavailable in a mother tongue context because of an accumulation of inherited assumptions and prejudices; and crucial because learners' errors and levels of success in a second language community can be recognised only in relation to a standard operating within that community. If no such standard is identified and defined there can be no rational distinction between unsuccessful learners' English and the English that represents the second language variety. This non-homogeneity is in fact a large difficulty in identifying a standard in a second language variety but it is also a crucial hurdle to overcome if the claim of a second language variety is to be sustained and, more importantly for the argument in this paper, if language learning in a second language community is to be fruitfully studied.

Disappointingly so far, second language varieties of English have been studied more in terms of their spread, penetration in the relevant speech communities, diversity of functions, adaptations, innovations, interactions with the mother tongue, etc., than in terms of an understanding that can help to define them more precisely or to teach them better. In particular, a principled distinction between language use that represents unsuccessful second language learning and language use that constitutes a standard second language variety—between learners' errors and accepted usage—does not seem to have been attempted or even seen as a goal. On the contrary, all use of language in a second language context is taken to be data of the second language variety, and learners' language is sometimes deliberately treated as an indistinguishable part of such data. The zeal to uphold the status of second language varieties thus seems to extend to a refusal to recognise unsuccessful learning in a second language context. This may have the advantage of avoiding difficult questions, but it also has the effect of undermining the search for knowledge about second language learning. Varied success and incomplete levels of achievement are clear characteristics of second language learning—they constitute the difference, as I said earlier, between learning one's mother tongue and learning a second language. It cannot possibly be maintained that once there is a community of second language variety, all learners of the variety within the community (who learn it, nevertheless, after learning their mother tongue) achieve the same uniform and complete success as learners do with their mother tongue—a cursory look at any second language situation would refute such a claim. The only material result of recognising a second language variety—from the point of view of understanding learning—is that learners are now seen to be learning the language variety they are exposed to, and their success and failure can now be assessed realistically in relation to whatever is the standard for that variety. If, however, no distinction is made, in a systematic way, between standard use and learners' use—between what learners aim at and what they are able to do—there can be no useful study of second language learning in that context, and any assessment of learners' achievements can only be in relation to an irrelevant, mother tongue variety of the language, as it in fact continues to be. The irony is thus complete: what sets out to be a remedy ends up being a reinforcement of the malady.

This leads me to the third problem, which is akin to the second. It relates to an ideological position often referred to as the postcolonial perspective on English. Not satisfied with the assertion of status for second language varieties just discussed, it takes the more radical view that the English language has been and continues to be both the medium and the means by which one part of the world unjustly dominates the rest. The linguistic part of the domination consists of the spread of English in the world, steadily diminishing and driving out of existence the other, less powerful languages along with the distinct cultures they represent. The effect of this particular line of thought is that those who are engaged in what I have called the ELT enterprise are led to think again of the ethicality of their profession and indeed to feel a sense of guilt for their part in the dissemination of English. They should either cease to work in ELT or find ways of atoning for their ELT work (by, for instance, giving support to the languages that are threatened by English). The lesson for what I have described as the search for knowledge seems to be that it should cease to use English as its data, and seek the necessary evidence in the learning and teaching of some other language as a second language, thus forgoing both the material support arising from the importance attached to English and the benefit of much accumulated information arising from past effort. They are not, that is to say, to seek to understand second language learning with the help of, and in a way helpful to, the most widespread activity of second language instruction taking place in the world.

Another, more inclusive, postcolonial view is that English represents not only the language of the colonial masters of many countries in the past and the linguistic wildfire that spread linguistic destruction across the world at present, but also the global vehicle of the capital–industrial system with its associated institutions and social structures, empirical scientific thought which provides intellectual scaffolding to the system, positivistic reasoning modes and perceptions of reality which favour the interest of those who define them, etc., not to speak of the more obvious interest of trade and profit in different forms. Since these coercive forces have already defined, created and consolidated the global order, so the argument runs, the victims of coercion are now obliged to employ the language of the coercion to try to recover or recreate a different, fairer order. This is why, it is claimed, second language varieties of English differ from mother tongue varieties—not because they initially arose from the learning of English as a second language or because their speakers now form independent speech communities maintaining the language endocentrically but because they are made up of a set of speakers who are all making their own meanings and using the language in the way that suits those meanings. They use English differently in order to express their own hitherto marginalised and silenced voices but not so differently that the prevailing English using global order fails to hear those voices. Nor is it right to say, we are told, that learners of English in these coerced communities attempt to replicate the system of the language they are learning with different degrees of success. That would mean that some or many of them make errors which show deficiency or fail to replicate the system fully, all of which are negative signifiers which devalue and subvert what they are actually doing. What these learners are actually doing, it is claimed, is creating and expressing new meanings, new identities and new world-views, using the language in a way that suits these purposes. They are, that is to say, not learning English, but creating new kinds of English to serve certain needs.

It is not entirely clear whether this view of second language learning applies only to the learning of a "coercive" language like English, or to the learning of any language as a second language, including those that are seen to be victims of the coercion, since a great many people in the world learn various languages in addition to their mother tongues. If it does not apply to the other, lesser languages, human beings must be using two quite different language learning processes, indeed different mental faculties, depending on whether they are learning a language of coercion or not. The search for knowledge in ELT can then be said to have chosen the wrong data for its study. If, on the other hand, this postcolonial view applies to the learning of any language as a second language, then there is no such thing as second language learning as outlined at the beginning of this paper, and no knowledge of the kind envisaged to seek. There is, by the same token, no basis left for regarding English as a coercive language—either all languages are coercive or none is. It is hard to think of a more negative, more reductionist view.

Let me conclude with one or two general points about the three arguments or movements I have dealt with. Notice, first, that the English language is more central to the three movements than it is to ELT. The three movements have all arisen from the status of English in the present day world, together with its causes or consequences. What I see as the essential search for understanding in ELT, however, relates to English only in that it uses English for the search; though it can in principle, use some other language instead. If some other language were used as the context and data, none of the arguments about native speaker standards, second language varieties and postcolonial perspectives would come in the way or cause any problem. ELT's intellectual concern is less with English than with second language learning, whereas the three movements are centred firmly on English. Secondly, it has not been my intention here to counter or criticise the three movements as such, though I do disagree wholly or partly with each of them. They have their views and agendas, just as others like me have our views of what ELT is about. I have discussed the three movements because they have the effect of distracting from, undermining or negating the intellectual content of ELT. The insistence on native speaker standards makes it difficult to study learners' success in relation to the actual language they can be expected to learn in second language contexts. The upholding of second language varieties frustrates the study by refusing to distinguish in a principled way between standard language and learners' errors in a second language community. The postcolonial argument, at least in one of its radical forms which I have outlined, has the effect of negating the value and validity of trying to understand second language learning and indeed making any such effort look like a part of a global injustice. These are all, to my mind, acts of appropriation.

24

Misapplied Linguistics

My purpose in this paper is to suggest that applied linguistics is not everything that is done with the aid of linguistics or in the form of relating language to some other field of concern. I would like to argue that there are intellectually more legitimate uses of linguistics as well as less legitimate ones, and that legitimate use involves a certain form of harmony or consistency between the nature of linguistics and the use that is made of it. I will point out some prevalent forms of activity which are lacking in this respect and which can therefore be regarded as misapplied linguistics.

Linguistics I take to be an attempt to understand the phenomenon of language, employing hypotheses such as that it is primarily a mental entity or that it is largely or solely a social construction. It is a knowledge-seeking enterprise, promoted by a fundamental human urge to make sense of the world one lives in and in that respect similar to other forms of knowledge-seeking such as science or philosophy. The form in which knowledge is perceived and sought can vary (and has varied) between cultures and between different periods of history, some of these forms being mythology, religion, poetic vision and occultism. Some forms, however, turn out to be more powerful than others—that is to say, more widely or deeply appealing, persuasive or influential—in a given period, and the form that has proved to be most powerful at this time is rational enquiry susceptible to empirical evidence. Linguistics is thus a rational enquiry into the nature of language,

---

This essay was first published in 2004. *Source*: Prabhu, N. S. (2004). Misapplied linguistics. In Ashok Kumar (Ed.), *Language, context and culture: Essays in honour of Prof. Shivendra Kumar* (pp. 175–82). Lucknow: Gurukul Publications.

the best outcome of the enquiry at a given time—that is to say, the conclusions most supported by available empirical evidence at the time—constituting knowledge or understanding of the phenomenon. Seen in this way, knowledge is not absolute—neither for all time nor independent of the assumptions and procedures that lead to it; it is knowledge only to the extent that the form in which it is perceived and pursued remains persuasive to those who produce and receive it.

What are the assumptions and characteristics of linguistics as rational enquiry? I would like to identify three of them for my purpose.

First, the enquiry is, or aims to be, objective and impersonal. It is not important who the enquirer is; what matters is how the enquiry is made and what it results in. This does not mean that ideas and outcomes are not attributed or credited to individuals, nor that the research carried out is uninfluenced by individual minds, temperaments or personalities. It means, rather, that the outcome of research is to be considered and judged by criteria that are unrelated to individual minds and, further, that these criteria have to do with the advancement of knowledge, not the advancement of individual or group interests. Linguistics, that is to say, is a knowledge-seeking enterprise, not a self-seeking one. Individuals engage in the enquiry in order to enhance their (and other people's) understanding of phenomena, not in order to fulfill their personal needs or ambitions.

Secondly, linguistics as a knowledge-seeking activity is open to all who care to engage in it. There may be variable access or opportunity for such engagement as with other forms of professional activity or research, but that variation has no bearing on the validity or value of the effort made or outcome arrived at. In particular, there is no ownership or privilege arising from social class or group affiliation; and it is not the aim of the activity to further or counter any class or group interest.

Thirdly, linguistic enquiry is not a social reform activity. It is not directed to showing what is wrong with the world or setting things right. It is not driven by any reformist or political ideal. It is driven, instead, by a deep-seated desire to know the world one is living in—or perhaps by an inability to live with the unknown, without even an effort at knowing or at any rate a way of persuading oneself that one knows. Linguistics, that is to say, is an ideational enterprise, not an ideological one. It involves developing ideas and conceptual structures that can account for the characteristics of language, not the espousal of an ideal or cause through the instrument of language.

Having stated my perception of linguistics, let me now state how I see applied linguistics. Some years ago, Widdowson made a distinction between linguistics applied and applied linguistics. He thought of linguistics applied as a matter of utilising the knowledge arising from linguistics in some field of practical activity such as language teaching, speech therapy or machine translation. The relationship between linguistics and linguistics applied is, on this view, similar to that between science and technology, or between theology and ritual. In contrast, applied linguistics was seen as a form of linguistics rather than an application of it. It involved the development of an understanding (or theory) of a particular aspect of language or of language seen from a particular angle. Applied linguistics, on this view, is similar to sociolinguistics, psycholinguistics or philosophical linguistics. I think this distinction of Widdowson's can be taken to point to two perceptions of what applied linguistics is about, instead of two distinct entities with different labels.

It is necessary to remember that applied linguistics on both these views is in consonance with what we have said about linguistics and its three characteristics. Forms of linguistics such as psycholinguistics and sociolinguistics are clearly knowledge-seeking activities, subject to a particular perception of what constitutes knowledge, as with all knowledge-seeking but, within that limit, objective, non-exclusive and ideational. Applied linguistics as an application of knowledge to an area of practical activity is no doubt utilitarian rather than ideational but the knowledge that is so applied is certainly ideational. It is not the case that a desire to use knowledge in a practical activity—or the nature of the practical activity concerned—influences the process by which knowledge is sought or the outcome of that process.

A distortion of linguistics occurs when the use to be made of knowledge exerts an influence on what is sought or seen as knowledge. Knowledge then is not a form of understanding but rather a device in achieving some other end. It is projected as knowledge only because it can then serve as a more effective or persuasive device. Purpose thus clouds the perception of knowledge, and what is approved or applied as knowledge is no longer an objective, non-exclusive, ideational entity. It is, instead, the pursuit of individual or class interests, or of a sociopolitical ideology. It is this form of activity that I am calling misapplied linguistics, to indicate that it is neither a form of linguistics nor an application of it, in the senses that I have attributed to those terms, but a misnomer for activities that are not concerned with knowledge. I go on to give one or two examples of such activity.

Linguistics as knowledge-seeking aims, among other things, to arrive at an understanding of what is involved in knowing a language—that is to say, what it is that the speaker of a given language knows (or has the ability to do) and a non-speaker of that language doesn't. Given the perception of knowledge-seeking as rational enquiry, the pursuit of this aim needs a notion of who knows a given language and who doesn't—or what constitutes evidence of a speaker's ability and what doesn't. This need is met by the concept of a native speaker—one who can be assumed, incontrovertibly, to be a speaker of the language in question. It is a concept representing an explicit assumption, neither an object of enquiry nor a claim to knowledge. But it is also a concept that can be used by some people to claim a privilege over others, especially when a language spreads to large parts of the world as English has done. Native speaker-hood then becomes a privilege by the circumstance of birth—inherent, unearned, inalienable. The privilege becomes even more exclusive when the concept of native speaker is combined with that of a standard variety within the range of varieties of a language. The native speakers of standard English thus become a highly privileged class, whose knowledge or use of English is more worthwhile describing or accounting for than other people's. It is easy to add to this argument such as usefulness to learners of English, especially those learners who are speakers of other languages—an argument which is very reasonable in itself but serves, nevertheless, to support or legitimise the exploitation of a concept in knowledge-seeking for claiming and perpetuating a social-class privilege globally. This seems to me a clear instance of misapplied linguistics, not because I approve or disapprove of such social-class privilege but because it makes unwarranted use of a concept of linguistics and projects itself as a form of linguistics. The special attention accorded to native speakers of standard English is not generally seen as acceptance of a privilege by birth; it is regarded widely (and wrongly) as a logical—or even rational—result of the concepts and procedures of linguistics.

Ironically, as it were, a recognition of and opposition to native speaker-hood as a social-class privilege does not just result in exposing a form of misapplied linguistics but often develops into another form of it. The procedure starts, reasonably enough, by regarding the forms of English used by large numbers of non-native speakers as varieties of English—new varieties as distinct from old varieties of the native speakers. But it does not stop at claiming for the new varieties the same status or legitimacy as accorded to the old varieties, including the one regarded as the standard. It goes on to claim special attention to the new varieties on grounds such as that their emergence and functioning indicate a complex and very distinct interaction between linguistic and social factors. It is then suggested that the study of this complex interaction needs to be different, in some unspecified ways, from that of the old varieties and that it can only be made by those who share this particular view of the new varieties. Moving in this way from one step to another, proponents of this view soon arrive at the position that not only is new knowledge called for about these new varieties but new forms and procedures of knowledge-seeking are called for and, once again, only those who subscribe to this series of assumptions and claims can legitimately engage in such knowledge-seeking. A movement against privilege and exclusiveness thus develops into an exclusive enterprise, with little time or tolerance for any attempt to question some of the steps in the argument or to suggest a different view of new varieties. It becomes a new kind of class interest, seeking to consolidate, expand and perpetuate its privilege as a form of linguistic enquiry. This too is an instance of misapplied linguistics in that it claims to be a form of linguistics but operates as a power- or privilege-seeking device.

My third example of misapplied linguistics is the effort to carry out linguistic analysis as an instrument of social justice. Human societies have always had unequal power relations, with various forms of domination and suppression, and it is natural for languages to carry a reflection of this power play in different ways. It is also the case that this reflection of power play can have a conditioning effect on unwary learners and users of a language, thus helping to perpetuate the existing forms of domination and suppression. It is therefore reasonable to argue that users and learners should be made aware of this particular aspect of language and thus alerted to the possible conditioning. But the argument put forward goes much further than this. It views language not just as a carrier of evidence about past power relations but as the actual site of current and ongoing struggles for power. It sees its analytic effort not just as a means of promoting awareness and reducing conditioning effects, but as a way of reversing unjust power relations and creating a more equal social order. And it goes on to claim that a demonstration of power relations in language is in fact a legitimate form of linguistics, under the label 'critical linguistics'. Ideology thus takes over from ideation, even to the point of denying that any analysis can be truly ideational, and declaring that all of linguistics is necessarily ideological. I see this as misapplied linguistics because it is an appropriation of linguistics—by a movement which is fiercely opposed to appropriations, ironically enough—through a replacement of ideation by ideology, of a need to understand by a wish to reform.

Let me now conclude by making two points. First, the activities which I have called misapplied linguistics are not so labelled because of what they deal with—that is to say, I am not saying that dealing with the native speaker/non-native speaker issue, or with the phenomenon of non-native varieties of a language, or with the relationship between language and societal power play, is by itself misapplied linguistics. It is quite possible, and potentially valuable, to try to understand what difference there is, if any, between the acquisition or use of one's mother tongue and those of an additional language, either in psychological or in social terms; and it is similarly possible to study the other two issues ideationally, with a desire to make sense through rational enquiry. What makes them misapplied linguistics is the fact that they are not genuine pursuits of knowledge or understanding but, instead, more or less camouflaged pursuits of individual or group interests or of sociopolitical ideologies.

Secondly, I am by no means saying that it is wrong to pursue individual or class interests, or to engage in ideological struggles. I think all of us have a right to decide what issues, aims and interests we pursue. What I am saying is that these particular pursuits do not constitute knowledge-seeking and, given the perception of linguistics as a knowledge-seeking activity, they can only be regarded as misapplied linguistics.

25

Teachers' Growth

In this paper, I want to outline a concept of language teachers' professional growth and speculate about what conditions or activities might be of value in furthering it.

I am thinking here of teachers' growth as something that arises from the ongoing activity of teaching—from the daily engagement in the classroom—rather than from any professional inputs to the teacher from the world of professional specialism. Specialist inputs to the teacher are generally meant to alter or improve the teaching that takes place and/or promote an understanding in the teacher of the nature of/need for such improvement, rather than start a process of growth based on whatever teaching happens to take place. Growth arises from and is sustained by experience, not training or knowledge.

It has been suggested that such growth is brought about by reflective teaching, that is to say, repeated reflection by teachers on their ongoing classroom experience. Reflective teaching is indeed a suggestive description, but it is not easy to see what would count as reflection and what circumstances are likely to bring it about. Reflection is not a process that one can bring about or engage in by intention—it is something that may happen, rather than something that one can do.

I think it is more useful to think of growth as a process of thinking about and making sense of one's classroom experience and bringing to bear the resulting understanding on one's further teaching. I wish to indicate four kinds of activity that are likely to start or prompt such a process.

This essay was first published in 2012. *Source*: Prabhu, N. S. (2012). Teacher's growth. In Francis Peter (Ed.) *Indian Voices in ELT* (pp. 1–6). New Delhi: Viva Books.

Viewing Instances of Teaching

The first activity is viewing someone else's teaching, either live or video-recorded. I do not mean classroom observation for the purpose of identifying, categorising or counting events of particular kinds, much less seeing someone's demonstration of a particular method of teaching. I mean just seeing classroom lessons as they take place, whichever the class and whoever the teacher. We all know that teachers hardly ever do this, probably because seeing other teachers teach is not a part of the prevailing concept of what is good or proper for a teacher to do. Equally, however, those of us who have seen a video lesson being played to teachers have been struck both by the immediate interest it evokes and by the effect it has in raising the level and quality of pedagogic discussion (Ramani, 1987). There seems to be something in the viewing of a lesson that touches a teacher in a way that talking about teaching does not. It links up with something in the teacher's pedagogic make-up, and brings to the fore some pieces of memory, past perception or understanding which are not otherwise open to recall.

I think there is an analogy between this and the reading of literature, especially fiction. What one reads is a depiction of life and one's interest in reading it stems from the fact that one has been living one's own life. The life one reads about makes connections in some way with the life one has been living, evoking elements in one's experience which are not normally open to retrieval. Reading fiction touches one's understanding or perception, though very inexplicit, of one's own life, with an immediacy and success that reading, say, philosophy does not.

Further, reading literature can be considered a way of living life vicariously, as it were, and, as a result, free of the immediate pressures and tensions that inevitably attend the actual living of one's life. There is, that is to say, both a similarity between life and fiction, which is essential, and a difference or distance which is equally helpful. I think this relationship holds between the teaching one does and the teaching one views: the distance and freedom from immediate pressures of decision-making or attendant feelings of anxiety, insecurity etc. are as productive as the linkages that can be made with one's own teaching.

Perhaps as a result of such freedom and distance, there is a likelihood of making more sense of what one reads or views than can be made of raw experience. By "making sense" I mean the occurrence of such things as seeing some new connection between one part and another, or a new significance to some event, or a pattern to the different parts or events that one had not seen before. One begins to see a shape to the sequence of events and consequently to develop an understanding of those events. Then, at some point, one begins to make sense of one's own experience in similar terms, thus achieving an understanding of what one has been doing and facing in the classroom. The meaning that is seen to what is vicariously experienced is then transferred to what is actually experienced.

I am of course not suggesting that the meaning that is seen in this way in either vicarious or actual experience is the "real" or "true" meaning in some sense. It is just the meaning that one is able to see—or simply happens to see—at a given time. Different persons can see quite different meanings, and the same person can see different meanings at different times. The important thing is that a meaning has been seen—an understanding has been achieved—or, even more importantly, a process of seeing, meaning or achieving understanding has begun. Further, the understanding one has of past teaching operates in one's present teaching, lending new meaning to ongoing classroom events and, equally, being influenced and modified by those events. A teacher's understanding of teaching is thus always in a state of development or change; when it is not, it is no longer active or alive. The important difference, then, is between teaching that is informed by an active and developing pedagogic understanding and that which is not so informed, rather than between true and false, or superior and inferior, understanding by some criterion. As far as I can see, the term "reflective teaching" can only mean teaching that engages an understanding of past teaching and has the effect of influencing/changing/developing that understanding.

Making Classroom Decisions

A second activity I wish to suggest is the teacher making pedagogic decisions in the classroom in the light of what happens and how he/she perceives it at the time. A lesson is normally based on a plan, and needs to be. But a plan is based on a prediction or expectation of how things develop in the classroom and how the learners respond at a particular stage or step. There are always instances of the actual events not matching the prediction and the teacher having to decide what to do differently from the plan. Such on-the-spot decisions are perhaps guided sometimes by alternatives envisaged in the plan itself, by memories of other things done on other occasions, or simply by opting for a course of minimal risk. But they can also be guided by a form of pedagogic intuition, that is to say, the significance the teacher perceives to the event concerned, the judgement he/she makes of the learners' current state or readiness for a possible activity, and the larger context of the pattern he/she can see to the progress of the lesson. This latter will involve an engagement of the understanding we have talked about in discussing the effect of viewing instances of teaching. Classroom decision-making can thus benefit from the teacher's pedagogic understanding and, more importantly, it can help to further such understanding—strengthening it, making it more and more readily accessible, adding to it and of course modifying it in different ways. The more decisions the teacher makes, the greater the chance that he engages and advances his current pedagogic understanding.

I am not assuming here that the decisions the teacher makes are likely to be pedagogically sound or good, by some accepted criteria—or even that the teacher herself will find them good or successful by her own standards, all or much of the time. Decisions will often prove to have been wrong in the teacher's own eyes, but that is likely to be a positive input to the further growth of the teacher's understanding. It is by making wrong decisions, and by perceiving them to have been wrong, that a capacity for making better decisions can emerge and strengthen itself. Also, making decisions differently from past decisions involves a modification of the pedagogic understanding that prompts such decisions, resulting in further growth of the understanding. Perhaps, as a teacher's understanding changes and develops in this way, it will come closer to other teachers' understanding of teaching, and the resultant decision-making will then approximate to what is good by more widely accepted standards—or, indeed, have an influence on those wider standards. Classroom decision-making by the teacher is thus productive both of learners' learning (in that, such decisions are responsive to the immediate classroom context, the learners' readiness, etc. instead of a prior prediction or pre-empting) and of the teacher's pedagogic understanding and growth. There is in fact a strong argument to be made for designing curricula in a way that minimises prediction and maximises the scope and need for teachers' classroom decisions.

Teachers are an immediate and constant presence at the place where learning takes place, even if it takes place occasionally, sporadically and not in keeping with the teachers' expectations. Such repeated presence, and continuous involvement in the contexts in which learning happens, often enables teachers to develop a sense or feel for the occurrence of learning—an ability to tell when things are going well and when they are not, quite independently of whether the teaching is going according to plan or not. Many teachers have the experience of coming away from a classroom with a sense of satisfaction or fulfillment on some occasions, and a sense of frustration or failure on others, for no clear reasons that they can see. When teachers make decisions in the classroom at variance with earlier plans and in response to their perception of the immediate context, at least some of those decisions are likely to be guided or influenced by their intuitive feel for the occurrence and non-occurrence of learning. Further, the perceived results of decisions so made are likely to be an influence on the feel for the occurrence of learning—firming it up, perhaps, or making it more readily accessible, or increasing a teacher's confidence in acting on it. Such a feel for learning is an input of great value to teachers' developing understanding of pedagogy and to their professional growth.

Articulating Pedagogic Perceptions

A third activity that can help teachers' growth is attempting to communicate one's current pedagogic understanding to a fellow teacher. This can be very difficult to do when one's understanding is still at a developing stage, perhaps dormant, uncertain and less than accessible. But that is in fact what gives value to an attempt to articulate it. The value is of two kinds. First, attempting to articulate a vague or half-formed idea, perception or understanding is a very good way of making it less vague, better-formed, more accessible to oneself and more open to articulation at the next attempt. Further, an attempt to articulate a half-formed idea often has the effect of making that idea grow and change, in the sense of being seen to be differently formed or differently interrelated to other ideas. As the literature on what is called "process writing" has brought out powerfully, attempting to say what one means is a very good way of realising more fully what one means and, equally, of realising that what one means is different from what one thought it was (Malderez, 2003). In a real sense, saying what one has in mind is a way of knowing what one has in mind and also of having more in the mind to say. A teacher's attempt to articulate his/her pedagogic understanding at a given time can thus be very useful both in clarifying that understanding and in furthering it. And there is also a second kind of value to it—the possibility of conveying it to a fellow teacher, leading to a gradual sharing of pedagogic perceptions between teachers. Here too the difficulty of articulating emerging perceptions can be a hurdle to success in communicating them, but it can also be a help. When what is being articulated is something genuinely felt or sensed and when it is being articulated with an effort or struggle, causing several tentative and varied rewordings, it tends to have a particular power to convey itself, especially to someone who similarly has half-felt or half-sensed pedagogic perceptions which are difficult to articulate. The communication that results will certainly fall short of academic standards for explicitness or rhetorical convention, but it will have the valuable effect of making different teachers' perceptions link up and exert an influence on each other, as well as strengthening each teacher's perceptions and helping them develop further.

Interacting with Specialists' Perceptions

The fourth and last activity I want to suggest is for teachers to try to interact with the more explicit pedagogic perceptions of specialists in the field as they appear in the professional literature. This can be regarded as an extension from a sharing of perceptions between teachers which we have just talked about, but there is a major difference and a further difficulty. Teachers' perceptions are not only in a formative, uncertain and inexplicit state but they are also, necessarily, personal and subjective. Although specialists' arguments and claims too are in many cases based ultimately on their own individual pedagogic perceptions, they are moulded to fit the conventions of academic discourse, and stated as part of a search for some more general, objective truth or knowledge. This makes the specialist's underlying, personal perceptions largely inaccessible to teachers, in addition to the fact that the appurtenances of academic discourse tend to have a discouraging, intimidating effect. The result is that specialist literature is looked on as a distant debate unrelated to teachers' personal experience in classrooms or at most as a body of superior knowledge to be received and retained as such. But teachers who have identified and developed their personal understandings over a period of time—those, that is to say, who have achieved some degree of growth—can perhaps approach the professional literature with a measure of confidence, withstanding the intimidation, working their way through the discoursal manners and making contact with the basic pedagogic perceptions. When this happens, teachers can truly interact with specialists, that is to say, identify the specialists' understandings, interpret them in the light of their own personal understandings and in the process sharpen or modify those personal understandings. The result is not that the teachers have absorbed some academic knowledge, nor that they have gained entry to some academic debate, but simply that they have used some academic literature to strengthen and further their individual pedagogic perceptions. I think this can be a valuable source of teachers' growth, well worth the difficulty involved and carrying the potential of bridging the current gap between teachers and specialists, or even perhaps influencing academic discourse so as to bring it closer to teachers' understandings and make it more directly relevant to teachers' growth.

References

Malderez, Angri. (2003). Alternative discourses—An interview with Julian Edge. *ELT Journal*, 57/4, 386–94.

Ramani, Esther. (1987). The role of classroom interaction in the integration of theory and practice. In Bikram K. Das (Ed.), *Communication and learning in the classroom community* (pp. 116–29). Singapore: Singapore University Press.

26

A Case against Practice

Most new thinking in ELT in the past century has given a high value to practice by the learner of different pieces of language structure. There has been a firm belief that the more a given structure is practised, the better it gets learnt, or gets 'established' in the learner's mind.

This paper is an attempt to question that belief and argue, instead, that practice may well be unhelpful and even detrimental to the learning of a second language.

First, however, I must make clear what I mean by practice—or what form of practice I am unhappy about. Although practice is broadly understood as something like "doing the same thing many times", it can, more specifically, be one of the following:

1. repeated attempts to perform the same piece of action, so that the performance becomes more and more easy, successful or perfect in the process. This is exemplified by the practising of a stroke in tennis, the playing or singing of a specific tune or musical phrase, or the pronunciation of a particular sound or word in a language. Practice is thus a form of rehearsal—that is to say, what is done as practice is an imperfect version of what is aimed at, and the perfection to be achieved is in terms of physical—neuromuscular—implementation.
2. doing something similar with a certain number of similar entities, so that one is able to do such things with all such entities later on. This is illustrated by the practice of

This paper was presented in 2012 at the Asia TEFL conference, 4–6 October 2012 in Gurgaon, India.

such arithmetical operations as multiplying and dividing numbers. Practice consists of applying the same procedure to different but similar entities so as to be able to apply it thereafter to any or all of them. The aim of doing things to different entities is to learn the general procedure of doing such things, the procedure itself being an abstract one, that is to say, operated by the mind.

3. encountering similar entities at different times, which results in a growing familiarity with them. This is represented by such things as getting to know different people, or the road system of a place, or the signs of an approaching storm, or the probable ending of a story. It does not involve any deliberate action as practice; learning results from recurrent experience of the same or similar things. What is learnt may be either physical (as in 1 above) or mental (as in 2).

The position I am taking is that practice in the first sense is useful only in learning the pronunciation (or handwriting) of a second language; practice in the third sense is not very relevant to a discussion of teaching (though it is highly relevant to the occurrence as well as an understanding of learning); and that practice in the second sense, which has been promoted and employed as a means of teaching grammatical structure, is not a useful activity.

I have three main arguments:

1. Structural practice essentially involves putting together a set of structurally similar sentences for the learner to work on, for instance, a set of six sentences with their verbs in the present perfect tense and with adverbs such as "so far", "since then" or "already". The learner is asked to change the adverbs to "last week", "long ago" or "this morning" and is expected to change the tense of the verbs accordingly. It is thought that an exercise like this will help to ensure that the learner will in future use the present perfect tense when referring to a duration, and the past simple tense when thinking of a point of time.

Notice, however, that a set of six sentences all in the present perfect tense and each with an adverb of duration is a "paradigmatic" arrangement which needs to be specially made by the teacher for this purpose. It does not normally occur as a continuing piece of text. Any sequence of six sentences in a continuing text is likely to be in a variety of tenses and often without any adverbs. Such a sequence or stretch of text does not serve the purpose of structural practice—we need a set of similar things, arranged as a "paradigm", not a sequence of varied things forming a continuity, or "syntagm". Members of a paradigmatic set are held together by their own structural similarity, while members of a syntagmatic sequence are linked together by something outside of them, such as meaning, topic, context, communicative purpose. Language practice is based on sets; language use has the form of sequences or "texts".

It follows that practice exposes learners to samples of language that constitute sets, not texts. The difference between the two is quite fundamental: sets are a way of displaying language structure, which is why books of grammar are full of them; and texts are the form in which language is employed in the business of exchanging meaning, which is why we do not find sets in them. Teaching a language through practice therefore necessarily involves giving the learner samples of the language that are fundamentally unlike language use in the world. It used to be argued that practice was much more relevant to language learning than an explanation of grammar because practice was closer to language use. It is now my argument that practice requires material which is much closer to language description than to language use and that it is as unlikely to promote language ability as grammatical explanation is.

2. My second argument has to do with the linguistic quality

of the sentences that make up the sets and the probable accuracy of the grammatical generalisations conveyed by the sets. I gave the example above of six sentences all in the present perfect tense and all with adverbs of duration. Now anyone who has made up such a set knows how difficult the job is. The difficulty arises from the fact that each sentence has to be self-contained, that is to say, contain within itself enough context and meaning to justify the use of the present perfect tense, in preference to any other tense. It also has to have an adverb that clearly indicates duration—an adverb that cannot go with the past simple tense, for instance. Now normal language use consists of sequences in which there is an extension of the context from one sentence to another, there is an interdependence of meaning between sentences and there are different degrees of precision or explicitness in wording at different points. In the absence of such connectedness, meeting the requirements of practice material leads to sentences that are over-independent in meaning, over-explicit in wording and overly constrained by grammatical rules, in comparison with normal language use. Add to this the expectation that the sentences in a set are to be roughly similar to one another in size and structural shape, thus highlighting the deliberate similarities/differences between them that constitute the teaching point. This too is different from the form of sentences in texts and makes the process of devising practice material that much more tricky and laboured. Anyone who has done it will recall the sigh of relief at arriving at the sixth sentence and not having to struggle any further.

There is a further dimension to this. If six sentences share a certain grammatical feature (one of two tenses in association with one of two types of adverb, for example), it does not follow that they share other grammatical features, even with regard to tenses and types of adverb. When, for instance, the lexical verb is a "process" verb, it does not follow the pattern of contrast between the present perfect and past simple. While some adverbs go clearly with one or the other tense, some others can go with either. A given lexical verb goes well with one adverb but not with another, even when both belong to the same category. In general, the grammar of any given sentence—or of any particular verb—is many-sided and similarity between certain sentences on one side does not indicate similarity on the others. We just ignore the dissimilarities—or remain unaware of them—in our pre-occupation with a particular similarity. In fact there is little else we can do since trying to make learners aware of the various qualifications and exceptions would completely obscure or undermine the generalisation we want them to absorb.

We thus have a paradox. The purpose of a practice exercise is to lead learners to see and learn a particular generalisation. But the practice exercise we put together is able to lead towards the generalisation only by hiding, ignoring or avoiding various facts of the language which come in the way of it. To deal honestly with those facts is to defeat the purpose of the practice exercise; but to leave them aside is to lead learners towards a generalisation that is of dubious or limited validity. Either we are prevented from teaching the rule, or we are made to teach a false rule.

3. My third argument has to do with our perception of language learning. Linguists have through the ages described the way language is structured by using a number of different models, among them the parsing of words in a sentence, a hierarchy of morpheme–word–phrase–clause–sentence, deep and surface structure, macro- and micro-functions, government and binding, and a lexical specification of syntax. It so happens that a certain model of description, which we can refer to as phrase-structure analysis, was widely prevalent at the time language

> learning was thought of as the learner's mind acquiring a representation of one structural pattern at a time, as a habit. The descriptive model suited the psychological model and this gave a central role to structural practice in language teaching. We must, however, bear in mind that both the model of description and the model of learning are just that—models (or claims or guesses). There are other models of description, such as lexical specification or functional analysis, as well as other models of learning, such as holistic, interlanguage development, which are commonly seen simply as ways of understanding or visualising the phenomenon concerned, not as the actual form, in some sense, of either language structure or its mental representation. In basing our teaching on structural practice, we implicitly treat the phrase-structure model of description as being both true and identical with the mental representation of language ability. This is a naive assumption, much more likely to be wrong than right.

There is a large difference between practice and experience. In learning a first language (or a second language untaught), one comes across a recurrence of similar sentences at various points, all as parts of sequences or "texts". It is very likely that this recurrent encounter leads to a gradual learning of different sentence types or structures. But it is not just recurrent encounter that happens. Each instance of a sentence type is encountered as part of a continuity of sentences constituting communication—it is encountered, that is to say, with all the context, meaning and grammar which it shares with other sentences; and it is perceived and interpreted in relation to those features, as a step towards its acquisition. This is learning through recurrent experience—what I listed as the third sense of practice at the beginning of this paper. In contrast, practice in the second sense gives great value to recurrence, attempting to increase it by artifice, but in the process loses all of the value of shared meaning and grammar in the context in a sequence. It provides practice in structures, but takes away the experience of language.

27

Evaluation in ELT: Six Levels

Education is commonly seen to be concerned with teaching, learning and evaluation. I want to look at the possible relationship between the three processes in English language education by discussing different forms of evaluation at different levels of the educational process.

First, when there are two competing "methodologies", each with its own concept of learning and procedures of teaching, an evaluation is undertaken to decide which of them is better. Such "method-comparison" is carried out by an external specialist or institution not involved in or partial to either of the methodologies and is expected to lead to an objective choice between the two.

Second, all students are given a final examination on completion of a course of study to decide which of them qualify for a degree, or promotion to the next level of study, and often to award a "class" to indicate the level of their achievement. The decisions are made by experienced teachers who can draw on their knowledge of many other students in the past in making the assessment.

Third, learners are periodically given "class tests" so that teachers can adjust the pace of their teaching and also give learners an idea of how they are progressing. The tests are also seen as a form of preparation or "rehearsal" for the more formal/final examination to come.

The fourth is concerned with what learners can do for themselves. Learning is a process of the learner increasing his understanding or ability a little at a time with an effort. Each time the learner makes

---

This paper is the summary of a plenary address given at the all-India seminar 'Trends in second language evaluation' in 2013 at the Regional Institute of English, South India, Bengaluru.

the effort, he hopes to succeed and add to his ability as well as his confidence on the next effort, but he also fears failure and the consequent loss of confidence or loss of face. He is therefore likely to try to assess the chances of his success on each occasion so that he can make the effort when success seems likely and opt out when failure threatens. His assessment of the chances of success can of course turn out to be right or wrong, but he is likely to learn from recurrent experience and get better and better at it, thus reducing instances of failure and increasing the frequency of success. That experience constitutes a process of productive self-evaluation.

The fifth is a somewhat similar process on the teacher's part, instead of the learner's. The teacher ideally wants the learners in her class to be attempting things that are difficult but attainable with an effort, since attaining it without an effort will mean they have not learnt anything new and not attaining it even with an effort can be disheartening. So she has to assess the level of difficulty of a classroom task in relation to the ability of the learners at a given time through trial and error in the course of her teaching. The more correctly she is able to make that assessment the easier it becomes for the learners in her class to make their own assessment and learn things faster. So the teacher has to evaluate her learners' ability in order to advance their learning.

The sixth level is also at the teacher's level but involves fellow-teachers rather than learners. As a teacher gathers experience and ability in assessing the suitability of a learning task to a given class at a given time, she is likely to ask herself at some point how she is able to make that assessment, when she is likely to make it better or more easily than at other times, what factors or indications seem to influence her assessment or make her more confident, less certain, etc. Such introspection, awareness and judgement can make it possible to articulate to fellow-teachers one's understanding of what leads to successful learning and teaching in the classroom, thus leading to a process of shared professional growth for teachers.

If we now look back at the six levels identified above, we will see that the first three of them treat teaching, learning and evaluation as three parts of education. In contrast, the next two levels treat evaluation as being internal and very integral to both teaching and learning; and the sixth level is wholly a matter of evaluation of classroom experience for professional progress.

Further, evaluation at the first and second levels is a form of external adjudication with an outcome which is something of a verdict. It is much less so at the third level but has the same general features. In contrast, evaluation at the fourth and fifth levels consists of processes of decision-making exercised by learners and teachers of their own accord for their own purposes, while at the sixth level it is a process of self-motivated interpretation, articulation and exchange between fellow-teachers

Broadly speaking, evaluation at the first three levels is top-down, geared to a conclusion and meant to mark a closure, while at the next three levels it is a self-motivated, self-controlled process of progress and achievement free to go on indefinitely.

28

Rethinking Language Pedagogy

This interview with the author (NSP) was conducted by the editor (GD), assisted by Deepesh Chandrasekharan on 17 March 2018. Its purpose was to provide an account of Dr Prabhu's most recent thinking on language pedagogy.

GD: *Good morning, Dr Prabhu. We are very happy that you have agreed to be interviewed by us. Let me begin with a very basic question. Many years ago, you were one of the few people in India who had very clear views on what language is, and how it can be learnt, and how it can be taught. I am referring to your Bangalore Project. Today, in 2018, what are your views on what is language first of all, and then, what is language learning for you?*

NSP: The Bangalore Project, as I see it now, was a kind of halfway house to where I think I am today. If I were to identify two or three stages or points in where I have arrived in my thinking, the Bangalore Project was definitely a prominent one, in that I was able to try out there a growing feeling I had at the time that we can achieve better results by letting language learning happen than by attempting to cause it. We can let it happen by identifying and creating conditions that might be most favourable to its happening, and I saw the most favourable condition as one where the learner's mind is focussed on meaning, content, knowledge, not the language itself. It is as though one is saying that a language is best learnt by the learner when it is least pointedly taught by the teacher. Instead, the classroom activity leads to an effort by the learner to make sense of a piece of language in order to get to a piece of meaning,

---

An earlier and shorter version of this interview was published in the July 2018 issue of *Language and Language Teaching*, 7/2(14), 38–42.

which is precisely the point of such activity. That was the idea. The Bangalore Project was an attempt to try this out and the way to get the learner's mind to focus on meaning was what I called task-based teaching. When there is a challenge to the mind in terms of meaning—a puzzle, something to be found out, a problem to be solved—then the mind is on that problem. And there is a sort of natural desire to solve the problem, partly to show that you can solve it, especially in young people but also at all ages. I want to solve the problem if I think I can and even more so if I think the other fellow cannot. It is a legitimate source of enhancing learners' effort. The learner's effort to understand brings about a kind of intensive exposure (I am coining this term), that is to say, focus on the meaning and in the process more sense is made of the language. And the more you do that, the better the learning. So that was the idea.

GD: *You said the Bangalore project was a sort of halfway house to where you are today. So, what are your views today on what language learning is? Are they the same? Would they be different? For example, in the Bangalore Project at that point, probably because it was at a time when the structural approach was in vogue, there was this focus that the forms of language need to be learnt. Have you changed from that argument that language learning is learning of form?*

NSP: It was a big change to move away from the Structural Approach in the context of the RIE (Regional Institute of English, South India, in Bangalore) because the RIE was the direct successor to the MELT (Madras English Language Teaching) Campaign which saw the first large-scale implementation of the Structural Approach in India. (Indeed, the first structural syllabus in the world, written by Dr Jean Forrester, a British lady who was Principal of a Teacher Training College in Madras, was published in the official Fort St George Gazette of Madras Presidency in 1952). The Structural Approach also loomed large in the Central Institute of English which came up in Hyderabad in 1958 and in the state-level ELTIs (English Language Teaching Institutes) that followed.

However, I wasn't particularly thinking of questioning the value of that approach while setting up the Bangalore Project. I was interested in seeing how far I can go with my line of thinking, that "form is best learnt when the mind is on meaning". It so happened that the director of the RIE at the time, Victor Devasundaram was a good friend of mine and had something of a personal trust in me, and we spent several evenings talking about it and he said: "Why don't you set it up here?" So, it happened there.

GD: *If we go back to the argument that we should let the learning of a language happen and not cause it to happen from the outside, how can we get this learning to happen? What should happen to English language teaching?*

NSP: What we do as teachers depends on how we conceptualise the learning process. If we see language learning as a matter of habit formation, then we get learners to repeat words or sentences so that the correct pronunciation or grammatical pattern becomes the correct habit. If instead you see learning a new language as a kind of moving over from the known language, then you first discover, through contrastive analysis, what the differences are between the learner's mother-tongue and the language to be taught and concentrate the learner's practice on those things which are different from the mother-tongue. Or if you see language learning as a kind of learning-by-doing, that is, rehearsing the use of given expressions, then you do "communicative" language teaching by getting learners to say such expressions in appropriately life-like contexts. You therefore have functional syllabuses—not structures, but functions in terms of what you are trying to achieve/do with the language. So it depends on how you visualise the learning process. Now to answer your question: how do I now see the learning process myself?

If you look at whatever has been possible to achieve with several of these pedagogic paradigms, as it were, the results show that there is a fundamental difference between the learning of the first language or mother-tongue and the learning that results from these teaching approaches and it is, once you begin to think about it, such a vast difference, such a fundamental difference, that you are forced to revisit past assumptions. What do I mean by fundamental? Look, the mother-tongue is learnt unfailingly by every human child regardless of what the language is or what the technological, civilisational or cultural level is etc. It makes no difference. No child fails and if we ignore the literate skills, it is not possible to say that one child has learnt its mother-tongue better than another child. Nobody fails and everybody succeeds equally. Put that way you can see that it is almost an impossible thing. There is hardly any other thing one can say that of. And in contrast, we have all these teaching approaches that we have tried. Typically results are varied, different degrees of dissatisfaction etc. Many fail, some succeed better than others. Hardly anybody seems to succeed fully. Typically the opposite of the mother-tongue. Now, that is a big puzzle. And, since the Bangalore Project, the one piece of thinking that has occurred to me has to do with it. If we look at L2 being learnt without any teaching, when people migrate to a foreign country, when a child encounters two different languages inside and outside the home or even within the family, when schooling happens in a language other than the mother tongue, even for only some of the school subjects, the L2 that is learnt is, if not at the same level as the L1, always higher than we can expect from L2 classrooms. In all these L2-learning contexts language is not the principle of organisation and the learners' minds are not focussed on the language. Language learning is not planned or caused, but happens. So what I now think is that a language is best acquired in the process of making sense of meaning or content. When you try to understand something, your understanding carries with it automatically the language in which it comes to you. That is to say, language encodes knowledge. It is a symbolic system that encodes meaning. Therefore, understanding any piece of knowledge is sorting out the code. Otherwise you don't understand it. So, the greater the effort and success in understanding the content, the more (or more thoroughly) you learn the language. People tend to think that, in mother-tongue acquisition, the child's language learning begins at about its first birthday when the first word is likely to be uttered, and the babbling that occurs earlier or later represents L1-learning through repetition and practice. I think it begins much, much earlier and silently, with the child beginning to make sense of this bewildering world, bit by bit, and goes on all the time over a year or so before enough has been learnt to produce a word. Then it takes another couple of years to engage in verbal communication. And the learning is full-time, not one hour a day! So mother-tongue knowledge is unique because getting to know a whole new world is unique. Knowledge of a second language begins to approach that level as the experience of understanding new things approaches that level.

GD: *To take you further on this statement, you have put together and shown us the differences between the way L2 is taught and L1 is learnt, and spoken about how, when L2 is taught in the ways it generally is, the results are varied but fall far short of not only those of L1 learning but even the levels reached in untaught L2 learning. Is this, then, an inevitable difference between taught and untaught language-learning, or do you see some way of closing or narrowing that gap? How would you want English to be taught today in Indian classrooms?*

NSP: The aim would be to get the learners' minds occupied with understanding pieces of a new language with effort. The most favourable condition is when learners have a strong desire or great need to make sense of something in a language they don't know. This happens most clearly and completely for newborn children who have to work out the world by working out the mother-tongue. Something less intensive but similar in nature happens when adults have to live and get by in a new language environment, when young people taste the pleasure of stories, games or activities accessible in a new language or when school subjects are taught in an L2: in all cases the effort is to acquire new knowledge by making sense of a new language. The result of such untaught L2 learning may be varied and below the level of L1 proficiency, but it is clearly and uniformly above the achievement of taught L2 acquisition.

[Dr Prabhu spoke at length at this point describing a small project he had been involved in at RIE Bangalore in the 1990s where, based on a government decision, and when requested by Dr Gayatri Devi, who was then the director of that Institute, he tried getting teachers to tell stories in English to mother-tongue medium students in classes 1, 2, 3 and 4 as a way of getting them to listen, understand and acquire English. My question to him, at the end of this was as follows.]

GD: *You have been talking to us about story-telling as a pedagogic practice to enable students to engage with language in the lower classes and how you also used stories in the Bangalore Project, but always as a puzzle where the story ends with a question for the child to answer. If we took the idea to higher classes, what would be other possible practices?*

NSP: Every child loves to listen to stories (perhaps because they present new worlds to be comprehended) but the attraction seems to wear out for a majority of them within a few years. Those who retain it get hooked on storybook writers such as Enid Blyton, with big gains to their English language ability. I am sure millions of young people in the world have learnt a lot of English from J. K. Rowling's Harry Potter novels, whose world is so vastly different. I think that young people are also attracted by problem-solving as a competitive activity, which was a major assumption in the Bangalore Project where we used, besides stories leading to a mystery to be solved, various other "tasks" where a problem has to be comprehended (from a linguistic description) and a solution worked out. I had discovered, while writing the book *English Through Reading* in the 1970s, that reading comprehension work can use inferential questions at different levels of challenge, thus providing similar problem-solving with older learners. I believe now that this is a very desirable activity in L2 instruction (at about the secondary level) for three reasons. First, texts are not just sequences of sentences; they are structured entities of language and logic: chunks of knowledge, reasoning, facts and opinion, with open as well as implied meanings, references back and forth, and so on. Comprehending a piece of text, therefore, has a dimension of depth, from superficial/general to thorough/detailed. There can, as a result, be comprehension questions at different levels of detail and depth, catering to learners of different levels of ability in a class. Second, being led to perceive the less obvious things in a text such as suggestions, implications, internal cross-references as well as logical relations such as cause–consequence, fact–conclusion etc., brings about what I would call a more intensive contact with the language than a mere reading with a general understanding, with correspondingly greater value for language-acquisition. Thirdly, such text-based work looks in line with past traditions of schooling and is fully respectable, instead of being threateningly innovative.

GD: *Dr Prabhu, what you are now saying is that instead of making reading easier for learners by explaining, paraphrasing, simplifying or summarising texts through the "lecture method", teachers should make things more difficult by asking such inferential questions and asking learners to read, re-read, search, weigh and risk giving wrong answers, in the course of an "in-depth" reading. This will be a major change from present practice. What kind of training do you think our teachers will need?*

NSP: The essence of task-based teaching is to get the learner to make an effort to comprehend. A task is successful when the learner manages to comprehend pieces of text a little more (or better) than he could before. Success in such an effort can result in raising both the confidence and (however slightly) the ability of the learner for the next effort, just as failure can be dispiriting. Therefore the effort demanded should be neither too low nor too high. It is of course very difficult to judge the right level of effort—as difficult for a teacher as it would be for anybody else. But the teacher has an advantage. She is teaching the same set of learners repeatedly and can learn by trial and error to judge their ability in relation to the effort called for by a task. Each error of judgement increases the chances of her judging better the next time, and each time she judges right, she becomes a little more confident and competent in making such judgements. The teacher, that is to say, trains herself in the course of her teaching, while the learners are getting used to such effort-making. And the teacher's training is not a one-time preparation for a career-long job but a career-long process of professional growth from practising the profession, as in other professions such as medicine or engineering.

GD: *If I have understood you correctly, your stance is that tasks must be fine-tuned to suit, or rather, if I may borrow a Vygotskian term, "zoned" to suit the level of the learner and that this can be done only by the teacher in the classroom. If such fine-tuning of tasks can happen, it would be fantastic, but it sounds almost too good to be true. Is this really achievable in our context?*

NSP: Well, it is something of a vision, an idealised view of the goal. In practice, not all learners in a class will be equal in ability, attention, motivation or even sincerity, and the same learner tends to progress faster sometimes than at other times. Our observation in the Bangalore Project was that a small minority tend to lag behind repeatedly while another minority tend to be consistently ahead, but a large majority are likely to be slow and fast at different times but make roughly equal progress over time. When I say "every effort", "next effort" etc., I don't mean that those things should or will happen with those results all the time; I am only pointing to the "Vygotskian" moments/occasions (when the learner is able to achieve a little more than he could before) which matter most and should be aimed at all the time. We should also remember that the teacher is not the only source of learning in a classroom. When some learners succeed and others don't in an effort/task, the unsuccessful ones want and try to learn by observing the successful ones—quietly, sheltered by anonymity. We noticed this too in the Bangalore Project.

GD: *So, you are saying that learners learn not only from their teachers but also from other learners and their peers. What about group work then? Wouldn't that be a better practice to follow to enable more learning to happen, particularly in the context of task-based teaching, where problems have to be solved for task achievement?*

NSP: Well, I know that group work has been promoted as a form of co-operative learning in a non-threatening ambiance, but it is more often the opposite. Small groups tend to encourage dominance/showing-off by the abler members, aggravating the diffidence of the others. While every learner fears a loss of face resulting from a wrong answer, a degree of anonymity in a larger group tends to reduce that fear. Also, a loss of face vis-à-vis the teacher is much easier to bear than one vis-à-vis a fellow learner. In addition, learners often do not have the maturity to protect fellow learners' pride while enjoying their own success.

***GD:** Can I then take you back to the other issue you spoke about, teaching materials—texts and tasks at the right levels? Do you think our teachers can themselves devise them?*

NSP: I wouldn't expect them to. We need to make materials available—not in the form of readymade coursebooks, stating what to do when, but rather as "sourcebooks", that is, a collection/compendium of many, many pieces of text at different levels with a variety of comprehension questions/tasks, also at different levels. The teacher's job is to select what she considers most suited for her class in each lesson or at each stage, judge afterwards how successful it was and use that experience in making the next selection. This way, we reduce the teacher's burden but ensure that each lesson she teaches involves her own judgement/decision and she is able to judge, select, adjust or modify given material better and better in the course of her teaching...perhaps arriving at a point where she prefers to devise (and build up a collection of) her own materials.

***GD:** So, what you are saying is that you would construct and provide materials to teachers and would have no problem if they modify, alter, or even, to use a harsher word, tamper with them?*

NSP: I would in fact welcome and encourage tampering by teachers, both because of what it can prevent and because of what it can promote. It will involve some thought or decision by the teacher and reduce the risk of teaching becoming a routine with little pedagogic awareness. More positively, the tampering will be done in order to make a given task more challenging or less, so as to match the learners' ability at a given point of time. The teacher has the most direct and immediate evidence of learners' ability and she also has the opportunity to learn to judge by trial and error. I think good materials should be easily tamperable in the interests of both learners' progress and teachers' professional growth.

GD: *Dr. Prabhu, your perspective of the teacher in the classroom is an extremely enabling one, for she is the only person in the classroom who can fine-tune tasks to suit her learners and she must have the freedom to modify and alter them as she sees fit. Can I take you back to what you said a while ago, about the need for using texts for reading with problem-solving activities, where the questions would require the learner to interpret the text and find answers. You said that this would be one of the best ways through which language can be learnt. Now if we take this as a base premise for language teaching, that we need to let language learning happen, I suspect that one of the big worries for present practitioners will be "What happens to the other skills?" What happens particularly to production, accepting that listening is similar to but different from, in some form, the kind of work that can happen with reading. What happens with the need for students being able to produce language? When will that happen? How can that be enabled?*

NSP: The four skills have been a part of modern ELT from the beginning—I think initially as a way of emphasising the oral aspects of listening and speaking in contrast to the earlier emphasis on reading and writing in grammar-translation procedures. But they seem to have quickly become something of a creed, expecting each lesson to be organised in an L-S-R-W sequence and, as the Structural Syllabus developed, asking for each single item of the syllabus to be practised in the form of listening, speaking, reading and writing, in that order. But that meant the attention was all on the sensory experiences of hearing and uttering, deciphering and transcribing, with little sustained attention given (or indeed possible) to meaning /content.

The Communicative Approaches that followed moved pedagogic attention to meaning (or purpose) but continued to ensure that learners employed the four different skills in their communicative practice, thus assuming that they can and should develop roughly in tandem. More regrettably, I think, they seemed to assume, as did the earlier Approaches, that repetition/reproduction by learners was the way to production ability.

***GD:** But, Dr Prabhu, how else would one develop learners' production ability, except by getting them to produce language?*

NSP: If we look at language ability not as four distinct abilities to listen, speak, read and write, but as simply the ability to understand and express information/thought, then there are only two sides of a single ability, namely, understanding and expression, and the two are necessarily sequential, not parallel. The Bangalore Project made the assumption that the development of comprehension was also an earlier stage of the ability to produce. No child learns to produce the mother-tongue before it can comprehend it. Instead, a child takes a whole year listening and making sense before uttering a single word, and a couple of years more before engaging in elementary meaning-exchange. When adults learn a second language from exposure, they take time understanding it gradually before venturing to speak it—just as children do in the mother-tongue. The way to enable second language learners to speak is to go on increasing their effort and success at understanding what is said. When they are ready to speak they will do so without any prodding; until then, they can only be made to repeat what is heard.

***GD:** So, what you are saying is that as teachers, we must just wait for students to begin speaking the language, without knowing when it is likely to happen. Isn't this something of a leap of faith, waiting for something without knowing when to expect it?*

NSP: That thought occurred to us on the Bangalore Project and we were asked that question repeatedly at the week-long review seminars that were held each year. We said that our task-based teaching provided us with continuous evidence of increasing comprehension ability in the form of increasing success on increasingly complex tasks and, at one such review seminar, I taught a lesson to one of the Project classes in front of the seminar participants telling the children a "whodunit" story which they had in fact been told some fifty lessons earlier and had failed to make sense of; but on this occasion there was a chorus of the solution to the mystery as soon as the story ended. The leap of faith is therefore much smaller if you see comprehension as an earlier stage of production and carry out task-based teaching so that you can see the progress in comprehension. I think such evidence is much better than making children repeat bits of language and creating something like an illusion of production.

Consider one other thing. As adults, we all comprehend a lot more language in our listening and reading than we produce in our speech and writing, in the mother-tongue as well as in any second language we know. This is captured in the statement that our "passive" vocabulary is always much larger than our "active" vocabulary in whichever language we know. It is also a fact that when memory begins to fade in one's old age, it becomes difficult to recall words for what we want to say earlier and faster than forgetting the meanings of familiar words. This means that comprehension not only precedes production in language learning but it remains larger in scope than production through one's life and lasts longer than production at the end. Does this not indicate that comprehension ability develops to a level at which a part of it operates as production ability and when memory begins to fail, production ability subsides sooner and faster than comprehension?

GD: *Dr Prabhu, your "small leap of faith" if I am not wrong, is with reference to spoken production. What happens to the other aspect, writing? Does that not have to be taught separately? Should it be given special attention?*

NSP: It does, but the written form, seen simply as an alternative medium to speech, can be learnt fairly soon after speech and relatively easily (as happens when children begin to read storybooks in the mother-tongue). But there is another, more profound, difference between speech and writing. In a 1985 book called *Spoken and Written Language,* Michael Halliday spoke about the "pragmatic" and "mathetic" functions of language, meaning roughly its transactional, "communicative" role in the ordinary business of living as against its role in the generation, representation and exchange of thought/knowledge in the world of learning. Writing, that is to say, is not just a graphic representation of speech; it is a valuable vehicle of thought. I think something like that is the concept behind the curricular provision in American Universities for courses of study taught by Departments of Writing to graduate/research students.

GD: *But then, what you are talking about, teaching writing as a vehicle of thought, seems to take us way beyond what we are doing with English at the secondary or even the undergraduate level. Do you think this is feasible in the Indian context?*

NSP: I spoke earlier about *English Through Reading* and my realisation of the potential of task-based reading comprehension by getting learners to dig texts for various facts, inferences, implications etc. A piece of text is a chunk of coherent meaning/knowledge essentially serving the "mathetic" function. It can of course provide what I called intensive exposure to the structure of the language when used in task-based teaching, but such exposure will also include the "mechanisms" of text-formation (what Halliday called "texture") which have to be perceived in some way in answering inferential questions. At some stage in the course of such teaching, one can perhaps lead learners to go beyond finding the answers to stating a justification for them, which will necessarily involve constructing coherent paragraphs. Learning to state one's reasoning as a coherent paragraph will be a major step towards participating in the mathetic function.

GD: *Dr Prabhu, learning to state one's reasoning coherently alone is not enough to enable a learner to write well. All of us know that it* *is common for learners to make many grammatical errors in a second language, though they hardly do so in the mother-tongue. This has led to the teaching and practice of grammatical rules or patterns as a remedy. Must this be done? Should grammar be taught, and if yes, how would you teach it?*

NSP: I think we should ask why it might be that grammatical errors occur so much in a second language but not in the mother-tongue. I have suggested that production emerges when comprehension rises to the level needed. But production in a second language tends to be expected or demanded in classroom instruction before comprehension has reached that level. Remember that comprehension in the mother-tongue develops as a whole-time activity over a couple of years, while second-language instruction in schools happens at most for an hour each weekday—perhaps about 300 classroom hours over two academic years. Teachers are likely to get impatient if production does not emerge over what looks like a long period of time, and begin to ask for or induce it. When comprehension in a second language is supported additionally by voluntary mind-engaging activities outside the school such as reading storybooks or pursuing hobbies or sports in the second language, production emerges much faster. When migration to a second-language environment happens for a whole family, the young who are free to make sense of what is heard without any pressure to produce begin to speak in due course without many errors, while the adults who need to make sense and put messages across at the same time tend to develop a pidgin. There is also the fact that the level of second-language comprehension achieved at school is likely to vary widely from school to school since the quality of teaching and learner-engagement are likely to vary widely. I think the teaching of grammar should be seen as an understandable attempt to make good the inadequate level of comprehension. Such teaching must, however, bear in mind that if something can still be done to raise learners' comprehension further, that deserves priority over remedial grammar because it is more natural, dependable and enduring. Perhaps comprehension is like nutrition leading to production while remedial grammar is like medication for ailments in production.

GD: *Let me ask you one last question, where I would like to move away from the specifics of teaching to your overall perspective. You have outlined a view of language learning and teaching which differs in several respects from most other views. How do you think teachers can be trained or, to use one of your terms, enabled to carry out such teaching?*

NSP: Since I haven't actually done such training, I will only state briefly what seem to me to be three important aspects. First, teachers need to understand the concept of language acquisition that informs the form of teaching to be done. Our concept is that a new language is best acquired in the process of comprehending new knowledge, in contrast to the concept of using existing knowledge to comprehend a new language. Attempting to comprehend new knowledge encoded in a new language necessarily involves some perception or getting the hang of the new language, thus beginning the acquisition of that language. This is likely to be what happens in first-language acquisition; and that indicates why second-language acquisition is clearly more successful when it is the medium of instruction, or when it is the language of a new environment which one has to cope with, than when it is taught and learnt as a second language. Language acquisition is driven, in such "immersion" and immigration situations, by a pressing need for the new knowledge. Similarly, when children make friends in a linguistically different neighbourhood or find pleasure in listening to stories/viewing cartoons/playing games in a different language, the attraction and enjoyment felt drives the acquisition of the new language. The most favourable circumstance for acquiring a new language therefore is a need or desire for knowledge encoded in that language.

Second, problem-solving is an activity that can be attractive and pleasurable to young learners—especially in groups so that a competitive element is added—and it can be productive of language acquisition. Such "task-based" teaching can be in the form of stories with a mystery to be solved, tracing someone's movement on a map from a verbal description of it, etc. Once learners are able to decipher writing, challenges of reading comprehension open up large opportunities for indirect, inferential comprehension involving interpreting cross-references and inter-relations of different bits of information within pieces of text. Effort at such comprehension of texts represents an intensive occupation with meaning, thus advancing acquisition of the language.

Third, a learner's engagement in problem-solving depends on the prospect of success perceived. Every learner desires the pleasure of success but fears a loss of face from failure. The motivation to make the effort can also depend on how likely fellow-learners are to succeed. A learner is most motivated when the task looks difficult (for others) but attainable (for oneself). That means that the teacher too needs to estimate the difficulty level of tasks to be set to a class of learners based on continual trial and error.

GD: *So, are you saying, that in effect, before every single lesson, the teacher must actually "look for the before and after" and then decide on the most suitable task and prepare that particular lesson?*

NSP: Ideally, yes, because what to do in each lesson is ideally decided in the light of what was attempted in the last lesson with what degree of success. In practice, a quick review of performance on the past lesson usually suggests a small adjustment in the level of challenge requiring a small change in the next task much of the time; and the teacher is able to do the review and make the adjustment more and more quickly and correctly with ongoing experience. The teacher's burden can be further reduced, as I said earlier, by providing her with a range of possible tasks and task-types—a repertoire of tasks, task-types and modes of adjusting difficulty levels (constituting "source" materials instead of "course" materials)—so that she has only to select the teaching material for a lesson instead of constructing it. The important point is that what the teacher does in each lesson should involve a judgement/decision made by the teacher herself so that each lesson can enhance her ability to make such judgements—a process that can truly be called professional growth.

***GD:** Dr Prabhu, academically, this has been one of the most challenging yet exhilarating and satisfying interviews. Thank you so much for this.*

29

Plausibility

I want to explain what a sense of plausibility means to me and will try to do so by recalling some events that specially influenced my thinking at different times and then attempting some generalisation.

In the summer of 1966, I attended a six-week course called Summer Institute of English meant to introduce some new methods of teaching English to Lecturers in undergraduate colleges. It was sponsored by the University Grants Commission of India, with support from The British Council and the Ford Foundation of America, both of which provided specialist staff to teach on the course. Such courses were first held in 1966 at six different locations in the country, including Mysore where I went. The specialists gave talks on linguistics, phonetics, grammar, stylistics, methodology and did demonstrations of language practice with children borrowed from a local school. The specialist in linguistics was an American who had studied the subject under C. C. Fries who, I learnt later, was a prominent figure in what was called Structural Linguistics. (We gathered that the new teaching method was called the Structural Approach.) In his last talk at the end of the course, he warned us with obvious concern against a new upstart school of linguistics called Transformational Grammar developed by a Noam Chomsky.

When, a few months later, I found myself at the Central Institute of English in Hyderabad starting on a year-long Diploma in Teaching English, I looked for "Chomsky" in the catalogue of the Institute's library, got hold of *Syntactic Structures* and read it overnight. I found the grammatical analysis extremely fascinating and

---

This essay has been written specially for this volume and has not been published elsewhere.

felt that the grammar of English was far deeper than anything that could be taught and learnt through the Structural Approach.

While at the Central Institute of English, I happened to hear Professor Gokak, Director of the Institute and an Oxford-educated scholar in English literature, say that all he knew about English language teaching came from a book by Harold Palmer called *The Principles of Language Study*. That made me get hold of the book and read it. There were many things roughly in line with the Structural Approach, but I was greatly struck by an undercurrent of something quite different, indicated by such statements as: (in learning a language) "we learn without knowing what we are learning"; or (we should) "design forms of work in which the learner's attention shall be directed towards the subject matter and away from the form in which it is expressed". I saw a convergence between Chomsky and Palmer and the result eventually led to the notion underlying the Bangalore Project, namely, that form is best learnt when the learner's attention is on meaning.

Professor Gokak himself argued for language teaching to be based on texts rather than sentences—simple paragraphs perhaps, but not sets of isolated sentences—and the Institute, under his guidance, produced a textbook called *Language Through Literature* using a careful selection of simple, enjoyable pieces of text from the literary canon. That book came to be widely prescribed for undergraduate classes in the country, perhaps because it offered language teaching in a form most acceptable to a long tradition of literature teaching. Soon thereafter, Macmillan Education in England approached W.W. S. Bhasker, faculty at the Institute who had done most of the actual work on *Language Through Literature,* to do a similar book for them (for the market in other ESL countries); and, at Bhasker's suggestion, I was invited to be his co-author and, in particular, to do the reading comprehension part of the work. That work made me intensely aware of what I saw as the semantic density of texts, on the one hand, and its potential value for language teaching, on the other. It seemed to indicate how one could move over from a tradition of teachers' explication of texts in the classroom to learners' effort to dig out particular pieces of meaning in texts.

In the years that followed, I continued to devise such comprehension tasks and tested them out on the short courses/seminars I was conducting for undergraduate college teachers as part of my work for the British Council in Madras. When I got an opportunity to advise teachers in Bombay University on devising a syllabus of language skills for undergraduates, I got those teachers to act as students and work through a quantity of such comprehension tasks, and felt rewarded when at the end they eagerly opted for a syllabus of such tasks.

During the course of the Bangalore Project, A. P. R. Howatt of Edinburgh University came to India on a British Council lecture tour and sat in on a task-based lesson being taught to a lower secondary class in Bangalore. He told me afterwards that he was very struck by how the children seemed suddenly energised on seeing the task of the day stated on the blackboard, and how keen and competitive they were in putting forward their answers. That made me recall how, in another lesson at a Primary School in Madras, a smallish boy used to get so excited on thinking up an answer that he compulsively walked to the blackboard and (since he could not reach the blackboard) raised his arms for me lift him up. I began to think that learning happens in something like "Eureka!" moments which are exciting. When, later, I was in Edinburgh writing *Second Language Pedagogy* and came across Vygotsky's concept of learning in small steps, each involving a successful effort, it seemed like an articulation of my feeling and a form of theoretical support to task-based pedagogy.

These half-dozen events happened over about a decade and influenced my understanding of language pedagogy in important ways. I have since wondered why I cannot recall any such event from a period prior to it, which was nearly a decade as a lecturer in English at the undergraduate level. I cannot believe it can be a difference between what I came across in the two periods. I think it was a difference in my preparedness to respond to such events.

In the earlier period, teaching meant carrying out a series of things before and during a lesson in the classroom; it was a routine one learnt to perform faithfully and efficiently to stay in the job and move up in due course. I think that such routinisation creates a veil of complacency, leaving not enough alertness to potentially suggestive events. Equally, however, when some event does happen to make one do some thinking, that fact makes it more likely that another event will do so too, or make one a little more alert to such events, gradually producing the cumulative effect of a larger view of the pedagogic process. There is also a steadily increasing pleasure in the process and confidence in the perceptions it leads to.

Towards the end of the Bangalore Project, Alan Beretta, a Ph.D. researcher at Edinburgh University, spent a few weeks in Madras carrying out an evaluation of the Project under the guidance of Alan Davies. I took him to the different schools where project teaching was going on at the time and we talked about the perceptions behind the project. Sometime after his return to Britain, he sent me a quote from an article called "Interpretation, understanding and educational research" by D. P. Ericson and F. S. Ellet in a 1983 issue of the renowned American journal *Teachers College Record*. It read: "Our coin of knowledge is not firm generalisations, but is more akin to the good measure of meanings: plausibility. In educational research, as in education as a whole, good judgement should be seen as the prized intellectual capacity."

I saw how well the term "plausibility" captured my own feeling and went on to use it.

Plausibility is not a fixed concept but a developing perception. As long as one maintains what I have called an alertness to events, such perceptions can gradually lead one to a clearer and more comprehensive view. When an event happens to start one thinking, that line of thinking is likely to continue and develop. The process can continue even without the stimulus of specific events, in the form of thoughts and concepts which had previously seemed discrete revealing their connectedness and cohering in a more complete view. Let me try to indicate how this happened with the events I have just recollected.

My fascination with transformational grammar continued over the next decade through a Master's degree and a Doctoral programme in Linguistics at the University of Reading and, while I wondered increasingly at the systematic complexity of grammatical structure, I was also struck by the contradiction between that and the fact that all babies learn their language by about the time they learn to walk. Grammatical structure had to be something that is acquired without being taught or learnt. That pointed directly to Palmer's perception of how a second language should be taught.

It seemed to me that the Structural Approach was essentially a form of disguised teaching of grammatical structure—by carefully arranging linguistic evidence so as to make learners infer the intended structure. But the structure which guided the arrangement of evidence, or could possibly be inferred from it, was far too simplistic and naive, as Chomsky's work had shown. I felt increasingly that better results might be obtained by getting learners to understand things such as stories and descriptions stated in English and likely to be understood by them with some effort. The process of making sense of—puzzling out—things said in English would necessarily involve perceiving (what we regard as) grammatical relations. Such teaching will not provide any direct evidence of the bits of grammar being learnt but it can provide evidence of success in inferring the semantic relations underlying grammar, that is to say, evidence of comprehension. The way to obtain such evidence is to make the teaching task-based.

When, later, I came across Vygotsky's concept of the "zone of proximal development", I saw even more value and potential in task-based teaching. Good teaching is assessing by trial and error how much a given class of learners can comprehend at a given time and setting the next task a little above that level. Those learners who feel they can succeed on the task will make an effort, while those who think they are unlikely to succeed will probably not make an effort at all. The teacher's aim is to set a task that calls for neither too much effort (since that may discourage any effort) nor too little effort (since success on it may not add to the learners' current ability). This struck me as a larger view of growth in general—each successful effort adding to one's ability to succeed in the next effort. And there is simultaneously a process of improving judgements on both sides: the learners grow gradually in their ability to assess their chances of success on a given task through trial and error, just as the teacher gets steadily better at judging the likely challenge of a task for the class in the light of the preceding lessons.

It occurred to me that the Vygotskian view was equally applicable to my work on reading comprehension. The semantic density of texts permits comprehension questions at different levels of challenge and the teacher can raise the challenge step by step as learners' ability grows, using both the evidence of learners' performance and the gradual growth of her own judgement as a teacher. I began to wonder if such a step-by-step process of effort, success and growth might in fact be the way the mother-tongue is acquired by the child, driven by the need to make sense of this world as well as of the words heard from adults. I began to wonder, that is to say, if the mother-tongue is so unfailingly learnt in childhood because of the child's intense preoccupation with understanding the world and, as a necessary part of it, the sequences of words which carry that knowledge. Perhaps making sense of a small bit of the world results in grasping a small bit of the language and vice versa, over a series of efforts. That would be similar to (though perhaps less pressurised than) an immigrant's acquisition of a new language in a new sociocultural environment, or to studying a new school subject in the medium of a new language. In the case of reading comprehension tasks demanding inference at different levels, learners are driven partly by the pleasure of searching for and finding newer /"deeper" pieces of meaning in the same piece of text and partly, I think, by the competition with peers in that process, the result being both an enlarging and a consolidation of language ability.

At the annual review seminars of the Bangalore Project, I saw a great deal of dissatisfaction about the concentration on learners' comprehension ability to the neglect of production ability. The progress seen in learners' comprehension seemed to lose some of its significance by not being matched by similar progress in production. I wasn't very surprised by such criticism from teachers trained on the L-S-R-W principle which I considered naive in equating repetition/reproduction with production, but I have wondered since about how comprehension might actually be related to production. It was obviously simplistic to think that comprehension and production are abilities that can develop in parallel. Even under the pressure of learning the mother-tongue, the child learns to understand quite a bit before it tries to speak; and in adult life, what one can understand from listening and reading is far more than what one can state in speech or writing, as a rule. It is a familiar truism that people's "passive" vocabulary is much larger than their "active" vocabulary all through life and in all the languages they know. And when one's language ability begins to decline in old age, it is recalling words to say things that becomes difficult before recalling the meaning of words does. The ability to comprehend, that is to say, develops over a period of time before production emerges, remains larger than the production ability through one's life, and lasts longer than the production ability. Production, in other words, develops later, stays more limited and declines earlier than comprehension. It seemed very plausible that there is in fact a single ability which develops as comprehension, rises to the level of production and recedes back from that level in due course. Comprehension, in short, is the path to production.

There appears to be a kind of mismatch between pedagogy and the nature of language acquisition. Teaching tends to seek evidence of learning at each stage but a large part of language learning has to happen invisibly as comprehension before visible evidence can appear in the form of production. I think earlier approaches chose to regard repetition/reproduction as evidence, while approaches such as the Bangalore Project look on progress in comprehension itself as evidence.

It occurred to me that, while comprehension in the mother-tongue is driven by the inescapable need to make sense of the world, comprehension in a second language needs to be driven by things like a need to get by in a second language environment, or the need to absorb new areas of knowledge, or the pleasure of getting into a different world in stories, or the challenge and pleasure of problem-solving. The need to make sense of the world is so powerful that comprehension in the mother-tongue develops and rises to the level of spontaneous production unfailingly, regardless of circumstances. But the need, desire or pleasure of comprehension in a second language is bound to be less pressing in a second language and the level of comprehension unlikely to have risen to spontaneous production when learners find themselves obliged to produce. This leads to grammatical errors in what they produce, prompting the teaching of remedial grammar.

The teaching of grammar in language pedagogy is thus remedial in nature, while acquisition through comprehension is in my view developmental. Acquiring grammar in the process of acquiring knowledge can be seen as linguistic nutrition, while learning to avoid errors by practising bits of grammar is linguistic medication. Continued comprehension (as in professional or recreational reading over years) can raise the level of comprehension further and reduce the need for grammar, just as improved nutrition can reduce the need for medicines.

We tend to think of plausibility as a state just short of certainty, but it also differs from certainty in significant ways. Certainty signals a finality, a culmination, a state of permanence, while plausibility is always a stage in a developing process resulting from and propelled by that process. It is formative, not summative. When a teacher feels certain, she is likely to become complacent, no longer alert to potentially suggestive events, and gradually settle into pedagogic routines.

Plausibility can be described as one's best judgement at a given time, "judgement" in the sense of assessment or evaluation, rather than conclusion or verdict.

In task-based pedagogy, a learner would most like to attempt a task that looks difficult but attainable, so as to feel pleased if he succeeds while avoiding the risk of failure. So he is likely to assess the difficulty level of a given task and the likelihood of his success on it, before he attempts it. He is also likely to use the actual success or failure that ensues to improve his assessment of the next task, and so on, thus increasing his ability to make such assessment. As he succeeds in tasks more and more often, he is improving both his language ability and his ability to assess tasks. That ability to assess can be regarded as his sense of plausibility as a learner.

The exercise of teachers' judgements and decisions in the classroom is not just a need but an opportunity for teachers to grow as teachers. At some point in her teaching, a teacher is likely to notice that some kinds of task are more successful than others, or more successful at one time than at another, or lose their ability to engage learners sooner than others, etc. The teacher, that is to say, develops a judgement about what types of classroom task are preferable to others, with one or another type of learners. She will thus be able to gauge the probable success of a task (or probable correctness of her pedagogic judgement) more and more clearly and confidently. She will, in other words, begin to develop a sense of plausibility about which set of learners will benefit most from which types of task, which is the best way to decide the suitability of a certain task to a certain group of learners, perhaps leading to some sense or feel of what learning is like and when it is happening or not happening.

A teacher can go further than developing a sense of plausibility in the course of her teaching. She can become more and more aware of it and begin to observe how it is influencing her teaching. She may begin to think about what it is like, what events or experiences seem to have specially influenced her thinking or helped to clarify her understanding. She may also notice how each strand of thought prompted by some context or event continues to get clearer over time, and different strands tend to coalesce into a larger, more inclusive perception in due course. Such ideation of experience is an articulation of plausibility which can be shared with others in the profession, perhaps awakening, influencing or interacting with their own pedagogic perceptions and generally adding to everyone's understanding and what may be called a sense of professional self-worth.

Index